Deadrise and Cross-planked

Deadrise and Cross-planked

Larry S. Chowning

Tidewater Publishers
Centreville, Maryland

Cover photo courtesy of Selden Richardson.

Library of Congress Cataloging-in-Publication Data

Chowning, Larry S., 1949-
  Deadrise and cross-planked / Larry S. Chowning.
     p. cm.
  Includes bibliographical references.
  ISBN 978-0-87033-588-4
  1. Boats and boating--Chesapeake Bay (Md. and Va.) I. Title.
  VM321.C48 2007
  623.82'31--dc22

                              2007031846

Manufactured in the United States of America
First Edition

Dedicated to the work of
Howard I. Chapelle

TABLE OF CONTENTS

INTRODUCTION

The construction of deadrise and cross-planked boats on the Chesapeake started in the 1880s. Earlier experiments with this style of construction had occurred in the North and Deep South on the Gulf of Mexico, but the style never became popular in these areas.

On the Chesapeake, however, water conditions; large, diverse inshore fisheries; availability of wood for planks; and talented backyard builders all came together at the right time so that the deadrise style was perfected and spread from one end of the Chesapeake to the other.

For more than a century, bay watermen and others revered this style of vessel. When other areas of the country had long since switched to fiberglass or steel-hull boats, the Chesapeake region was one of the last strongholds in America of wooden boat construction. In the 1980s and 1990s, wooden boats were still the vessels of choice of many bay watermen.

Some say watermen would not make the switch to fiberglass simply because they were slow to change, while others say that watermen could repair and work on a wooden boat themselves, which made them more attractive than fiberglass, steel, and aluminum vessels. There is probably some truth to both thoughts, but the main reason for the extended life of wooden boat construction on the bay is that the hull shape of the bay deadrise, combined with the water conditions of the bay, was a marriage made in heaven. The vee in the bow of the hull that flattens out in the run aft, the wide beam, and the shallow draft were just right to contend with the short, choppy seas and shoal waters of the Chesapeake.

It was not until the lack of availability of good wood, the decline of the bay's commercial fisheries, and the price of building a wooden boat began to catch up with the cost of fiberglass boats in the late 1980s that bay watermen began to turn to other boats. Even then they wanted a similar boat, and fiberglass hulls were designed after the time-tested wooden deadrise hull.

The era of wooden deadrise construction was a grand era on the bay. The Chesapeake Bay deadrise became so prominent that Virginia legislators voted on March 25, 1988 to make the Chesapeake deadrise the official boat of the state. The skipjack, with its deadrise and cross-planked bottom, became the official boat of the state of Maryland in 1985.

The technical definition of deadrise is the "dead" straight rise of the wood from the keel rabbet to the chine. This usually includes all bottom planking from the bow staving to near the stern.

Over time, the use of the word deadrise became more associated with the entire boat than in the vee-planking in the bottom. That is why today people refer to the vee-bottom and cross-planked boat, in a general way, as the Chesapeake Bay Deadrise.

FOREWORD

In 1980, Greg McCandless came by my home in Urbanna, Virginia, and we sat on my front porch and talked. At the time, McCandless was building a steel-hull commercial fishing boat in Wake, Virginia, about fourteen miles from my home.

He had read several of my articles on Tangier Island waterman Elmer Crockett in *Chesapeake Bay Magazine* and wanted me to do a story for *National Fisherman Magazine* on the boat he was building.

I wrote the story, submitted it, and the article was published in February 1981. Chris Cornell, then Atlantic Editor for the publication, wrote me a letter requesting more stories for their boatbuilding pages.

The next story was on Deltaville boatbuilder Grover Lee Owens, and that was the first of many articles I was to write on Chesapeake Bay wooden deadrise boatbuilders.

I have continued to write for *National Fisherman* (NF) and all of those years of writing for NF on boats and boatbuilders laid the foundation for *Deadrise and Cross-planked*.

However, I was well acquainted with deadrise boats long before I wrote that first article. As a boy, I had gotten my Boy Scout boating merit badge in my father's wooden deadrise boat. She was built in the 1950s in Mathews County and used as an oyster-ground watch boat. She had a six-cylinder flat head Gray engine for power.

She made a great family boat. The *Miss Susan*, named after my sister, had high sides and provided a very stable platform for Saturday hook-and-line fishing trips. She had a large engine box, which provided a great lunch table.

We had a large family on my mother's side and we often took a boatload of cousins, aunts, and uncles bottom fishing on the *Miss Susan*. One Saturday afternoon we were off Hog House Bar and a summer squall came up. Everyone ran for the cabin. We had not yet installed a canopy and my father stood in the pouring rain at the helmsman station.

I might have been eight or nine years old and my uncle, Harry Bray, who was on the stout side, jumped into the cabin first to get out the rain. As the rest of us piled in, we noticed we were not moving very fast. My mother stuck her head through the cabin door and asked, "Shep, what's the problem with the boat?"

My father yelled into the cabin, "She won't go with the prop out of the water. Some of you need to get out here in the rain with me to balance the weight and push it back down." As I recall, my uncle stayed inside and several of the ladies stepped out into the rain.

When I was a boy, wooden deadrise boats were everywhere on Urbanna Creek. In the 1950s and 1960s, the Rappahannock River oyster fishery was thriving and wooden deadrise vessels

Deadrise and Cross-planked

from Tangier Island, Mathews, and Gloucester counties came to Urbanna every October at the start of oyster season.

In 1966, there was a bad snowstorm and freeze, and school was out for more than a week. Urbanna Creek froze solid and most oystermen left their boats and went home. I remember going down to the docks at J. W. Hurley and Son Seafood and walking from one boat to another and looking back at my footprints in the snow on the stern decks. I remember the hush and stillness over the creek and the beauty of the harbor with snow-covered boats.

This book was written in about a year, but the research spanned twenty-five years. Many people who helped me with it are dead now. Neither they nor I knew at the time I would be writing this work. There are so many, I would be afraid to start a list.

I do, however, want to mention the late Hugh and Dorothy Norris. Hugh was a Deltaville boatbuilder who built boats in his side yard on Lovers Lane. In the 1980s I interviewed Hugh and Dorothy probably a dozen times. Whenever I arrived, everything stopped so we could visit. We would go out on their front porch and sit in rocking chairs overlooking Jackson Creek.

Dorothy would stop her work and serve us ice tea and we would all chat. I loved her garden tennis shoes that were always just inside their front porch. They were faded pink and both shoes had a hole worn through from her big toe. Once I called and said I was coming down for a visit and we all sat on the porch and talked of old times. I found out later that Dorothy had canceled a doctor's appointment to be a part of our visit.

Hugh built boats under a tree in his yard, and beside it he had a band saw that was covered with a canvas tarp when he

was not using it. Many of his boats were dragged down to the creek bank on Jackson Creek and launched right there. My inspiration to write this book came from men and women like Hugh and Dorothy, who represented a very special bay maritime culture that is almost gone today.

I need to thank many people. John and Vera England have spent hours working on this project. John has read every word for content and Vera edited the copy. Because of them, it is a much better book than I could have produced by myself. My lifelong friend Ray Rodgers contributed line drawings, as he has in other books of mine. Ray's attention to detail always makes my books better.

Individuals who have taken an interest in the work and provided photos, information, and books beyond the call of duty are Gary Thimsen, Bill Hight, Joe Conboy, Craig O'Donnell, Selden Richardson, Arthur Lee Walden, Wit Garrett, Raynell Smith, Janet Surrett, Jody Anglin, Pete Lesher, and Jonesey Payne.

The Deltaville Maritime Museum in Deltaville, Virginia; Calvert Marine Museum in Solomons, Maryland; Chesapeake Bay Maritime Museum in St. Michaels, Maryland; and the Captain Avery Salem House Museum in Shady Side, Maryland were extremely helpful by providing photos, boatbuilders names, and other information.

Calvert Marine Museum Curator of Maritime History, Richard J. Dodds, contributed greatly to the chapter on Potomac River dories. His assistance made the chapter much more credible.

The works of Howard Chapelle, M. V. Brewington, Paula Johnson, and Robert Burgess provided the literary foundation for this work. I thank them all for having taken the time to write down the history of the boats of the Chesapeake Bay.

Finally, I want to thank my wife, Dee, who has been my soul mate, and my best friend through all of life's ups and downs. She has put up with my passion to write about things that only a few dedicated folks are interested in.

The history of wooden deadrise boats spans every nook and cranny of the thousands of nautical shoreline miles of Chesapeake Bay. I assume that I have most certainly overlooked some aspects of the history of deadrise boats. I hope that this volume will inspire others to write about the region and the things I have missed.

Larry S. Chowning

A SKIPJACK PRAYER

The Blessing of the Fleet is a tradition that has started every Deal Island, Maryland, skipjack race for forty-two years. In 2001, United Methodist Minister Rev. Zollin Hofer offered a prayer for the captains, mates, and skipjacks down on the dock just before the race began. This prayer is a fitting beginning to the start of a book on Chesapeake Bay deadrises.

"Our Father and Creator of the sea who has sent the stars to guide our course, the sun for our daytime, the moon for our watch in the night, help us navigate again today . . .

"Take us over shoals and waves. Take us into pleasant seas in a free, fair wind to sail again with our captains, vessels, and crews. Help us to be worthy seamen upon your waters and may we honorably apply our skills and [may those skills] bravely bring us to victory . . .

"Keep us vigilant and sober in judgment, fair sportsmen and competitors as we were as oystermen of years gone by. May we sail today by the grace along these bay shores of beauty and bounty—free of storm or calamity, but always aware of the great and beautiful environment in which we sail.

"We remember the captains and the vessels and the crews as a memorial of which we represent today. You have surely given us favor by their heroics and their labor over fog, sand and bars. . .

"In respect, we sail today under your divine power and your beautiful sky. We praise you and we ask a blessing for the victor and the vanquished.

"We all sail today as victors. A fleet that has won—won from worm and rot and rust, and wrestled with time and machine and storm and calm and regulations. We are the victor and today we sail again. Amen."

one
WOOD AND WATER

For most of the time that English descendants have lived along the shores of the Chesapeake Bay, wood and water have been the main ingredients that have shaped the rhythm of bay life.

The first settlers marveled over the giant virgin timber in the forests and the great bounty of the waters of the Chesapeake. A land-water culture grew from the water and shores. From the seventeenth through the mid-twentieth century, wood extensively helped shape the lifestyles of those who lived in the region.

Ash, red cedar, poplar, sassafras, catalpa, cypress, white oak, locust, hickory, spruce, and rosemary pine trees and limbs were shaped and used so that fundamental needs of life could be met. Canvasback duck decoys made from red cedar; oyster nipper handles shaped out of ash; log canoes made from a mixture of poplar, spruce and rosemary pine; white oak

Francis and Esther Haynie at their home on Cod Creek on the Little Wicomico River.

sculling paddles; shad skiff knees shaped from sassafras and catalpa; canoe trunnels whittled from locust; and oyster mops made from hickory—all came from local forests and were part of a culture that is all but gone today.

Esther and Francis Haynie live on Cod Creek, a tributary of the Little Wicomico River, at the mouth of the Potomac River in Northumberland County, Virginia. Their lifestyle is almost as unusual as the presence of codfish on the bay, the namesake of the creek on which they live. The writings of Captain John Smith of Jamestown in the early 1600s of cod fish sightings, and "The Year of the Cod" in 1936 are the only two documented writings of cod fish schooling this far south.

Esther and Francis live a gentle Tidewater style of life that was once commonplace on the Northern Neck. They enjoy turnip and mustard greens and sweet potatoes from their fall garden. They have fresh eggs from the hen house and tomatoes, string, and lima beans from spring and summer gardens. They catch crabs and oysters from the Little Wicomico and Potomac rivers and, what is even more symbolic of a bygone age, their lives center around wooden boats. There are three boats at their dock and two underway in Francis's boat-building shed. Stacks of wood planks and timbers, some as wide as 22", and several 12" x 12" pine keel logs are scattered around the yard. Outside are stacks of planks with metal roofing sheets laid across to keep the rain and snow from reaching the wood.

Deadrise and Cross-planked

Francis Haynie, above, is at the helmsman station of a thirty-two-foot wooden deadrise he recently built. Haynie is one of the last bay boatbuilders who goes out into the woods and selects and cuts his own boat lumber.

The cry of wooden builders for the past half-century has been that very little good wood is available anymore for building boats, and they blame the housing industry for using up the best of the crop. Well, that is probably true if you want to buy wood from someone else, particularly someone who doesn't know the first thing about good boat wood. But it's not true if you are willing and able to go into the woods of Tidewater Virginia and Maryland, find good wood, cut the trees down at the right time, and air dry it for two to four years. Francis Haynie is proof that it still can be done.

Francis is truly unique today, in that he learned the boat-building trade from an old-time Northern Neck builder who taught him how to recognize good trees in the woods and how to dry and care for boat lumber.

Jim Battleson built boats across Cod Creek from where Francis grew up. Francis was born in 1929, and around 1934 he began paddling across the creek to watch the "old man" build cross-planked, deadrise boats. By selecting and cutting his own wood, Battleson was already a product of a time gone by.

By 1900, West Coast fir, which was used to build boats and shafts for oyster tongs, had arrived in the Tidewater area via steamboat from Baltimore. Steam- and gasoline-powered sawmills were around and good lumber was being cut and hauled all over the bay in sailing schooners. Battleson also lived close to a steamboat landing and could get good lumber out of Baltimore or from local sawmills.

Perhaps the reason Battleson stuck to the old ways of getting wood is because he built a boat every two or three years for friends and family in his backyard. He did not have a railway, nor was he a prolific enough builder that he would have used much boat lumber. The old-timer was a carryback to how the boatbuilding industry started on the Chesapeake. Wood was cut from the land and boats were built in the backyard, usually for a relative or friend.

The neighborhoods that grew along the bay's creeks and riverbanks usually had one or two or three good boat carpenters who could build a good boat, make a sculling paddle, or shape a good pair of tong shafts. Battleson was a neighborhood builder who built the occasional boat, and out of tradition, and possibly economics, selected, cut, and cured his own lumber. In the 1920s and 1930s small backyard builders like Battleson were scattered here and yonder at the headwaters of creeks and guts, and at the end of back roads and footpaths. Their boats were not widely known outside of the neighborhood, but these backwater boatbuilders were important to the local economy and the water-based lifestyle of that area.

Perfections in Chesapeake Bay deadrise construction evolved over a century of trial and error. The neighborhood builder built in the same style of his uncle, father, or neighbor who had taught him with some of the same imperfections passed down from generation to generation.

By the 1920s, there were boatbuilding centers around the bay where cross-planked, deadrise boats were built in volume. By then, many imperfections in the boats were being fine-tuned. A waterman would go here and yonder to have a specific builder build a boat. Yet there were still builders in isolated spots that catered to their neighborhood clientele of watermen.

Francis Haynie is a carryback to the days when log canoes and plank boats were built in the backyard, and on a Sunday walk in the spring through the wood, a man would look for a tree just right for a straight keel or curved knee. He often would mark the tree and come back in November or December, when the sap was down, and saw the tree and have it cut into planks, so that in two to four years the wood would be ready for building a boat.

As long as planks were pit-sawed (cut by hand with one man up top and another in a dug out pit) boats built of logs were the preferred style of construction on the bay. Sawing planks from a trunk of a large tree with a two-man cross-cut saw was much more work than going out and cutting down a good log and shaping it with a foot adz and broadaxe.

Around the late nineteenth and early twentieth centuries, demand for wooden boats skyrocketed. It was good timing too, because steam-, and later, gasoline-powered engines came along to run sawmills. This made it much easier to cut planks for boat and house lumber. The demand continued to escalate as the population grew along the shores of the bay. More people needed a reliable means of transportation, and

Haynie has plenty of wide twenty-two-inch planks for side and bottom planking.

After the wood is stacked and each layer stripped, it takes one year per inch thick before white oak is ready to be used to build a boat. Spruce pine takes three to four years. Haynie always uses pine or popular to strip oak and oak strips on pine stacks. He said to always use softwood to strip oak and hardwood strips to strip pine or popular. Pine against pine or oak against oak causes wood to rot.

good roads and automobiles were still decades away. Commercial fishermen also were using all types of wooden boats.

By 1920, many builders had gotten away from selecting and cutting their own wood. There was a living in building boats, such as it was, and eliminating the time it took to find, cut, and cure lumber could be put into building boats. Some watermen still built their own boats, and many small builders, like Battleson, were carrying on the tradition of selecting, cutting, and curing their wood from local forests.

Francis Haynie is now the old-timer, and he is perhaps the last traditional bay boatbuilder who goes out in the woods to get his lumber. Typical of many boatbuilders, Francis started as a commercial watermen and discovered he had a talent for working in wood. He fished crab pots in the spring and summer, oystered in the winter, and built boats on bad weather days and between seasons.

When he was fourteen years old, he quit school and went to work for James Lewis, of Walnut Point, Virginia. Lewis ran a large vegetable-canning factory, a herring-cutting house, and an oyster-shucking business, and owned several well-known bay boats. These included the eighty-one-foot planked bugeye (converted to power) *Gladys L.,* which was built in 1903 by Joseph W. Brooks, of Madison, Maryland, and the sail-carrying bugeye *Matilda*, built in 1887. In 1929, Lewis had E. C. Rice and Son Boatyard at Fairpoint, Virginia build the *Andrew J. Lewis*, a well-known deck boat.

Francis's work with Lewis gave Francis valuable experience in the ways of the water and in building and working on boats. He soon realized he was pretty good with wood and moved on to a boatyard. His first boatyard job was for Henry Stephens of Stephens's Railway on Virginia's Coan River. Francis worked there full-time for ten years, learning from old-time boatbuilders and honing his skills.

After Francis's stint at Stephens's Railway, he went home and worked the water and built boats in his backyard. He patent-tonged for oysters in the winter and ran crab pots in the spring on the Potomac and Rappahannock rivers.

I interviewed Francis on November 11, 2005, inside his boatshed at his home on Cod Creek. There were two boats underway in his two-room dirt floor boatshed, a thirty-foot deadrise crab boat, and a twenty-foot deadrise seine skiff.

Seventy-eight years old in 2007, Haynie annually turns out three wooden deadrise boats, like this one launched in 2005 at his home on Cod Creek.

Wood Selection

"I go out into the wood and pick my trees for building my boats and I cut it anytime from middle part of November to mid-February," said Francis, leaning against the white oak stern of the thirty-foot deadrise. "The sap goes down the tree in November, December, and January. You don't cut boat lumber trees when the sap starts going back up around the middle of February. Now every year is not the same. You catch a warm year, the sap starts going down a little later.

"Jim Battleson, who has been dead for quite a few years now, used to tell me the best time to cut boat timber is when the sap is down. Mr. Battleson built boats right across the creek from where I lived. When I was seven or eight years old, I would sit there and watch him work, but you didn't put your hands on his tools. He kept his tools shining and his hatchet was razor sharp.

"He built a workboat, but he didn't build many—one every two or three years. His boats were cross-planked and deadrise.

"He didn't have a railway. Mr. Battleson just built boats in his yard all by himself. Now his wife would come down to hold this or hand him that, but mostly he worked alone. He had three or four sons, and I remember him building boats for two of his sons. In those days, when it came time for a son to go work the water on his own, a father often had a boat built for him. A good workboat was necessary to success in a watermen's life and a father wanted his sons to survive as best as could.

"When I was a boy, I'd get in a skiff daddy kept around the shore and paddle over in the afternoon and just watch Mr. Battleson. It was real interesting. I guess that was around 1935 or so. He made models too—not to build boats by, but for us children to play with.

"He also made decoys. I used to watch Mr. Battleson make them and I learned from him. He always used red cedar. He'd

One of the most used tools on traditional wooden deadrise boats is a foot adz. Haynie keeps one close by to smooth the sides of bottoms.

Haynie demonstrates his technique of caulking the side seams of his wooden deadrise boats. He uses one-hundred-year-old caulking maul and caulking irons, and caulks his seams with cotton.

These caulking irons belonged to pound net fisherman Smith Clark, who fished pound nets in Potomac River the early part of the twentieth century. Haynie still uses these irons to drive cotton into the side plank seams.

Deadrise and Cross-planked

These caulking irons are more than 125 years old and used regularly by Haynie.

Haynie uses these caulking hammers regularly. Over the years, he has collected old tools from builders who have gone into retirement or who are deceased.

Maryland side, but that's not so. [See chapter eight.] Giles Headley, who lived up on Coan River, built a pretty dory. I built one myself around 1960 and it was a good boat, but I'm use to building cross-planked and I think cross-planked boats are stronger, and I know it takes less lumber. You put them boards cross ways with a keelson into it, you've got all the support you need. You put the board long ways with a keelson, you still got to put little timbers into her up and down the sides, back and forth to hold it. When fasteners go bad, the next thing you know the boats come apart.

Chesapeake Bay tradition is to build deadrise and cross-planked bottoms upside down, then flip the hull over and build the rest of the boat right side up. This hole drilled through the bilge clamp is used to attach a block and tackle to flip the hull over when it is complete.

say that was the best wood for a decoy. I've still got the buck saw that I used to make my decoys with. I don't have my old hatchet, but I wish I did. I'd go around the shore in a skiff and I'd cut blocks of wood for decoys. Later, when I got so I could make a pretty good decoy, I'd go down to the old sawmill and pick up blocks of red cedar they'd cut off, and I'd make my decoys from that.

"I really learned to build my first boat by watching Mr. Battleson. Now I build cross-planked boats because that's the way he did it, but when I got older I went around and saw other ways. [Potomac River] Dories were built on both sides of the Potomac. Most people think they were all built on the

"Not only did we have dory builders, but we had log canoe [cunoe] builders around here when I was a boy too. Giles Jones built log canoes. He'd go out in the wood, cut the tree down, and build it right there in the wood. He had a brother who worked with him.

"On my boats most all the wood is cut from the woods. Rosemary and spruce pine and white oak are the main wood. Rosemary is a short leaf pine and is full of resin and mostly heartwood. I think rosemary and spruce pine are about as good as the other.

"I used to get Chester Haislip and Earl Withers, who had sawmills, to cut my wood. I would select what I wanted. I'd walk down into timber they were cutting and find old trees like I wanted, and they'd notch it to mark it. The sawyer would cut the tree down and they'd drag it out and saw it out and bring it to me. I wasn't the only one that did that. In the 1950s, it was a common practice for a boatbuilder to go in the wood and pick his own wood and have someone cut it down and saw it up.

"Chester and Earl had two different mills and they sold a lot of lumber to boatbuilders. They would haul wood to Deltaville, Virginia, where there was a boatbuilder in most every backyard. Those boys didn't select trees like I did though. They bought what they could get. Don't get me wrong, they got good lumber, but I think I got better wood by selecting my own trees. Now, I wasn't building as many boats as they were because I was working the water too.

"In the 1950s, I'd buy wood for seven to eight cents a running board foot. Nowdays you can't buy the bark for that price."

Today, Francis selects his wood from the forest, has a sawyer cut it down, and has the trunk hauled to his home. A portable mill is brought in and planks are cut from the trees. Once the planks are cut, they are stacked for curing.

"The real problem today with boat lumber is that most of what you can buy is loaded with sap. When I go out in the woods, I

Francis Lee Haynie has the distinction of building the last Chesapeake Bay deck boat on the Bay. The *Francis L*, above, was completed in 2004. The 42' x 12' x 2.5' deadrise deck boat carries Haynie's own name.

look for an old white oak tree. You don't want to get a young oak tree because it's got a whole lot of sap in it. I can look at a white oak that's just right and I can see in my mind stringers, beams, and knees. You don't cut oak usually until January because sap takes longer to go down in oak than pine. If there are many leaves on the tree, it's not ready to cut. The best time to cut it is when most of leaves are down and the straighter the trunk of the tree, the better the lumber turns out."

Francis uses white oak and sometimes rosemary pine in the stern, but has installed mahogany sterns in workboats. In the 1970s and 1980s, watermen began to request finished mahogany in the sterns. "I have used mahogany, but that's real expensive. I figured out an alternative for the boys that didn't cost as much. I can take rosemary pine or white oak and treat it and you will swear it is mahogany. I put shoe polish, a little turpentine and stain on the stern and you can hardly tell that it is not mahogany."

White oak is used in the stern, sister keelsons, guards, knees and bilge stringers. The side and bottom planks, keel and solid piece horn timber are made from spruce pine.

"Once I get logs here, I bring the mill in and saw it up in a couple or so weeks because when you cut a log in hot weather with all that bark on it the log will go in heat and it ain't no good. I like to get it here, saw it, and stack it with strips. You don't use pine strips between pine boards because pine against pine will turn black and rot. Always use oak or any hardwood strips between pine boards. I always use pine or poplar when I strip oak planks.

"Also, I get all the bark off the board, because if you don't, drywood worms gets in it and eat up the side edges, and if that happens you lose two inches off the side of the board. A drywood worm is something like a little termite.

"Once you got it staked and stripped, it takes one year per inch thick for oak to dry. If it's two-inches thick, it takes two years to dry to make good boatbuilding lumber. Now oak doesn't shrink, so you can use it early if you are in a bind, but you put spruce pine in before it is cured and it will shrink and open up. I usually cure pine three to four years.

"There was a builder in Deltaville who built all his boat out of green wood and they used to say one ole boy bought one of his boats and when it was delivered the wood was so green there was a squirrel leg stuck in the seam. Now that was green wood, won't it?"

Francis cuts about 20,000 board feet of lumber each year and some of the trees are more than 100 years old. It takes about 2,000 board feet to build a 22-foot skiff.

He is perhaps the last of his kind.

two
HOW THE MODERN DEADRISE WOODEN BOAT EVOLVED

Howard Chapelle, in his book *American Small Sailing Craft,* wrote that V-bottom or deadrise-hull forms in America came late in the nineteenth century.

Chapelle and others state that the origin and evolution has been lost to time. Chapelle wrote that a variation that appears to be a V-bottom-style boat was built during the Revolutionary War on Lake Champlain and the St. Lawrence.

Most of the evolution appears to be in the middle and end of the nineteenth century. Chapelle notes that V-bottom boats started in New York around 1860. There is also evidence that V-bottom boats were built on the Gulf of Mexico before 1886, where Creole builders were turning out "cats and luggers."

Chapelle and other maritime historians confirm that Chesapeake Bay boatbuilders took up V-bottom construction in the late 1880s, and from this time on the bay became the acknowledged home of the V-bottom or deadrise, as it is known around the bay today.

Historically, the 1880s would make sense as being a good time for the evolution of a new style boat on the bay. In 1884, in San Francisco, steam engine designers at Union Engine Works built the first marine engine in this country, and the internal combustion engine paralleled the evolution of V-bottom boats on the Chesapeake. The two complemented one another, as motors worked well in these boats, and the deadrise hull shape was perfect for the waters of the bay. Also,

the bay's commercial blue crab fishery in the 1880s took on bay-wide significance and this affected the need for a new style of hull.

Prior to the 1880s, the bay had two major fisheries, oysters and finfish. In Colonial days, shad and herring were caught and salted down, then sold domestically or shipped to the West Indies. Fishermen did not venture far offshore and caught the fish in primitive haul seines, which were worked from the shoreline. A log canoe, round-hull skiff, or a blunted-end punt worked fine.

Log canoes evolved as the main vessel of choice for bay watermen. The double-ender (pointed at both ends) canoe had a vee shape in the bow and stern. This allowed the vessel to cut though the short, choppy waves of the Chesapeake when moving forward, and the sharp-ended stern cut through wave action from following seas. Oystermen standing on washboards out on the water in the middle of winter wanted to control the up-and-down motion of the boat as much as possible. The vee in the stern helped minimize the effect of following seas beating against it. Bay watermen and log canoe builders knew early on the value of sharp-ended boats.

Round-bilge boats work well in areas where the wave movement rolls, but on the Chesapeake, a deadrise V-hull was ideal for the bay's choppy seas. This in part led to the creation and success of the vessel on the bay.

Deadrise and Cross-planked

Captain Columbus (Lum) Burton, a Confederate Civil War veteran and owner of Burton's Steamboat Wharf in Urbanna, Virginia, bought the log canoe *Spray* in the early 1900s for $75, and used it as a family boat to harvest oysters and catch fish on hook and line. The boat is an excellent example of an early engine-powered canoe, with the motor mounted as far aft as it will go with an outside rudder/steering rig on the stern. The motor-powered log canoe was the forerunner to the modern day deadrise boat. (Courtesy of Betty Burton.)

transportation, Chesapeake Bay crabbers established markets in cities, and the booming crab fishery needed a new kind of hull.

Although no one knows for sure, it is believed the origin of the deadrise hull used on Chesapeake Bay boats today may have started from small sailing crab skiffs built on the Eastern Shore of Maryland and Virginia. Some of the most fertile crabbing grounds on the bay are in Tangier Sound, around Smith Island, Maryland, and Tangier Island, Virginia. As watermen in those areas began to exploit the new crab market, the watermen may have begun to experiment with V-bottom sailing skiffs. It makes sense. They needed a skiff with a shallow draft to catch crabs in the grassy shoals of Tangier Sound. Yet, they needed the sharp vee shape in the hull to cut through choppy seas as they traveled in deeper water.

Other circumstances made the time right for the development of the deadrise hull. Prior to the 1880s, soft-shell crabs, unlike salted finfish and oysters in the shell, were a local delicacy that did not extend far beyond the region where they were harvested. Soft-shell crabs were extremely perishable, and the culinary art of steaming hard crabs was not widely known then. Prior to the era of steamed crabs, early generations on the bay wanted little to do with the feisty jimmie crab. Also, unless the market for crabs was just down the road, it was difficult to get hard crabs live to market. As markets developed, watermen began to experiment with ways to keep hard crabs alive and found that crape myrtle branches stuffed into a basket full of jimmies allowed the crabs space to breathe and kept them from biting one another. But the crab fishery remained localized until the mid- to late 1800s, when the steamboat and railroad came along. With improvements in

Another factor that may have come into play is that right after the Civil War the Virginia portion of the bay experienced an influx of northerners coming down to collect the spoils of war. Most of the war had been fought in Virginia and the state had suffered greatly. Because so many Virginian men had been killed in battle, the population of eligible brides was high. The loss of slave labor had caused many farms to fail, so inexpensive land was available.

These northern men, some of whom were craftsmen and boatbuilders, migrated into the Chesapeake Bay region and may have played a role in the evolution of the bay deadrise boat. Styles of fore-and-aft boats have been built in the North for years. Chapelle stated that V-bottom boats were being built in New York in the 1860s. He also wrote that several early bay boats in the 1870s resembled the New Haven sharpie, and that, "a V-bottomed skiff, once built at Tangier Island, showed strong resemblance to the Connecticut sharpie." By then, several New England small fore-and-aft planked boats had made their way into the Chesapeake region, including the Long Island "Yankee skiff," which was used extensively on the York River.

Even though the Yankee skiff was round bilge and not deadrise, it is a good bet that the skills of northern boatbuilders combined with the skills of area log canoe boatbuilders could have led to developing the modern Chesapeake Bay deadrise.

Just as the crab fishery had much to do with the development of the bottom of the deadrise bay-built boats, the oyster fishery had just as much or more to do with the development of the boat from the chine up. In fact, the oyster probably had more to do with the overall development of nineteenth- and twentieth-century watercraft on the bay than any other fishery. It is fair to say that such craft as bugeyes, skipjacks, brogans, and motor-powered buyboats evolved out of the growth of the Chesapeake's oyster business. Many features found today in Chesapeake Bay deadrise craft evolved out of the specific needs of oystermen, some of which had been built into working sailboats. Some of the same shape, style, and features on sail-powered log canoes, bateaux, coastal canoes, and brogans can be found today on the modern Chesapeake Bay deadrise workboat.

The oyster hand-tong fishery created special needs in a boat for oystermen. An example is wide twelve- to fourteen-inch washboards, which allowed a man with large feet to stand and work a pair of hand tongs. Watermen wanted wide washboards because most could not swim. Many fell overboard and drowned in winter, because hypothermia would kill them before they could reach the boat or their oilskins would drag them under. They needed a wide, sturdy platform on which to stand and tong oysters.

Today, wide washboards are standard on most deadrise boats, even though most of the boats are no longer used in the hand-tong fishery. As styles of boats evolved for different fisheries, wide washboards became a norm.

Attached to the washboard is the "toe rail," a two- to three-inch-wide strip set atop the washboard on the water's edge

The Chesapeake deadrise evolved from bay watermens' need to have a sturdy, strong platform from which to work. This photo of two James River oystermen shows how close watermen often have to get to the water while working. A snag in a dredge line means jumping up on the wide washboards and fixing it. A stable platform is much desired in this case, especially on a cold December day.

side of the boat. When tonging, oystermen stand on the washboard and put the point of their boot on top of the toe rail. This does two things. It helps with leverage when they pull the tongs to the surface, and it telegraphs where they are on the washboard without looking down. These features also were found on early sail-powered canoes and bateaux.

In the late 1800s, the wintertime oyster fishery employed many men living on rivers that produced market-size oysters. The twenty-four- to thirty-foot open canoe and bateau probably would have sufficed had hand tonging remained the main method of harvesting oysters.

The introduction and use of the oyster dredge, or drudge, as the watermen called it, to harvest oysters created the need for new and different features in bay workboats.

The *Miss Katie* and *Miss June E* are classic Chesapeake Bay deadrise and cross-planked boats. The boats are shown here working in the Virginia dredge fishery. It took 120 years of trial and error by thousands of bay boatbuilders for this style to evolve.

The device was introduced to the bay in 1808 by New York oystermen and was far more efficient than hand tongs. Once Virginia and Maryland oystermen saw it in action they quickly tried to adapt it to their canoe fishing. (See more on the history of the dredge in chapter six.)

Maryland and Virginia dredge laws had a great effect on the evolution of nineteenth- and twentieth-century bay watercraft. Maryland laws require that the dredge be worked under sail power. This has helped to preserve the last commercial sailing fleet in America.

Virginia laws allowed the use of motor-powered boats on private (leased from the state) oyster grounds. Since almost half of the oyster beds in Virginia could be leased by private individuals, this gave rise to a large, motor-powered deadrise known as a buyboat. (See chapter seven.)

It is well documented that Maryland boatbuilders were more prolific in the construction of larger sail-powered boats, such as log and planked bugeyes, deadrise, and cross-planked skipjacks. Yet it also is evident that Virginia builders excelled in the construction of the motorized deadrise buyboat. The fact that boatbuilders in a particular state excelled in a certain style had little to do with the builders' skills and more to do with the laws that regulated the use of the dredge. This dictated the style of boat needed by oystermen in that state. If sail had been required for dredging in Virginia, most likely more skipjacks would have been built there. If motor-powered dredge boats had been allowed in Maryland, most likely more would have been built in that state.

When bay watermen started using the dredge in the 1800s, it created a need for larger boats. The dredge allowed oystermen to catch more oysters and included a more spacious platform to work the apparatus. Larger canoes were built and were known as coasting canoes and brogans. Some of these boats were built with two masts and rigs and a small "hunting" cabin installed in the bow. M. V. Brewington wrote, "A hunting cabin contained two built-in wooden bunks and a small wood stove at the forward end. The cabin occupied all the space between the washboards beginning just abaft the foremast and extending aft some six feet."

This Hooper Island draketail deadrise is being used in the oyster hand-tong fishery. The craft has a house but no booby house or pilothouse. The earliest deadrise boats started as open boats without house accommodations. The next stage was adding a house, and the final development was the standard house/ pilothouse configuration. (Courtesy of Ben Williams.)

The forward layout of the house on early brogans was to become the model for the inside and outside house configuration on early motorized deadrise boats. Similar styles would be used on later deadrise workboats. The booby house or pilothouse configuration came along in the 1940s, but the trunk cabin configuration on the boats was similar to early styles built into earlier sailing craft.

Several variations of pilothouses evolved on deadrise boats. Few pilothouses were installed on deadrise boats until around 1945. Some of the very early style pilothouses were quite interesting. This round pilothouse on the crab boat *Beverley Ann* is fairly unique.

Early small sail-powered bateaux and canoes were mostly open boats, but when gasoline and diesel engines began to

replace sail, the boats took on a different look. Watermen began to install small cabins for storage and bedding, and motor boxes to protect the motor from the elements.

Some early motorized boats, from 1900 to around 1915, had motors installed as far back toward the stern as possible and engines were exposed to the elements. A hand guard mounted on the engine kept passengers from falling into the motor. Eventually, houses or motor boxes were built over the motor. Some houses were large enough to cover the motor and provide storage.

The early experiments with houses had some mounted aft, while others were mounted forward in the bow. The aft configuration went on to became the norm for bay buyboat-style boats, while the forward house became the style of choice for smaller bay deadrise boats. Many early workboats had the house aft, sitting down on the ceiling. (Ceiling is the same as floorboards in boats.) When the boats were converted to buyboats or deckboats, the house was raised off the ceiling onto a deck. The early style, with the house on the ceiling, was particularly popular on the Western Shore of Maryland near Shady Side, Edgewater, Galesville, and Annapolis.

Watermen wanted a house built on their boat for various reasons, but the most obvious was to provide a place to get out of the weather. When weather conditions got rough on the water or watermen had to stay on the boat for extended periods, a house was a blessed feature.

Wit Garrett, of Center Cross, Virginia, explained why his father put a house on his motor-powered log canoe. "My father had an open canoe named the *Clipper,* and at first he used it for hand tonging," Wit said.

"In later years, there was so much trouble with people stealing oysters off my father's oyster grounds in the Rappahannock River that he had a trunk cabin installed up in the bow. We hired a man to watch our oysters at night and he used the house to get in out of the weather. Believe me, it would get cold out there at night."

Cold was often the main factor for installing a house. During the winter oyster season, watermen would travel to rivers that were having the best oyster harvest. As overnight transportation to and from home was impractical, some watermen would rent an oyster shanty in small "oyster towns" built by entrepreneurs who owned land near fertile public oyster rocks, while others stayed on their boats and crammed into small houses on their boats.

Oysterman Bobby Shackelford, of Water View, Virginia, worked in the Potomac River hand-tong fishery in the 1960s. He would work the river by day and live on his boat at night. "I've slept on the boat when the covers would freeze to the side of the boat," he recalls. "If you pulled it, you could hear the covers ripping. Now that was cold."

Early houses allowed just enough room for storage and for the men to crawl inside and sleep. Old-timers speak of

snowy nights and having to sleep with their feet sticking out the house door, because the house was not long enough to accommodate their height. Usually there were three men to a boat, two tongers and a culling boy, and they would stuff themselves inside the cabin for the night. Five-gallon buckets were the only heads on the boats, and watermen would make sure to relieve themselves before crawling inside, to avoid having to get up during the night.

As time passed, the boats got longer and wider, and trunk cabin/pilothouse configurations were installed with bunks, a small galley, and heating systems. A Shipmate wood stove was a welcomed addition to the boats for heat and cooking.

The introduction of the booby house or pilothouse was a major change in the looks and style of bay deadrise boats. All kinds of interesting variations of pilothouses were installed on bay boats. In the 1930s, the standard bay workboat carried a house, but few had pilothouses. Early boats had all shapes and sizes of steering rigs, most mounted outside. This meant that in foul weather the helmsman stood in the elements.

When engines first came along, Chesapeake Bay watermen and boatbuilders spent years experimenting to find the right marriage of boat and motor. This log canoe has some early features that show how the boats evolved. Note the yoke attached to the top of the rudder in the stern. The tiller system for steering the boat was replaced with a yoke and ropes that run from the yoke to some type of steering mechanism inside the boat. A trunk cabin without a pilothouse has been installed and the engine is pushed all the way aft. This photo also shows the reason for the engine placement. The waterman needs as much room as possible in the center of the boat for his oyster culling board, storing his catch, and working his tongs. The low freeboard also shows why when larger engines came along many watermen had to switch to larger deadrise and cross-planked hulls to accommodate the size of the engine and the horsepower it produced. This boat speaks to another interesting problem. The four-cylinder Model T Ford engine was a step up from the old one and two lunger engines, but some boats were not large enough to accommodate a Model T engine. Instead of upsizing the boat, some watermen cut the engines in two, plugged the water cooler with a piece of wood, and operated their boats with a two-cylinder Model T engine. The configuration of the boat was not the only thing watermen experimented with. (Courtesy of John Frye.)

Windowed pilothouses gave height to the house and allowed the helmsman to stand and control the boat from inside. It also gave him visibility to see where he was going. Some pilothouses were makeshift, to say the least, while others took the shape of the modern boats.

Getting up on Plane

Just before the turn of the twentieth century, log canoes were still the main platform used on the bay, but gasoline and diesel engines created a need for another hull style. As engines evolved from small one- and two-cylinder power plants to larger and more powerful motors, a hull was needed that could get up on plane. Gradually, builders realized they could produce more speed from a boat by installing a larger engine and building a hull shape to accommodate that engine. It was a simple concept. When a boat skims across the water, it eliminates drag and goes faster.

It took bay builders sixty years to perfect the modern deadrise hull, and through the trial and error period some interesting variations were built. Some early motorized vessels had strong sailboat features on the topside and in the hull.

The first marine engine was built in America in 1884, and it was an exciting time for mariners. One of the first articles written on the new internal combustion engine was in a 1903 issue of *Rudder* magazine, where E. W. Roberts explained how to make a three-horsepower engine. Just two years later, *Rudder* carried ads for sixty-three different makes of gasoline engines for boats.

Sail power was great, but during a calm period a sailboat could sit for days and have no way to move other than by oars. Motorized boats could go from point A to point B in a specified period. Experiments in converting sailboats to power began throughout the Chesapeake Bay region.

The *Edna Florence*, above, is an early deadrise built in 1933 by Perry Rogers, of Shady Side, Maryland. She has several features that were found on early bay sailing craft. The first deadrise and cross-planked vessels built for power had several sailboat features built into the boats. Builders experimented for years to find the right hull and deck style to accommodate gasoline and diesel engines. As time passed, most of the sailing features were removed from the boats. The *Edna Florence* has a bridge deck built right behind the house and has a tuck stern known in that area of Maryland as a West River tuck stern. Both these features evolved from sailboats. As motors grew in size, tuck sterns had a tendency to squat or drag in the water when the boat was underway. Several styles of sterns evolved to replace the tuck stern. The bridge deck is the only one this author has ever seen on a workboat, but it was probably a standard feature on Rogers's boats. Rogers was a renowned and innovative builder on the Western Shore of Maryland. The *Edna Florence* was built for Captain H. E. Sadler Sr., of Annapolis, Maryland, and is now owned by the Captain Salem Avery House Museum in Shady Side. (Photo Courtesy of the Captain Salem Avery House Museum.)

Deadrise and Cross-planked

A race between the *Comet* and *Jenette*, a sail-powered log canoe against a motor-powered canoe. When gasoline engines arrived on the bay in boats, skeptics believed the traditional sail-powered log canoe would never be replaced. Early on there was competition and bragging rights as to what was the fastest—sailboats or powerboats. This might seem ridiculous, but in the beginning a sailboat with a good breeze in the right direction could beat a powerboat any day. The problem was there was not good wind every day in the right direction, and as motors got larger to accommodate the boats it became obvious that combustion engines in boats was here to stay. (Photo courtesy Viola Jackson.)

Perry Rogers's early experiments with engines and boat construction are examples of what probably went on throughout the bay. Around 1901, Rogers, of Shadyside, Maryland, began experimenting with gasoline engines in log canoes. Many builders began to experiment with making changes on canoes to make the engines more compatible. Others, like Rogers, began experimenting with V-bottom cross-planked boats.

Rogers built deadrise boats on Parrish Creek at Shadyside from the early 1900s to the 1930s. He came from a sail-powered log canoe background and built many sailing features into his deadrise and cross-planked workboats.

Perhaps one of his most unique features was a bridge deck aft of the house. Generally, sailboats going forward on the boat have a cockpit, bridge deck, and cabin. The bridge deck is a platform for entering and exiting the cabin. It is an extremely unique feature for an oyster boat. Experiments like Rogers's were going on throughout the bay region. Since there was little communication between folks in different areas, construction information was passed along when boats from one area traveled into another area. Local builders took notice of

these different boats and often incorporated features from those boats into their own. Over time the best features were being used up and down the bay.

As late as 1933, Rogers was building forty-five- to fifty-foot deadrise boats for Shadyside watermen and installing bridge decks. The Captain Salem Avery House Museum in Shadyside has one of his boats on display. The *Edna Florence* is a classic Rogers's model. It has a Rogers's design stern called a West River Tuck Stern and an extremely raked stem line; a wide, long stern deck; low freeboard; and narrow beam; all similar to early bay sailing craft. The house also sits on the ceiling.

The *Edna Florence* is a fine example of a wooden deadrise workboat that has many aspects of a displacement sailing hull and shows in part the evolution that took place by bay boatbuilders to come up with today's modern deadrise planning hull.

This photo, taken in 1964 in Tom Trevilian's backyard in Urbanna, Virginia, shows a nearly completed deadrise bottom about to be flipped over. Chesapeake Bay boat builders, who built under the sky rather than in a shed, usually built their boats under a large tree. They would use a block and fall placed on a hefty branch to help flip the bottom. In this case, the bottom also is a playground for a young boy, and the forks of the tree are used for stacking a few planks. (Courtesy of Joe Conboy.)

Flared Sides

Early builders designed and built their boats to accommodate the area and waters where the boat was being used. At first, watermen did not go far from home. This changed as fisheries expanded and waterman began fishing in waters throughout the bay. Some local features, however, remained in boats. This is evident in the many styles of sterns built into boats and, to some degree, in the bow shape.

In the 1960s, some Maryland and Virginia builders went to strip-planking and laminating hull sides to produce more flare in the bow. Customarily, Maryland boats have more flare in the sides toward the bow than Virginia boats. Flared sides are not, however, a new style to the bay region, as evidenced by the Sinepuxent Skiff or Seaside Bateau, as it is called by most. This was a style of sailing skiff used on the seaside of the Eastern Shore in the late 1800s. Some were flat-bottom, while later styles had V-bottom hulls. Chapelle mentions the boat in his book, *American Small Sailing Craft*.

This photo of a deadrise boat being built on Tangier Island, Virginia, in the 1980s by Mickey Parks, shows the bottom being built upside down. Note the stem hole that has been dug into the ground to get the stem down low enough so the bottom can be built level. When the bottom is completed, it is flipped over and frames, side and bottom planking, decks, and house/pilothouse are installed.

Joe Conboy, a nationally known bay boatbuilder, grew up near Accomack on Virginia's Eastern Shore, and as a thirteen-year-old boy restored a sixteen-foot Seaside Bateau. He said that two sizes of the V-bottom bateau were most prominent, sixteen- and thirty-footers. The thirty-footer was used in the Atlantic Ocean to commercial fish with nets for finfish, and the sixteen-footer was used to travel to and from where the larger boat was moored.

"The Seaside Bateau was very popular in the inlets between Chincoteague to Cape Charles, where you needed a boat with more flare," said Conboy. "If you didn't have a boat with flare, the waves coming into Metomkin Inlet would fill the boat up with water. Flare helps knock the wave action down and throw water away from the boat. You have four- and five-foot rise in tide over there. The bateau had a lot of flair to accommodate ocean water."

The attributes of flare in the sailing bateau were recognized by modern builders and many, particularly oceangoing deadrise boat owners, found that they wanted more flare in the hulls of their boats. Hooper's Island, Maryland, builders found this style to be very popular, but some Virginia builders built flare into the sides of their boats as well.

Chunk or Head Block Bows and Outside Rudders

Prior to V-bottom, deadrise construction, log canoe builders had for years been shaping the vee in the bow and stern of log boats from chunks of wood, referred to as "head blocks." In the experimental years with V-bottom construction, many bay builders used chunks to shape the deadrise in the hull. The use of chunks in the bow did not last very long as boatbuilders realized that pronounced vee bows could be shaped more easily with staves. Staves also were easier to replace than chunks when there was a repair problem.

Deadrise and Cross-planked

Another canoe feature on early motor-powered boats was the use of outside rudders and steering tiller. As builders and watermen converted log canoes and sailing bateaux to power, many took the sailboat steering configuration and mounted

The Ruby was built by Odis Cockrell of Burgess Store. Cockrell used a tumblehome construction technique in his sides. As the side planking goes aft it changes from flaring out to leaning inboard as it rises. This technique also is used on Hooper Island draketail vessels.

Installing a cross-planked staving in a deadrise hull. Deadrise is the straight angle from the chine to the keel rabbit. The angle forms a vee shape, which allows the boat to cut through the choppy seas of the Chesapeake. The wood used to shape the vee in the bow is called staving, while further aft the wood is referred to as planks. Early builders used chunks of wood instead of staving in the bow. (Courtesy of Joe Conboy.)

The *Maid King* was built by Lennie Smith on Pepper Creek in Mathews County in the 1920s. This style boat was built extensively early in the evolution of the deadrise and cross-planked boats on the Chesapeake. Note the sailboat style outside rudder and tiller configuration. The *Maid King* was used in Virginia's pound net fishery and the pile driver up near the bow was used to drive pound poles into the bottom. Around 1998, the vessel was towed to Deltaville from Gwynn's Island and put on a burn pile. She was one of the last of her kind left on the bay.

it over the stern of their powerboats. As the evolution progressed, yokes were mounted to the top of sailing style rudders and ropes were attached to the yoke. The ropes ran to a steering system in the boat.

Wheels and side-mounted sticks (called Guinea sticks in some areas of Virginia) took the place of the tiller and outside rudder steering system. Inside rudders mounted under the boat took the place of the outside rudder.

The Deadrise Hull

In the early years of deadrise construction, engines were not powerful enough to get the boats up on plane, so builders continued to build displacement-type sailing hulls.

Skeptics believed that sail-powered log canoes would never be replaced, and there were documented races between powerboats and canoes. If the wind was right, a good sailor and a good sailboat could hold their own and often won these races.

However, as engines became more powerful, the era of sail-powered workboats came to an end. Deadrise builders started building hulls that could get up on plane and go faster.

It took years of experiments and trial and error for the Chesapeake Bay builders to perfect the deadrise hull. The most efficient style deadrise boats really did not completely evolve until the mid-1960s. Much of the experiments dealt with sterns.

The squat or settling or wing board was one of the most-used methods on deadrise boats to keep the stern from dragging in the water.

When the throttle was pushed down for speed, sterns on displacement hulls settle or drag, which often keeps a boat from getting up on plane. For years builders up and down the bay experimented with building a stern that complemented the power plant, so the hull would level off on plane and reach maximum speed.

As engine power increased in motors and more efficient boat styles developed, there was less need for squat boards to help keep the stern from going down in the water when getting the boat up on plane. Some boats still needed a system, but not one that extended out as far off the stern as a squat board. Boatbuilders began installing smaller wedges, as seen here, to keep the stern from sinking down. These wedges were on the boat *Only Son*, a forty-five-foot deadrise boat.

All kinds of variations were created to keep the stern from dragging in the water. The squat or settling board attached to the stern was the most common method. Later, as construction techniques improved, wedges were nailed to the bottom of the stern, extending out about three inches to keep the stern from dragging.

The best solution to the problem was the curved-shaped horn timber. In wooden boat construction, the horn timber ties the keel and transom together, with the propeller shaft running through the timber from the reverse gear. In the typical deadrise construction, a reverse curve in the horn timber gives the boat a concave bottom at the stern. This feature helps to keep the stern down, just touching the water, and makes the boat lie level in the water.

In wooden boat construction, the horn timber ties the keel and transom together, with the propeller shaft running down through the timber from the reverse gear. A reverse curve in the horn timber gives a boat a concave bottom at the stern. This feature helps to keep the stern down, just touching the water, and makes the boat lie level in the water. The horn timber, above, is a standard-pieced horn timber. In later years, this style was improved with the introduction of the solid-piece horn timber. Over time, the pieced-horn timber had a tendency to leak in areas that it was pieced together. (Courtesy of Joe Conboy.)

The solid-piece horn timber was the final evolutional in creating a stern that could accommodate the deadrise and cross-planked planning hull. The concave shape to the stern area of the bottom section created a smoother ride when the boat was up on plane. This photo shows a solid-piece horn timber turned upside down. Some call this style of horn timber a Guinea horn timber, named after an area in Gloucester County, Virginia, where it is believed it was first developed. (Courtesy of Thomas R. Marshall.)

Curved-horn timbers were in use in deadrise boats probably as early as the 1920s, but they were pieced together. A curved two-sided channel was shaped, and sometimes as many as five chunks, also called filler blocks, were installed between the channels to finish off the horn timber. The traditional method of construction involved fitting the horn timber around the

shaft in five different pieces, resulting in leak-prone joints where the shaft log was drilled through the structure.

In the 1940s, Gloucester County, Virginia builder Frank Smith and others started using solid-piece horn timbers. Francis Smith, of Bena, Virginia, an area also called Guinea, said his father Frank was the first to develop this style of horn timber. He also coined the name, Guinea Horn Timber, after the area in which he lived.

Francis Smith said his father was commissioned to build a forty-five-foot trawler for a New Jersey fisherman. The owner wanted to swing a big wheel but still work in shallow water. Smith developed the solid-piece horn timber to raise the wheel up, allowing the forty-five footer to get into shallow water. The concave shape of the stern area's bottom section also creates a smoother ride when the boat is planing. The design became a standard for Chesapeake Bay deadrise workboats.

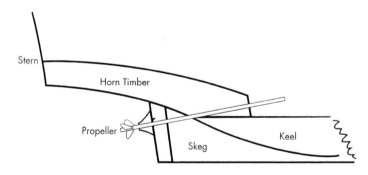

A drawing of the layout of a modern deadrise stern, showing how the horn timber is installed to form a concave bottom from the end of the skeg aft. Note how the shaft is installed through the horn timber and skeg. (Drawing by Francis Smith.)

Another improved building technique called step planking was introduced in the 1960s. This procedure eliminates any squareness where the bottom butts to the sides at the chine. Planking the sides at the chine starts by select-

A deadrise that has recently been flipped over and the builder has started installing frames along the bilge clamp. On the inside of the bottom is the keelson, sister keelsons, and shaft log. A horn timber creates the rise and a concave bottom in the stern, shown in the foreground of the photo. This style of construction eliminated the use of wing boards, wedges, and other techniques used to keep the stern up, while getting up on plane. (Courtesy of Thomas R. Marshall.)

The step plank between the chine and first side plank. The tapered step plank eliminates any squareness where the bottom butts to the sides at the chine. It gives the hull a smooth, straight appearance. (Courtesy of Thomas R. Marshall.)

ing a nine-foot-long fir plank measuring six inches wide. The step plank is tapered down to three inches at one end and fastened just above the chine. The six-inch-wide end butts up to the stem, while the three-inch end goes aft. When the rest of the side planking is nailed to the frames (above the step plank), it lies straight and smooth over the length of the boat.

Since the experiment of deadrise V-bottom boats began on the bay around 1880, it took nearly eighty years for the classic bay deadrise cross-planked style to completely evolve. Later builders perfected the process, but they had the advantage of engines large enough to bring the boats up on plane.

37

Deadrise and Cross-planked

Those who started the experiment used broadax, foot adz, and other hand tools to shape their hulls. In the final years, electricity and modern tools made a world of difference in the final shape and looks of the modern deadrise.

Ironically, when builders finally perfected the deadrise style of Chesapeake Bay wooden boats, the demand for wooden boats bottomed out. As the oyster fishery declined from disease, pollution, and overfishing, watermen did not have enough work to justify building forty-two- to forty-five-foot wooden workboats.

Many crab fishermen turned to fiberglass outboard boats that were less expensive to operate than the larger wooden deadrise. As the cost of wooden boat construction began to come close to the cost of fiberglass construction, those who felt they could justify building a larger deadrise turned to fiberglass, which required less maintenance.

Just as the sail-powered log canoe yielded to changing times, so did the wooden Chesapeake Bay deadrise.

Grover Lee Owens, of Deltaville, Virginia, built this Chesapeake Bay deadrise in 1981. It has a solid-piece horn timber, step planks in the sides, and all the ingredients of a modern bay deadrise. It took more than a hundred years of experimenting with cross-planked construction for this style of boat to be perfected by wooden boatbuilders on the bay. (Courtesy of Thomas R. Marshall.)

three
STERNS ON DEADRISE BOATS

Perhaps the most interesting aspect of the evolution of the Chesapeake Bay deadrise was the development of the stern. Early on, deadrise boatbuilders had the double-ended log canoe as a model of a stern that worked well in a following sea. The outboard rudder with a tiller mounted at the stern enabled the helmsman to guide the canoe with relative ease when underway.

The pointed stern worked fine in a canoe, but log canoes were built for sail. When internal-combustion engines became the main source of power, early boatbuilders and mechanics began to experiment with engines in log canoes. The mast was taken out, the centerboard hole plugged, and engines were installed, usually as far aft as possible in the boat.

The one- and two-cylinder engines, called one and two lungers, actually worked well in canoes because they provided about as much power as a windy day. However, as engines got larger and produced more horsepower, the log canoe hull, designed for sail, was not adequate. Although V-bottom hulls were being built into sailboats in the Chesapeake region as early as the 1880s, and maybe before, advanced evolution of the modern deadrise hull came with the advent of engine power.

In the 1800s, different styles of sterns were being built into large and small sailing craft. The pointed, or ducktail stern, as it was called, was found in the sailing bugeye and the tuck stern was found on sailing schooners. Long before engines came along, bay boatbuilders had perfected these sterns in sailing craft. Many of the early deadrise and cross-planked

boatbuilders learned the trade as log canoe builders. They already knew what worked well in sailboats. When the great experiment started on the Chesapeake with engines in boats, they already had several models to go by.

The problem was that as the engines got larger, the hull and sterns needed variations to keep the boats from squatting or dragging in the water. Sailboat features were built into the early motor-powered boats because many builders simply did not realize a boat with sufficient power could get up on plane and go faster. As they installed larger engines in the early deadrise hulls, the sterns sat down in the water.

The early builders had no reason to think that the hull type would be any different from a sailboat hull because motors were not powerful enough to get a boat up on plane. As motor power became more effective in boats, boatbuilders created some very interesting sterns on bay boats.

Lennie Smith, of Mathews County, was building this tucked V-stern, similar to sterns on sailing vessels in the early 1900s. Smith and his son Alton went on to become two of the most productive deadrise boatbuilders on the lower bay. (Courtesy of Mildred Stillman.)

Tuck Stern

An early style stern built into V-bottom, fore-on-aft planked boats was the tuck stern. This style had been used for years on schooners and small sailing skiffs. The stern deck line on the tuck stern extends farther aft than the waterline. These sterns worked well on sailing schooners, particularly in water conditions with strong following seas. As water hit against the stern, the extended deck would knock the water back into the bay and keep it from coming into the boat.

The problem with the tuck stern and engine power is that early motors did not have enough power to get a boat up on plane and to level it out in the water. When the boat is going forward, the bow goes up and the stern goes down or drags in the water.

To keep the tuck stern up, boatbuilders began experimenting with squat or settling boards and wedges built into the sterns. Squat boards and wedges attached to the stern extended the waterline and gave buoyancy to that area. These features were built into boats as late as the 1980s and were found in tuck sterns and on round- and square-stern boats.

A 1940s boat may have been built to accommodate a certain size engine and did not need a squat board. However, when the boat was refitted with a new, larger engine in the 1960s, features had to be built into the boat to accommodate that larger engine. Often squat boards and wedges had to be added to keep the stern up and help get the boat up on plane. In later years, the squat board was referred to as a planing board. Early on, it simply kept the boat from squatting down in the waters. Later on, with the advent of more power, it helped keep the boat level in the water so that it could lift up on plane.

The tuck stern was one of the earliest experiments by bay boatbuilders on deadrise boats. Wittman, Maryland, nicknamed Pot Pie, and Shady Side, Maryland, were areas where boatbuilders experimented with tuck sterns. Wittman is in

Perry Rogers, of Shadyside, Maryland, built this West River tuck stern into his cross-planked deadrise boats starting from around 1904, well into the 1930s. A similar style was used in early sailboats throughout the bay region and elsewhere. When motors came along, boatbuilders accustomed to building sailing hulls continued to build sailboat features into motorized boats. The tuck stern was a style seen on large sailing schooners down to small racing sailing skiffs built on the Eastern Shore of Maryland and Virginia as far back as the mid-1800s. This is a classic tuck stern that has a vee in the bottom from just forward of the end of the keel to the stern. As motors became larger in boats, this style had a tendency to squat in the water creating a drag. Squat boards or planing boards were attached to the stern to help keep the stern from settling.

Miss Cecelia is a good example of a Pot Pie tuck stern where the deck line extends farther aft than the waterline. Note it does not have a vee shape as the West River tuck stern. There were several builders around Wittman, Maryland, on the Eastern Shore, that built this style of tuck stern.

Talbot County, on the way to Tilghman Island on the Eastern Shore. Shady Side is on the West River on the western shore in Anne Arundel County. Interestingly, Wittman and Shady Side are almost directly across the bay from one another. The

Note the similarities on the stern on the *Robert Leo* to the West River tuck stern built by Perry Rogers in the early 1900s. The vessel was on the rails for repair in 2000.

tuck stern built by Wittman boatbuilders was called a Pot Pie Stern and the Shady Side version was known as the West River Tuck Stern.

Many in Shady Side believe that around 1904 boatbuilder Perry Rogers built and developed the first tuck stern in deadrise motorized boats. He built a deadrise boat named the *Princess* for pound net fisherman, Bernard Hallock.

Rogers built the forty-foot-by-eight-foot deadrise vessel *Princess,* which was an example of a very early motorized semi-deck boat. It was laid out like a traditional bay buyboat with the house aft, but the house sat on the ceiling and not on deck. This was a style popular on Maryland's Western Shore. Old photos taken in the early part of the twentieth century show Annapolis Harbor with many boats of this style.

Howard Shenton, of Shady Side, described Rogers's stern style in a 1986 interview: "The *Princess* was the first motor powerboat that I know of that was built with a tuck stern. The traditional box stern goes straight down from the stern deck to the water. The tuck stern angled up from the keel to the stern and Captain Perry's boats had a vee shape in the stern."

As previously mentioned, the deck line on a tuck stern extends farther aft than the waterline. On a Pot Pie Stern the angle from under the boat to the stern is square, while the West River tuck stern has a vee shape built into the angle.

Shenton says that the advantage to the tuck stern compared to a box stern is that it lays better in the water when working in a strong following sea. "When hand-tong oystermen anchored the boat stern to sea, the tuck stern gave them better stability. The boat would lay better that way and it would keep spray out of the boat. Now, if it was real rough, you would get some spray but not as much as in a box stern boat."

In a 1980s interview, Rogers's son, Elliott Rogers, says his father designed the West River Tuck Stern and Eastern Shore builders copied his style.

The tuck stern was a standard style on sail-powered Potomac River dories in the mid-1870s. When motors came along, the tuck stern was one of several styles used on engine-powered dories.

Poquoson or Diamond Stern

The diamond or pointed stern is a mirror style to the vee built into sterns of log canoes. It is a Virginia style that probably grew out of Poquoson, Virginia.

Many Chesapeake watermen refer to this type of stern as the "Poquoson stern," and M. V. Brewington notes in his writings that Poquoson was the center of log canoe building in Virginia.

It certainly makes sense that as log canoe builders began to experiment with deadrise construction they would incorporate the best features of the log canoe style into the boats. They certainly knew the benefits of a pointed stern in a strong following sea.

The late William Rollins, of Poquoson, builder of the *Holly June*, the last log canoe in that area, said in a 1987 interview that he thought the diamond stern was built for haul seine fishermen and clammers. "The vee makes it easy to bring in a net over the stern. It also works well for clammers, who often have to work stern to sea."

Deadrise and Cross-planked

The pointed style was also used by oystermen and pound net fishermen and was built not just in the Poquoson area. Mathews County boatbuilders Lennie and Alton Smith, Freeman Hudgins, and Boney Diggs each built an extremely rare diamond-stern deck boat.

The vee stern was often referred to as a Poquoson stern. It is believed that the vee stern on the Cheseapeake Bay log canoe was a carryover to this style of sterns on bay deadrise boats.

Most diamond-stern deadrise boats were built in thirty-eight- to forty-two-foot lengths, but Smith built the V-stern, fifty-five-foot *Elizabeth D.* in 1926 for Stanley Pritchett for $800.

The V-stern deck boats, referred to as trap boats, were extremely unusual and were mostly built for use in the pound net fishery. Like haul seine fishermen, pound net watermen wanted a boat that made it easy to work a net over the stern. Pritchett was a pound net fisherman.

Hudgins and Diggs built boats in Laban, Virginia, in Mathews County. They built the V-stern *East Hampton* as an open-trap boat in 1924 at Eldridge Diggs's landing in Laban for pound

net fisherman Curtis Hudgins. The *East Hampton* is still alive today, but has been converted from an open boat to a deck boat and sports a "pretty" round stern.

Round or Elliptical Sterns

As log canoe builders began to experiment with deadrise and cross-planked construction, the round stern was a natural evolution, since canoe builders for years had been shaping the V-stern in canoes with chunks of wood. The method of shaping a V-stern was similar to the way the round or elliptical sterns were built into deadrise boats. In fact, watermen and boatbuilders called early round-stern deadrise boats round-stern canoes.

Round sterns provide the same attributes as a V-stern boat in a strong following sea. The advantage over the V-stern is that the rounded stern provides more space on the stern deck. As the fisheries evolved throughout the bay region, watermen tonged and worked fishnets off the stern. They needed more space on which to stand and the round stern provided it.

The pound net "trap" boat *Pet* has a narrow, spoon-shaped stern. This style of boat was used mostly in the pound net fishery for setting and removing pound poles and other aspects of the fishery. These boats carried a small trunk cabin for storage.

Early deadrise boats with rounded sterns had more of an elliptical (spoon) shape. This was because of the narrow beam in early boats, which made it difficult to get a full round stern. Also, log canoe builders needed some trial and error time to perfect the construction methods in building round-stern boats.

Gilbert White was born in Mathews County, Virginia, in 1869. He started out building log canoes in the 1880s. He later moved to Foxwells in Lancaster County, Virginia, where he became a well-known deadrise builder. He is an example of a log canoe builder turned deadrise builder, who was noted for his spoon-shaped sterns.

Early versions of round sterns on wooden boats often had more of an elliptical shape than round. This photo above shows a spoon-shaped stern being built by boatbuilder Gilbert White, of Lancaster County, Virginia. White started his boat-building career in Mathews County, Virginia, as a log canoe builder. The elliptical stern was a direct carryback to the vee in log canoes, and many early deadrise builders who started as log boat builders tried to keep some vee in the stern. As time passed and more beam was added to boats, the elliptical stern became a more rounded stern. (Courtesy of Ella Jo Henderson.)

Coast Guard documentation concerning White's boats states that he built his boats with elliptical sterns. White's style came from his experience in shaping the vee in the stern of a log canoe with chunks of wood, rather than staves.

White creates the spoon shape by rabbeting the bottom edge of the bottom chunks and setting the bottom plank in the rabbet. "He gets a unique canoe-type stern," said George M. Butler, a longtime boatbuilder in Reedville, Virginia. "Particularly on his early boats, he comes way forward and has a long, gradual, round shape."

He also sets the chunks differently from most round-stern boatbuilders. White does not use the traditional brick-work style, where the chunks appear to be laid like bricks in a wall. "His chunks do not seem to follow a plan," said Butler. "But when you look at several of his sterns, you can see that he builds them all the same with different size chunks located in specific places. The way he has them arranged helps to create the long spoon shape. He knew exactly what he was doing."

Over the years, two types of construction methods evolved for the round stern. Builders with log canoe backgrounds built logged or chunked sterns, while other builders built round sterns out of staves. Both styles were popular in Virginia.

Deltaville, Virginia builders specialized in logged-stern construction, while Tom Trevilian, who lived just seventeen miles up the road in Urbanna, was noted for his round, staved sterns. It was not unusual for builders just one town over to have different styles and techniques.

Willard Norris, a noted Deltaville boatbuilder, said the logged stern was the most popular in his area. "We would shape the pieces from large timbers. It takes five pieces laid horizontally for the bottom rim. The second layer was set on top of that rim and lapped over the butts. Each piece was then bolted down." This was continued until the stern reached the desired height. The transverse layers were then bolted down.

The staved style started like the logged stern, using bottom and top rims, but each rim was rabbeted out. Planks were then fastened vertically to the two rims to fill in the stern.

Deadrise and Cross-planked

This round chunk stern built by Alfred Norris, of Deltaville, Virginia, shows the layered chunks placed so that the seams from the next layer do not overlap. Before electricity, log canoe builders were employed at boatyards to "dress" the stern down with a foot adz. A good adz man could dress chunks down so smooth they did not need sanding. With electricity came powered sanders and planes, which enabled most anyone to finish off a stern. The chunk stern was the most popular style of round stern construction on Virginia's Western Shore.

This photo shows the round-staved stern with the staves installed on a forty-foot Virginia-built deadrise boat. The round stern on deadrise boats was extremely popular in Virginia and in portions of lower Maryland. The staved style, however, was not as popular in some areas as the chunked or logged round stern. (Courtesy of Joe Conboy.)

The advantage of the chunk stern was that it was thicker than the staved stern. Watermen working oyster or crabs dredges from the stern wanted a thick stern in case the dredge banged against it. Oystermen working hand tongs, and crabbers or trotliners fishing crabs from the side of the boat, were less concerned about the thickness of the stern.

This photo shows how the rim is built to shape a staved-round stern boat. Boatbuilder Tom Trevillan was building this forty-foot round stern deadrise boat in Urbanna, Virginia in 1964, in his backyard at the corner of Howard and Cross streets. Trevillan was an example of a backyard builder who specialized in staved-round sterns. The rounded rims on the boat have been setup and staves will be fastened soon. (Courtesy of Joe Conboy.)

Staved sterns were easier to repair than logged sterns. Since watermen were inclined to work on their own boats, many commercial fishermen preferred their sterns staved.

Norris said his uncle, Lee Deagle, built some staved round-stern boats, but he feels the chunk stern method of construction creates a "prettier" stern on a boat.

"With the staved method, you could not get the true shape because you had to cut a round piece at the top and a round piece at the bottom to nail the staves to, and seldom did they come out exactly the same," he said.

Round-stern boats were extremely popular in the lower bay and hundreds were built there. Deltaville boatbuilders most likely turned out more round-stern deadrise boats than any other area on the Chesapeake Bay. On the Potomac River, watermen went so far as to distinguish where in Deltaville their round-stern boats were built. "Jackson Creek" and "Broad Creek" round sterns were names watermen used with pride to identify their boats. These are the two main creeks in Deltaville where deadrise construction took place. Even today, there are watermen who will tell you, "Yeah, I got a Chesapeake Bay deadrise, but it's also a Jackson Creek round stern."

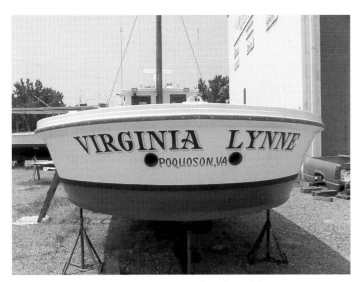

When finished off, the chunk round stern makes a beautiful stern. Grover Lee Owens, of Deltaville, built the *Virginia Lynne* in the 1980s. Chunk-round stern boats were made of wood thicker than the wood used in staved-round stern boats. Watermen working dredges off the stern wanted plenty of wood back there to accommodate a dredge banging up against it. Oyster hand tongers often preferred staved sterns because the style was easier to repair than having to pull out and reinstall chunks of wood.

Interestingly, the round stern was also found on some fore-and-aft planked Potomac River dories. As the dory began to lose some of its sailboat characteristics builders began to build into the boats features they liked. The round stern was attractive and functional.

Hooper Island Draketail

Maryland's example of a staved-style stern can be found in the Hooper Island draketail. The draketail also is referred to as dovetail and ducktail. The original Hooper Island craft had a long, narrow hull of lightweight and shallow draft. The boats sported a rounded, fantail stern with a reverse rake, and a chine that followed the waterline throughout the length of the boat.

Built predominantly at Hooper Island, Maryland, these boats were modeled after early racing launches and torpedo boats. Many of the early draketails were easily driven up to ten knots with the five- to fifteen-horsepower engines available

The Hooper Island draketail is a rounded, staved stern with a reverse rake. This style of boat was modeled after early 1920s racing launches and torpedo boats. The style of stern was used on boats from twenty-foot in length to fifty-five-foot Chesapeake Bay buyboats.

before the 1930s. The style of stern also kept the stern from squatting without having to install a squat board.

The early versions were generally very narrow, with the beam at the waterline less than one-sixth of the length of the vessel. As the engines got larger, so did the beam.

In later years, the style was adapted to Chesapeake Bay buyboats, and these boats, like the diamond-stern deck boats, were unique. Irving F. and Walter B. Cannon were two well-known builders who constructed classic draketail deck boats at Fishing Creek on Hooper Island.

Maryland and Virginia boatbuilders around the bay were capable of building almost any style of stern. Although few

This Hooper Island draketail workboat was still working in the Potomac River crab fishery in 2006. These boats were built extremely narrow for speed.

draketails were built in Virginia, a few were built on the lower bay, and in 2006 a classic draketail was working as a crab boat on the Potomac River.

William E. Wright, yard foreman at Deagle and Son Marine Railway in Deltaville, starting in 1935, said in a 2001 interview that he once built a deadrise with a draketail at the yard for a man who requested it.

"We hadn't done it before, but we had worked on a lot of draketails," said Wright. "I knew how they worked and I told Captain Lee [Deagle] that we could do it. We built the drake-tail and the owner took it back to Maryland.

"He probably told everyone he had it built at Hooper Island," Wright said with a laugh.

Potomac River dory builder John Cheseldine built what he called a ducktail dory, which was similar to the Hooper's Island draketail. As styles of sterns evolved on deadrise boats on the bay, builders built to customer demand. Edwin W. Beitzell in his book *Life on the Potomac River* had a photo of one of Cheseldine's ducktail sterns on a dory. It looks very similar to the Hooper Island version on a cross-planked bottom boat.

Square or Box Sterns

The final evolution of the stern on bay-built boats was the square or box stern. In the 1970s, the box stern became the predominant style of stern built by bay boatbuilders.

In the 1960s, Virginia watermen began experimenting in the crab dredge fishery by working two dredges off of sterns of thirty-eight- to forty-two-foot deadrise boats. Prior to this, the fishery was exclusively worked with fifty-five- to sixty-five-foot Chesapeake Bay deckboats, with dredges worked from port and starboard sides. By the early 1970s, the cost of fueling and maintaining the larger deck boats was becoming a factor in the fishery.

Over time, the squared-off box stern became a standard on deadrise boats. Once boatbuilders figured out how to keep the stern from squatting with an S-shaped horn timber, the square stern evolved into the style of choice for most watermen. The square or box stern provided the maximum amount of room available for a boat of its size. As engines became larger and gear required more space, watermen needed as much room as possible inside the boat to work.

The use of the smaller boats opened the fishery to more watermen, but the forty-two footers really were not big enough, and the top decks on round sterns did not provide enough space for two dredges. This led to construction of forty-five to fifty classic deadrise boats to accommodate the crabbers, and the only stern that worked well in this fishery was the square stern.

Crabbers needed a longer and wider boat to work two eight-foot dredges from the stern. Boatbuilders widened the boats to fourteen and fifteen feet, but sterns still were not wide enough to accommodate two dredges and room to work, so platforms wider than the sterns were built onto the already widened sterns to accommodate the workspace.

The other ingredient that made the square stern popular was the introduction of the S-shaped horn timber. (See chapter two.) As stated earlier, a reverse curve in the horn timber gives the boat a concave bottom at the stern. The raised stern fairs water into the propeller, giving the vessel more thrust and contributing to smooth cruising by keeping the boat level.

The box stern on the *Ann French* is the preferred style of bay watermen working in Virginia's winter crab and conk dredge fishery. Crab dredgers need a wide square stern to accommodate a platform and two dredges. The stern is made of mahogany and varnished seven to eight times. Watermen build this style stern on their boats to make the stern look pretty. Many of the boats built in the 1980s and '90s have sterns and trim on the boat made of mahogany. Jerry Pruitt of Tangier Island built the *Ann French*.

Before S-horn timbers, square sterns that went from the top deck to the water without the concave bottom in the stern were not as efficient as other bay-built stern variations.

Willard Norris says that the solid-piece horn timber led to the decline of round-stern vessels on the bay. Since the logged and staved round sterns were structurally weaker than the box stern, the raised square-stern vessels resulted in a very efficient style.

This deadrise boat used for crab scraping is called a barcat on Tangier Island. It has a box or square stern. This style of boat evolved from the days of sail and in earlier times would have carried a raked stern with an outside rudder and steering stick mounted to the rudder. When engine power was introduced, the raked stern on these boats had a tendency to squat in the water. Therefore, outboard rudders were replaced with inboard rudders and squat boards had to be mounted to the sterns to help hold the stern up in the water. The broader beam aft that accompanies the square stern on the modern barcat creates buoyancy aft, which eliminates the need for a squat board.

Deadrise and Cross-planked

In 1985, Norris said, "Watermen don't even consider a round-stern boat anymore. But before the solid-piece horn timber, I was building round sterns all the time."

The last phenomena that took place in the evolution of sterns was the introduction of varnished mahogany planks in sterns on bay workboats, a feature normally seen in yachts. The draketail, diamond, tuck, and round sterns were all visually prettier styles of sterns than the standard box stern. Mahogany sterns made the boats pretty again.

Watermen take great pride in their boats. The mahogany stern was a way to reinforce that pride. When watermen look at a deadrise workboat, the first thing they notice is the stern. The sterns on the bay boats have evolved as a result of the sea conditions associated with the Chesapeake and from the methods of harvesting seafood while working in these conditions.

But there's another reason: Watermen just plain like a pretty stern.

four
BAY BOATBUILDERS

Throughout the bay region, isolated waterfront landings, neighborhoods, and towns had either a boatbuilder or someone nearby capable of working on wooden boats. The wooden boatbuilder was as necessary to a Tidewater community in the late nineteenth and early twentieth centuries as the automobile mechanic is today.

The builders profiled in this chapter speak for generations of wooden boatbuilders who, with broadax and adz, shaped the hulls of thousands of bay watercraft.

Since little has been written down, we have no way of knowing how many boatbuilders there have been from the Susquehanna to Cape Henry, but it is a good bet that wherever there was a landing used by commercial fishermen, or another type of water commerce, a wooden boatbuilder was somewhere close by.

William Lomax
Nesting, Virginia

There were many African-American builders on the bay, but most of the evidence of this is through oral history. Large numbers of African-Americans were working in the bay's oyster and finfish fisheries from the late 1800s to the mid-twentieth century, and black boatbuilders were a part of that heritage and culture.

It is well documented that Virginia plantation owners allowed some black slaves to learn carpentry. White planters needed

Right after the Civil War, African-American boatbuilders, like William Lomax, of Nestings, Virginia, built boats for other former slaves. The black boatbuilder played an important role in helping to create economic independence for African-American watermen. A good boat and a willingness to work was all anyone needed to generate income from the bay. (Courtesy of J. D. Davis.)

skilled laborers to maintain the many wooden structures on plantations, and capable slaves often were hired out to others to provide income for the owner. Knowing this, it is logical to assume that if slaves were able to shape plow handles, ox bows, tobacco sticks, corncribs, barns, and houses, they could build boats.

William Lomax was born a slave and became a boatbuilder after slavery ended. The Lomax family was enslaved to Joseph and Lucy Eubank, of Nesting Plantation. Nesting, one of the oldest plantations in America, is located in Middlesex County, Virginia, on the Rappahannock River.

Ancestors of William Dickerson, of Pittsburgh, Pennsylvania, also were slaves at Nesting. Dickerson, who was eighty-one years old in 2006, grew up in the Nesting area. As a small boy in the 1920s, he saw William Lomax building three-and-five log canoes and flat-bottom, cross-planked skiffs on an isolated landing on Parrotts Creek known as Burnt House Landing.

"These little landings were places along creek shores where there was deep enough water for boats to get in close to offload oysters and fish," said Dickerson. "As much as possible, boats were moored behind the safety of a creek bank. As watermen and their boats congregated in an area, waterfront commerce evolved. Mr. Lomax was the main boatbuilder and woodworker for Burnt House Landing and Percifull Landing, which were on the same creek.

"Mr. Lomax built sail-powered canoes for most of the black watermen in the community, and if they couldn't afford a canoe, he would build them a skiff," he said.

"My grandmother, Lucy Crump, was born a slave on Nesting Plantation and was a good seamstress. She was the community sailmaker," he said. "She and one of my cousins made sails for most of the boats built by Mr. Lomax."

Parrotts Creek, near Water View, Virginia, had a large population of black watermen working out of isolated landings toward the headwaters of the creek. These landings are gone now, and forest, vines, and crop fields hide their remains.

After slavery, some white planters encouraged their former slaves to stay close to the farm, in hopes they would stay and work. The planters could pay their former slaves little other than food and a room in the dirt floor shanties the slaves had been living in all along.

The former slaves were well aware that promises were not always kept. The river, however, provided a promise that could. Former slaves willing to work on the river could provide some economic independence for themselves and their families and hope of a better future. They turned to the river for food and money made from harvesting oysters, fish, and crabs.

As commerce expanded and more people turned to the river for their livelihoods, competition for good boats grew. The segregated society that grew and flourished in the post-Civil War era forced many African-Americans boatbuilders to build their boats exclusively for their race.

Creek bank landings where African-Americans congregated and worked were located on the James, York, Rappahannock, and Potomac rivers. The isolation of these landings provided cover for former slaves to work and live as freemen, and to nurture a free enterprise system without race being so much of an issue.

The river was fair. The price offered for a bushel of oysters on any given day was the same for a black man as for a white man. Boatbuilders like Lomax kept the playing field even by offering a stable platform from which these former slaves and their children could work.

It is probably fair to say that many black American boatbuilders, just like Lomax, provided a service to the area in which they lived. Although there is no evidence that Lomax built deadrise boats, he did build skiffs, and it was the next generation of boatbuilders that turned to the cross-planked deadrise style of boat.

Luther James Hackett Amburg, Virginia

Luther Hackett was an African-American log canoe boatbuilder from Amburg, Virginia. Many log canoe builders made the transition from logs to plank construction. Luther is an example of a canoe builder who continued to use his talent as a new era of deadrise boatbuilding evolved. Luther's skills in shaping chunks in round-stern deadrise boats was a talent

Luther Hackett was known for his work with a foot adz. Whenever there was a round chunk stern to be smoothed down, Hackett was the best around with an adz. (Courtesy of Deltaville Maritime Museum.)

needed in Deltaville, Virginia, because chunk round-sterns on boats were much in demand.

Luther learned log canoe building from his father, Samuel Hackett. The Hacketts lived on Cores Creek, off the Pianka-tank River, in an area called Pace's Neck. Luther and Samuel had reputations for building sailing canoes that "sat on the water like a leaf."

When the boatbuilding explosion hit Deltaville in the 1920s, Luther first went to work for Linwood Price, and later for Lee Deagle at Deagle's and Son Marine Railway on Fishing Bay.

Like many builders in that area, Price and Deagle specialized in building and repairing chunk round-stern boats. Luther was a master with the foot adz and could dress down a stern with an adz so smooth it required little sanding.

In the evolution of deadrise construction, chunk-stern construction was a carryback to log canoe building. In log canoe construction, "raising" wood used to create height in the sides, and the log chunks to form the hull were shaped with broadax and adz. The technique used was similar to the way chunk sterns were shaped before electric power tools changed the way boats were built and finished.

The best canoe builders were very efficient with an adz. Of the fifty men working at Deagle's yard, Luther was one of two black men working there and the best of any of the men with an adz.

Ed Deagle, who worked with Luther at his father's yard for many years, said, "Luther wasn't the best carpenter we had, but he was an expert man with an adz and that goes back to what he learned as a young man building log canoes.

"He was a valuable person because we needed his talents when building and repairing chunk sterns," he said. "This was particularly true before electricity came because planes and sanders allowed most anybody to be able to dress the chunks down.

"I can see him now working an adz, just like it was yesterday," said Ed. "It was an art to it and Luther was the best. He would take his right hand and place it on the handle up near the blade. He would place his left hand a little further up the handle. Then he would take the end of the handle and brace in the bend of his right arm. He then braced his elbow against his body.

"Luther would then work the adz up and down, and in no time he would have that stern dressed right down. It was so smooth you did not need to touch it with a piece of sandpaper. He was the best!"

At his home, Luther built and repaired log canoes for friends and neighbors who made their living fishing and oystering. The use of log canoes did not stop right after the deadrise and cross-planked boats became popular. Many old-timers continued to use their motorized canoes into the 1960s. Men like Luther kept these boats repaired and seaworthy.

He was highly respected by blacks and whites in a time when segregation was part of every day life in Virginia. His talent as a canoe builder and his industrious nature were respected throughout the community, but the key to his success was his nature.

"He was old when I knew him—at least he seemed old," said Ed. "Even being old, he was the best we had with an adz. He was also one of the finest men we had on the yard. He was a good, churchgoing man who nobody ever had a bad word to say about."

Captain Perry Rogers
Shady Side, Maryland

Captain Perry Rogers, of Shady Side, Maryland (on the right), was an early deadrise boatbuilder who specialized in building deadrise boat with a tuck stern, which became known as the West River tuck stern. (Courtesy of the Captain Salem Avery House Museum.)

Many around Shady Side, Maryland, believe that Captain Perry Rogers was the father of deadrise construction on the Chesapeake Bay. They believe Rogers developed the V-style deadrise bottom at his boatyard on Parrish Creek, and the style spread from there to the Eastern Shore and throughout the bay.

Certainly Rogers was a forerunner in the design of motor-powered deadrise boats, and his style is as unique as any on the bay. He was building boats right at the beginning of the introduction of power. His boats feature some unique elements on early deadrise boats that were eventually eliminated as construction evolved on the bay.

Around the turn of the century, Rogers's boatyard was a busy place. His brothers, Frank and Oliver Rogers, and his nephews, Porter, Benjamin, Leonard, and Clarence Rogers, all worked at the yard.

Perry's son Elliott said in a 1986 interview that his father started building motor-powered deadrise boats around 1903, when automobiles started coming into use.

"The deadrise boat familiar to the West River country for over fifty years was designed by my father and it was later copied by Eastern Shore builders," he said.

"When my father started building frame boats, most watermen on the West River were using log canoes that were heavy, lumbering affairs. They were sail propelled and when there was no wind the operators had to fall back on oars.

"My father saw a future in gasoline engines," said Elliott. "He bought an early engine and tried to fit it into a canoe, but it wouldn't work good. He realized that the boat was too heavy for the power plant, so he went about fashioning a lighter craft.

"He bought fir from North Carolina for the hull and used standing poplar for the keel. While he was felling a poplar tree it crashed on him and broke his leg.

"While in convalescence, he continued to work on plans for his boat and it was during this time that he designed his first deadrise boat," said Elliott.

"The canoes then in use had flat-bottoms, which, of course, provided the maximum resistance to propulsion. The sides came straight down flush with the keel, which was below the water line.

"My father worked to design a bottom that would cut through the water instead of dragging, which would work much better for engines.

"He hit on the idea of a V-type bottom fitted into the super-structure of the boat. This vee swept back from the bow, which is known now as streamlining. He added a flat stern, which would give the boat more stability. The cabin was then fitted and the engine installed."

In 1904, Captain Rogers built his first deadrise boat named *Princess,* which was discussed in the chapter three. The construction of deadrise motorized deck boats or buyboats started between 1900 and 1910, as gasoline engines became popular. His 1904 model was a fairly early style boat.

However, it should be noted that by 1904 builders throughout the region were constructing buyboat-style boats, with the house aft and decks installed everywhere except over the hold. They also were building variations of deadrise hulls and cross-planking bottoms. Fred Ward, of Urbanna, Virginia, built the buyboat *Crescent* in 1904, and certainly many other builders were experimenting.

The *Crescent* actually had the house up on deck, while the Rogers's house on the *Princess* sat on the ceiling. Ward's variation was closer to the modern buyboat style than Rogers's.

This is not taking anything away from Perry Rogers. When he started building the experiment with V-hull boats on the Chesapeake was just beginning, and he was a major pioneer in deadrise construction on Maryland's Western Shore.

In late winter of 1930, Captain Rogers told a reporter for the *Washington Evening Star* that the *Princess* had outlasted four engines and was equipped with its fifth. The original poplar keel was replaced, but the rest of the boat had not changed.

As time passed, Captain Rogers built his boats with Oregon pine for the keel and sides, oak ribs, and cypress bottoms. The *Princess* was forty-feet long with an eight-foot beam. His later boats were forty-five and forty-nine-feet long.

Most of Captain Rogers's deadrise boats had what came to be known as West River Tuck Sterns built into his boats. (See chapter three on sterns on deadrise boats.)

Elliott said he never used a blueprint and always used hand tools. "The pattern was always the same. First the hull was put together, then the keel was fitted, and finally the cabin and engine installed."

In a 1986 oral interview, conducted by a member of Captain Salem Avery House Museum in Shady Side, Maryland, Howard Shenton talked about Captain Rogers and his boats.

"Captain Rogers built the *Princess* in 1904," Shenton said. "She is what we call a deadrise boat. That means she's got a V-bottom and is frame built.

"She was approximately forty-feet long. The reason they built the boats that length is because of the length of the seas that usually run in Chesapeake Bay.

"Out in the bay, when the wind is blowing fifteen knots or more, the seas run in a series of three. The first sea is smaller than the other two as they build up. The third sea is higher than the others. They built the boats so they ride the three seas more comfortably and have more stability," said Shenton.

Shenton believes that the *Princess* was named for Rogers's daughter, Amy Rogers Leatherbury. She was born in 1904, the same year the boat was built.

Captain Lawson (Lawes) Tyler

If we were to consider the greatest boatbuilding generation as it pertains to deadrise and cross-planked motorized boats on the Chesapeake, it would have to be those builders who were born in the decades after the Civil War.

Deadrise and Cross-planked

The 1870s to 1900s were transitional years, as builders born in that period struggled with how to make the combustible engine effective enough to replace sail. They had to refigure the hull configuration to accommodate the motor, shafts, propellers, and rudder. Yet they still wanted to retain the seakeeping ability of the sailing hulls that worked so well on the bay. They also had to shift from log canoe building to deadrise construction, which was an entirely different technique.

As previously stated, Chapelle and other maritime historians believe that deadrise, cross-planked bottoms on boats evolved from V-bottom crabbing skiffs on the Eastern Shore. At turn of the twentieth century, many bay boatbuilders experimented with different construction techniques.

It was not unusual for a builder, such as Ladd Wright, of Deltaville, to experiment with cross- and longitudinal-bottom planking in an attempt to find the best style of boat for his customers. His first deck boat, the fifty-five-foot *C. E. Wright,* was fore and aft planked, whereas everything he built in later years had cross-planked bottoms.

Lepron Johnson, of Crittenden, Virginia, was noted for his longitudinally planked buyboats. His boats were mistakenly referred to as Carolina Boats, as many long-time bay watermen thought they were built in North Carolina.

Johnson built the *Chesapeake,* the second-largest buyboat ever built. It had a round bilge and was planked fore and aft, yet Johnson built numerous small deadrise hulls with cross-planked bottoms.

Potomac River dories were known for their fore-and-aft bottoms, yet Francis Haynie, of Northumberland County, Virginia, was capable of building a dory or classic cross-planked deadrise.

Born in 1882, on Smith Island, Maryland, Captain Lawes Tyler was one of those builders who could go either way. He could build a classic deadrise cross-planked crab scraping boat, called a barcat on Tangier Island, or a longitudinally planked Smith Island speedboat.

The late Edmond Harrison had Captain Lawes build him a classic cross-planked crab scrape boat. In a 1989 interview at his home on the island he talked about his boat and Captain Lawes.

"Captain Lawes built me the *Margaret H.* and he was one of the nicest fellows who ever lived," he said. "He built mine and he built my brother's too."

The *Margaret H.,* named after Captain Harrison's youngest daughter, is a classic crab scraping boat with low sides,

Captain Lawse Tyler, of Smith Island, Maryland, built this classic barcat for Edmond Harrison in the late 1950s. This style of deadrise and cross-planked boat generally is used to scrape for peeler and soft-shell crabs in Tangier Sound. It was also used in the days of sail, which makes it a very early Chesapeake Bay deadrise style. On Tangier Island these boats are called barcats. Smith Island watermen refer to the boats as scrape boats.

shallow draft and a cross-planked, deadrise bottom. Measuring twenty-eight feet by ten feet by one-and-a-half feet, she is the second crab scraping boat he has owned.

His first, powered by sail, was built in Norfolk. "The first one I got cost me $330, and that was for sail, mast, boat, and I even got the scrapes for that. Didn't have no [engine] power when I got my first one. I never would have gotten rid of her, but she got some bad wood in her and Captain Lawes told me, 'Time I build you a new one.'"

Captain Lawes was noted for building classic crab scrape boats, but he also specialized in constructing extremely fast Smith Island speedboats.

The Smith Island speedboat was built to accommodate the growing soft-shell crab fishery around the turn of the twentieth century. The skiff is narrow and fore and aft planked for speed. Boatbuilders throughout the bay region admit that longitudinally planked boats normally can generate more speed than cross-planked boats because more friction is created on the bottom from the many cross-planked seams.

Soft-crab fishermen who worked the grassy shoal waters of Tangier Sound used these skiffs. They needed a small, speedy boat to get to and from the fishing grounds.

Right after the 1933 August Storm that flooded Smith and Tangier Islands, many islanders moved to the higher ground of the Western and Eastern Shores of Maryland and Virginia. Tangiermen loaded their thirty-two- to thirty-eight-foot boats with furniture, food, and family. What they could not get into the big boats they loaded into skiffs that they towed. Some families had as many as six skiffs loaded down with everything they had in the world.

Interestingly, this is how several Smith Island speedboats, Hoopers Island drake-tails, Eastern Shore gunning skiffs, and other styles of boats built in isolated locations around the Chesapeake spread throughout the bay region.

Several of Captain Lawes speedboats found their way to Urbanna, Virginia, right after the 1933 storm. Ed Payne was born on Tangier Island and moved to Urbanna with his mother and father after the August Storm. "When we came from Tangier, we had a sharp-ended skiff, a gunning skiff, and a little rowboat. Saul Dize and Elmer Shores brought a Smith Island Speedboat with them. Captain Lawes built Saul's. She was about twenty-feet long and about four-feet wide with a live box in the middle of the boat for storing soft-crabs. They were fast for the day and she had a big bow for standing on. They were built for poling around the grass catching soft-crabs," said Ed.

"The bottom planks ran stem to stern and she was pretty much flat-bottom. There was a little vee in the bow."

A Tangier Island bootlegger named Willie used one of Captain Lawes's speedboats to transport whiskey from Crisfield to Tangier Island. William (Bill) Pruitt, former commissioner of Virginia Marine Resources Commission, was born on Tangier and he recalls how it was done.

"Those skiffs made good little bootlegging boats and they were fast. On a calm day, Willie could go to Crisfield in thirty-five minutes.

"Tangier Island was a dry island and had strict Methodist rules when it came to alcohol," Pruitt recalls. "Willie would go to Crisfield in the skiff and get whiskey in half-pints. It was all store bought. Well, the Smith Island speedboat has a long deck over the bow and a seat with sides that went down to the floorboard of the skiff.

"Willie took crab pot rubbers, the kind used to keep the opening closed on the pot, and installed them under the bow and seat. He stretched them tight, nailed each end. The rubber would hold it tight so it wouldn't break in rough water. He had a board that he slid under the bow deck that covered the whiskey. It looked like it was just part of the boat.

"The seat was midway in the boat and he did the same thing under that. He could get under the seat from one side by pulling up the side and then he would nail it down and it looked normal.

"The town cop, who was the mayor of Tangier, would try to catch him. He would go on that boat and look in the baskets and under the oilskins and he never did figure out how Willie was hiding that whiskey.

"Finally, the church people came down hard on Willie and forced the mayor to do something," said Pruitt. "Willie never sold to a minor and you had to be right for him to sell to. He was real careful.

"The mayor was forced to do something. Even though he never found any whiskey, he charged Willie and took him to court and found him guilty. In those days, the mayor could hold court himself.

"'Willie, you owe the court $25 and if we catch you again it will be more,' the mayor said.

"They say the mayor paid his fine," laughed Pruitt.

Another time one of Willie's customers got caught and went before Willie Cook Crockett, who was mayor then. Mr. Cook, as everyone called him, was tough on drinking. Mr. Cook asked the man if he had taken a drink.

"I just took one, Mr. Cook."

"He pounded the table and yelled, 'One drink drunk! Pay $25. Next one come on up here'," he said.

J. Bailey Cornelius
Poet Laureate of Bay Boatbuilders

Jim Cornelius was a Deltaville boatbuilder and a poet. (Courtesy of Edna Shackelford.)

"Give me a trial and save money. I will treat you square," is the handwritten advertisement on an old post-card advertising Jim Cornelius's boats and motors.

James (Jim) Bailey Cornelius was born on Jackson Creek in Deltaville, Virginia, on March 22, 1862. He and his father, Bezelle, known as "Bez," were wooden boatbuilders in that area.

It is unknown whether Jim built in today's modern cross-planked deadrise style, but it is known that he was not a log canoe builder, as shown in the photo of his boat on the postcard.

Deltaville lore has Bez and a man named Ike Thomas as the men who brought the modern style of boatbuilding to Deltaville, and perhaps Jim learned the trade from his father.

In an 1880 United States census, Bez is listed as fifty-one years old and his occupation as waterman/farmer, with no mention of boatbuilding. However, being a waterman could have easily meant that he built boats too.

Jim owned a small railway next to Jackson Creek public dock. He was there from the late 1800s to around 1917. Lee Deagle purchased it from him in the mid-1920s and ran a railway business there, specializing in repairing and installing engines. Deagle was there until he bought a much larger railway on Fishing Bay in 1935.

This handwritten postcard with a photo was used as an advertisement by Jim Cornelius to sell his boats and motors. Cornelius later moved to Baltimore and published an anthology of poetry in 1920. His father Bezelle, known as Bez, first introduced fore-and-aft plank boatbuilding to the Deltaville area. He and Ike Thomas are considered the fathers of boatbuilding in that area. (Courtesy of Selden Richardson.)

Jim Cornelius moved to Baltimore and was working in a shipyard when he published an anthology of poetry in 1920 entitled, *Spare Moments*. The price of his anthology was sixty cents. Edna Deagle Shackelford, ninety years old in 2006, said she found a copy of the poems in her mother's things shortly after her death.

Edna, who was born in 1916, said she never knew Jim Cornelius because he was gone by the time she could remember much, but her mother and father were good friends with Jim and his wife Ida.

"They lived right across the road from us," she said. "I remember mother talking about Jim's wife.

"She said Ida was one of the most meticulous women around. When you went there, she always had linen tablecloths and everything was just right.

"Mamma told me this story. He had the railway and he had a black man working for him. One day, Mrs. Cornelius called for her husband to come and get lunch. Well, Jim invited the black man to come and eat. Back in those days it was unheard of for a black man to come inside and eat with whites."

This little story speaks to the fact Cornelius and his wife were far advanced in their attitude towards race and that Jim Cornelius was a thinking man. His poems tell us little about his boatbuilding skills, but speak volumes on his thoughts on life. The anthology contains seventy-five poems, which address everything from booze to women's suffrage. Here are two from the book.

Molly Coddled

I remember well, when a boy
    My father, used to say
Don't you smoke, play ball or fight
    When you go out today;
Take off your hat and stay behind,
    And be polite as you can.
Don't run up and butt right in,
    But act just like a man.
Don't try to learn what others do.
    Don't take hold until told.
Don't hang around too close
    Nor act so very bold.
Don't catch a hold, first think, my son,
    First let others try their hand.
Be polite, keep out of sight
    And act just like a man.
Do things after others have,
    And follow a good man's way;
Keep mum, don't ask no quiz,
    It will help you all your days.
Don't never preach up nothing new
    As you travel through the land,
But keep in mind what others do.
    And act just like a man.

Don't never stay out late at night

    Nor touch old rock and rye,

Don't look at things unsightly, lad,

    Nor ask what for and why.

I tried to observe this all my life.

    And looked at things quite blind;

No doubt it's kept me out of strife,

    But I ride sti'l in the coach behind.

Home Ties

Here's to the shores of Jackson Creek,

    Where I first saw light of day,

With its bright and sparkling waters

    That unites it with the bay,

Where we hear the seagull screaming,

    And the waves roar, ring with mirth,

I wonder could I give it up

    For another spot on earth.

Where we see the white winged vessels

    Darting, glancing—a pretty sight;

The white and shining beaches

    Stand out boldly to left and right,

And the broad Chesapeake that wash them

    With its pale green waters and surf,

It would break my heart to exchange it

    For another spot on earth.

Here's where friends and kindred,

    And the wild fowl come and go;

I take my summer evening's rest

    Where the cool southeaster blows;

With sand diamond studded beaches,

    And the breakers dance with mirth,

Shall I ever have to leave it

For another spot on earth?

    Oh, for a thousand years right here,

With friends that come and go,

    And view the sunbeam sparkles

On the tide that ebbs and flows,

    And hear the gladsome laughter

Mingled with the roaring surf;

    Lord, I pray thee let me live,

My last day, here, on earth.

Lewis G. Wright
Boatbuilder / Artist

Lewis Wright was the son of Tom Wright, one of the early pioneers in Deltaville deadrise and cross-planked construction. Lewis probably built as many boats as anyone in Deltaville, and as a sideline he was an artist. Here he is in a 1984 photo at his home on Jackson Creek, standing beside his favorite painting that he did of President Dwight Eisenhower with a Stetson hat and a horse.

When Lewis Wright built his first boat, Woodrow Wilson was president of the United States and America had not yet entered World War I. The first L. G. Wright-built boat left Deltaville in 1916, on his uncle's sailing schooner *Esther A. Waters*, bound for Baltimore.

The fourteen-year-old boatbuilder collected $20 for the flat-bottom, sixteen-foot skiff and started a career in bay boatbuilding that spanned a half-century.

Lewis grew up on Lover's Lane in Deltaville, the son of boatbuilder Tom Wright. Tom was brother to John, Ladd, and Tollie Wright. Tom, John, and Ladd were early bateaux builders in Deltaville.

As a boy, Lewis got his feet wet early in the boatbuilding trade, as backyard boatbuilding was just beginning to become a major part of the area economy.

In an interview in 1982, Lewis said, "When I built my first skiff things were some kind of tight. My daddy was building houses around and he was making $1.25 a day. So, you see, when I got $20, I thought I was something.

"Before I got old, I built mostly thirty-six- and thirty-eight-foot round-stern boats," he said. "I just about filled the Potomac River up with them. I like an old round-stern boat. It's mighty pretty, but it's a lot of work getting that stern in, and that's why the boys put the square stern on today."

The term Jackson Creek Round Stern was used up and down the bay, and many of those round-stern early bateaux came from the Wright's on Jackson Creek.

Wright built a traditional chunk round stern and he worked with his father and uncle, John Wright, for many years. They built boats on the banks of Jackson Creek.

After Lewis's father and uncle died, he continued to build boats until 1986 on his own, in a cinderblock boatshed on Jackson Creek, not far from where he learned.

Among the vessels Lewis recalled as watermark boats that he was involved in building were the *City of Crisfield*, *Thelma Earl*, and the *Tilly*.

The *City of Crisfield* was a 59' 4" x 16' 6" x 5' Chesapeake Bay buyboat, completed in 1923. John and Tom were listed as the builders, and Lewis helped them. She was renamed the *Etta Marie* in 1931, and was last documented in 1972.

The *Thelma Earl* was completed in 1924 and the vessel's documentation lists Tom and Lewis Wright as the builders. The buyboat measured 47.1' x 12.3' x 4.3'.

Wright was very proud of the *Tilly* for her speed. She was a classic bay round-stern boat, built for a waterman who lived on Carter Creek. Three years in a row, he won a workboat race with the *Tilley*.

"I built one the same size as the *Tilly* for Calvin Barrick of Irvington, and he put the same size motor in her. She took the cup away from the *Tilly*," said Wright with a laugh. "I built a fast boat."

Wright was eighty years old when he was interviewed in 1982. He had a flat-bottom and a deadrise skiff in his shop nearly completed. Between them was a blunted bow, scow-type skiff that was already sold. The scow was the first he had built.

The skiff rested on blocks and poles worn from previous boats in the same positions. The old blocks were covered in white and copper paint, matching the spots dotting Wright's pants. Boards were stacked neatly on the sawdust-heaped floor, awaiting Wright's next endeavor. A saw leaned against a sawhorse and the rest of his tools were strewn around the shop in an order known only to their owner.

Three corners of the shop were in apparent disarray with sawdust, several old broken blocks and tackles, and wood chips piled high. At the top of one pile was an unfinished canvas painting with sky and water apparent. An old buyboat was pictured moored in the channel. Dust covered the painting.

"I've always liked to paint pictures, but there isn't any money in it," said Wright, although he has had some success in the field. "I did right many paintings of old Stingray Point Lighthouse."

One of his paintings of the lighthouse hangs in the Deltaville Maritime Museum, and many homes in Deltaville have his paintings on the wall. In 1966, Nimcock Gallery opened in Urbanna, Virginia, and sold Wright's paintings, which were very popular.

Longtime Deltaville boatbuilder Hugh Norris, a competitor of Wright, never owned a Wright-built boat, but he had the Stingray Point Lighthouse painting by Lewis on his living-room wall.

Inside Wright's shop were several other unfinished paintings of water scenes scattered around and many finished paintings hung on the walls.

"Now this one is my favorite," he said, pointing to a picture hanging on the wall inside his home of President Dwight Eisenhower with a Stetson hat and a horse.

When asked if he would rather have been a full-time boatbuilder or a full-time artist, he answered, "I love to do both."

Wright died in the 1990s and his home and boat shop were torn down to make way for a waterfront home. The boatbuilding era of the Wright family spanned nearly a hundred years on Lovers Lane in Deltaville. Lewis's death marked the end of that era.

Grover Lee Owens
Deltaville, Virginia

Classic Owens forty-two- and forty-five-foot wooden workboats are considered to be some of the most polished and well-built boats on the Chesapeake Bay.

Grover Lee Owens was born in Mathews County, Virginia, and first got the notion that he might be able to build a boat in 1960. "I can tell you exactly when I thought about

Grover Lee Owens is a Deltaville boatbuilder respected up and down the bay.

becoming a boatbuilder," he said in June 2006, while working on a wooden round-stern boat in the boatyard of Norview Marina in Deltaville.

"I had a good chance then to get into this right. My first wife and I had just separated and I was up at Joe Davis's beer joint drinking a beer when Captain Alton [Smith] came in and sat right down next to me and asked me if I wanted to work at his boatyard," he said.

In 1960, Alton Smith, a renowned bay boatbuilder, was just seven years from retiring. There was a world of knowledge there for Grover Lee to learn from.

Alton's grandfather, Peter Smith, was a boatbuilder and most noted for building the logged bugeye *White Wing* in 1896. Peter's father had built log boats in Poquoson. Alton's father, Lennie, learned the trade from Peter, and Alton learned boatbuilding from Lennie.

"If I'd had any sense I would have gone to work for Captain Alton," said Grover Lee. "It was not a good time in my life, with just being separated from my wife, and for whatever reason, I didn't do it."

Grover Lee had a reputation as a good house builder, but he also was known for his cabinetry. "I don't know why Captain Alton came to me. I guess he knew I was a good woodworker on houses and thought I'd do good."

The offer planted a seed in Grover Lee that blossomed a few years later. "In 1963, I remarried and moved to Del-taville. Over here everybody was building boats in their backyard," he said.

"I remembered that Captain Alton thought I could build boats, so I decided I was going to build one for myself. I went down to Captain Earl Weston's. He built boats and he had a boatshed he wasn't using. So, I started a thirty-eight-footer. I didn't know how it was supposed to go, but Captain Earl showed me a few things. He chopped her down for me. I faired her down, put the bottom on her, flipped her over, and went on and put raisin (sideboards) on her.

"I kept her for a while, but I soon decided I'd sell her. I was still house carpentering when a fellow from Tangier Island came by the house and asked if he could take her to island to sell her for me. He called back that night and said she was sold.

"I decided then that I'd build a boatshed at my house," he said. "I'd given anything in the world now if I had gone to work for Captain Alton. Lord knows, I could have picked up so much information.

"Alton Smith was just about the greatest man that's ever built a boat," he said. "When I would get in a jam and couldn't figure something out, I'd go to him. He would explain it to you so easy, that you would think you'd gotten it out of a book. When I had a question, he never failed to give me an answer."

Grover Lee had a knack for building boats, and by 1980 he was providing the majority of the wooden hulls for the Tangier Island fishing fleet. He was building four to five boats annually in the forty-two-foot range.

A typical vessel was one he launched in 1981 for Strickland Crockett of Tangier Island. The forty-one footer was 10 1/2' wide at the stern and 12 1/2' wide at amidships. She was powered by a 4-53 Detroit Diesel engine, working through a 2:1 Warner gear to turn a three-bladed, 26" x 16" Columbian Bronze propeller.

Grover Lee's experience as a cabinetmaker certainly contributed to the polished look he put into a finished boat. The stern on Crockett's vessel, the door on the house, the door trim and the wood around the windows were all made of mahogany and finished with clear varnish. The rest of the boat was painted with Z-spar white paint, except for the bright-finished toe rail and back of the house, which were made from fir and tongue-and-groove pine.

The construction of the boat was pretty much standard, but Grover Lee incorporated two methods of construction that evolved from years of trial and error by boatbuilders around the bay. He used a solid-piece horn timber in the stern and a method of creating a finished look in the sides called step planking. (See chapter two.)

By the time Grover Lee got into the boatbuilding business, the methods of construction had evolved to its finest level and he became a master of the craft. Owners of Grover Lee Owens boats anywhere on the Chesapeake Bay often remark, with great pride, "Grover Lee built her and he builds the prettiest damn boat on the bay."

Jerry Pruitt
Tangier Island, Virginia

Boatbuilder Jerry Pruitt is the third generation of his family to build boats on Tangier Island. His boatbuilding heritage goes back to the 1880s, when early V-bottom crab skiffs were first being built on the Chesapeake.

Deadrise and Cross-planked

Jerry Pruitt is a third-generation Tangier Island boatbuilder, whose great-grand-father was building deadrise crab skiffs before the turn of the twentieth century. Raymond Thomas Pruitt could have been one of the first deadrise boatbuilders on the Chesapeake. It is believed the deadrise and cross-planked style started here in the 1880s.

Tangier Island lies in Virginia waters, midway between the Western Shore of the Virginia mainland and the Eastern Shore, and about ten miles from the Maryland-Virginia state line. Commercial fishing is the main occupation of watermen on the island, and boatbuilding is a tradition that goes back to the early settlement of Tangier in the 1700s.

Before the turn of the twentieth century, Pruitt's great-grandfather, Raymond Thomas Pruitt, built speedy sixteen-to twenty-foot V-bottom sail-powered barcats for watermen crabbing Tangier Sound.

"When I was a boy, I remember my grandfather and father talking about it, and I recall when there were a few of my great-grandfather's skiffs still around," said Pruitt. "His boats were V-bottom, but unlike the way I build boats, his had length-ways [longitudinal] bottom planking, and they were real speedy in their day. They had a catboat sail rig."

Perhaps Raymond's style V-bottom skiff resembled that New Haven sharpie Chapelle saw on Tangier in the 1950s and

mentioned in his book *American Small Sailing Craft*. It gives further credibility to Chapelle's theory that V-bottom construction on the bay came from up north.

As a boy, Jerry received his first schooling in the trade from his grandfather, Willie Frank Pruitt, who built flat-bottom and deadrise skiffs on Tangier.

"He showed me how to make the bends, and after a while I just picked it up from him," said Jerry.

Jerry also learned techniques in building from Leon Marsh, a renowned barcat builder on Smith Island, Maryland. "He is a very kind man," said Jerry, "and years back, he and his father, Lawrence, were well known for their barcats. Leon and his son Larry are just as good. They are as good builders as any on the Chesapeake."

The *Inez* was built by Jerry Pruitt, of Tangier Island, and named after his wife. Jerry is one of the last traditional wooden boatbuilders on the island.

Leon gave Jerry tips on building the classic Smith Island crab scraping boat. At his boatyard on Tangier, Jerry has built twenty-eight- to thirty-four-foot barcats, standard forty-two to forty-five-foot deadrise workboats and skiffs of all sizes. Traditionally, Jerry builds a couple boats a year and does an extensive amount of repair work to the aging wooden boat fleet on the island. A boat is as important to an islander as a car is to mainlanders.

As the seafood business has declined in the bay region, so has the demand for new boat construction. In 2002, Jerry received no orders for new boats, so he built the *Inez*, a thirty-four-foot deadrise named after his wife and owned by Jerry, but fished by a Tangier Island waterman. This is a tradition on the bay that goes back to the days of sail-powered schooners, where a third party owns the boat and the profits are split between owner, captain, and crew. After expenses, the cut is 60 percent to the watermen and 40 percent to the owner.

"It cost so much to build a new boat now that many of the boys just can't afford one," said Jerry. "This is an option that works well for them and allows me to keep building."

The island has provided a challenge for Jerry as a boatbuilder and he admits it is a "one-handed place" to build boats.

"In Deltaville, they used to have sawmills right down the road that would deliver a forty-five-foot long keel log right to their door or a tractor tailor would deliver it from Baltimore," he said. "We have to get it to Reedville or Crisfield and float it across by dragging it behind a boat. I've gotten a lot of my plank lumber from Snow Hill, Maryland. They put it on a truck, carry it to Crisfield, where it is loaded by hand onto a boat, and then we have to unload it by hand when it gets here. The only way anything comes or goes is by water. If we are out of something and it's not on the island, we've got to get in a boat and go get it."

Even though it is a lot of work, Jerry longs for the days when customers were standing in line for his wooden boats. "Now so many of the boys are going to fiberglass boats," he said. "Give me the wood—but the wood boat is dying. My great-grandfather saw the beginning of the wooden deadrise on the bay and it looks like I just might see the end of it."

Molly "Crab" Weston
A Boatbuilder's Wife

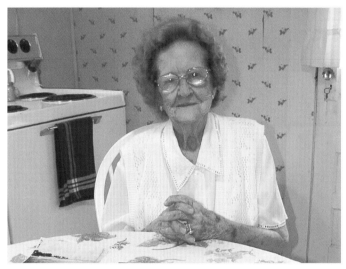

Molly "Crab" Weston was wife to Deltaville boatbuilder Johnny "Crab" Weston. She once had to build a boat because her husband had cut his hand so he could not work. "He helped me set it all up . . . and I nailed it together," she said.

The role of the wife and daughter in a boatbuilding family cannot be overlooked. Molly (Jackson) Weston was born in 1909, in Amburg, Virginia. She was the wife of Johnny W. Weston, of Deltaville, a backyard boatbuilder. In her youth, she often worked right alongside her husband.

Johnny W., also known as "Johnny Crab," and Johnny C. Weston, known as "Big Johnny," moved from Westmoreland County, Virginia, to Deltaville and learned the boatbuilding craft from boatbuilder John Wright.

Molly and Johnny first met in 1924 at the Deltaville skating rink. Johnny was nineteen years old and had recently moved to Deltaville. Molly was fifteen, and after a short courtship they married.

The couple settled in a house not far from where John Wright was building boats. Big Johnny and Johnny Crab got jobs as boatwrights at the yard and learned how to build V-bottom, cross-planked boats from the master builder.

Once Johnny Crab and Molly married, she was nicknamed "Molly Crab" after her husband who had gotten the name, "Johnny Crab," for being such a skilled crabber. Many attributed his success to the crab pots Molly made for him.

Molly also made pots to sell. In a 2003 interview at her home in Deltaville, she said, "There was a man in the neighborhood that always got me to make crab pots. He would call me 'Molly gal' and say, 'Molly gal, I want you to make me some crab patches [pots], just like Johnny Crab's. Johnny Crab can catch more crabs than anyone in the county and it's got to be those crab patches you make.' I made and sold 'em for thirty-five cents a pot," she said.

"Johnny would get up at 4:00 a.m. to go work the water and I'd get up and fix him breakfast. I cooked three meals a day, and a bag of flour wouldn't last a week. We always had a cow. Just about everyone in Deltaville had a cow. My son Herman said there were two things he never wanted around the house—a wood cook stove and a cow.

"I made my own butter out of cream and used the clabber in my bread and would also eat the clabber with sugar on top," she said. "We raised three hogs a year and Johnny wouldn't kill them. He had too soft a heart. We'd have to get someone to come in and kill the hogs. We had one grow to six hundred pounds and we used everything but the oink. We always had country ham and thick bacon around the house.

"I had a chicken house and we had our own eggs. I'd kill chickens most every week. We ate a lot of chicken," she said.

"I'd work all day and into the night and wouldn't stop until I got my work done and Johnny would say, 'You better slow down because you are going to wake up dead one day.' I told him, 'If I was dead I wouldn't wake up,'" Molly said with a laugh.

Once Johnny Crab had mastered building boats, he constructed a boatbuilding shed in his backyard and started building deadrise boats. It was not unusual to see Molly out there with a hammer, fastening nails.

"Johnny cut his hand bad one time and he had a boat order and told me he was going to have to let it go. I told him we can't do that, we need the money too bad, so I got out there and, with his help, I built the boat.

"He helped me set it all up—that's the hard part—and I nailed it together," she said. "I started out helping Johnny by passing him lumber and nails. I'd pick up a big heavy plank and rest it on my stomach and then pass it over to him.

"I don't guess you can say I was a boatbuilder, but I know where every piece of a deadrise boat goes," she said. "Johnny built a lot of boats, but between boats he worked the water in his own boat. Dredged crabs in the winter in Captain Johnny Ward's boat, and when things really got tight, he'd work at Lee Deagle's railway for fifteen cents an hour.

"It took doing a lot of things to keep us going," she said. "I stayed home and did what it took there so Johnny could make us a living."

Cathy (Winegar) Davenport
Railway Owner

Cathy Davenport owns and operates Winegar's Marine Railway and Dymer Creek Seafood with her husband, Ray, and son, Bill. In 1982, Cathy's father, Joseph David Winegar, died and she suddenly inherited one of the oldest railways on the Northern Neck.

Winegar's Railway in Ocran, Virginia, was started in 1911 by Cathy's grandfather, John Joseph Winegar. Shortly after

Cathy Davenport took over her father's railway and boatbuilding business when he passed away in 1982. She still operates the business her grandfather started in 1911. The windlass in the foreground was hand and mule operated to haul boats when Cathy's grandfather ran the business. She uses a 1929 Model A Ford engine to haul boats at the railway.

the Civil War, her great-grandfather and four other Winegar brothers moved to Virginia from New Jersey. Many northerners came down after the war with greenbacks and were able to purchase large tracts of land. The Winegars purchased several hundred acres on Dymer Creek.

The five brothers, artisans of German descent, built a large barn on the property and opened a wheelwright, blacksmith, and carpenter shop.

The enterprise eventually led the next generation to building a railway for maintenance and boatbuilding. Her grandfather ran the business until 1939, when he died. Her father took it over and ran it until his death.

When Cathy's father died, she had no idea she would take over the business. The day of her father's funeral, the family went down to the creek and spread his ashes and several roses just out from the railway. Wind and current pushed the ashes and rose petals out towards the bay, as the family gathered and mourned along the shore.

The next day Cathy walked down to the railway alone. She paused to watch the first swan of the year alight onto the creek, and then she noticed one of the rosebuds had returned. It was floating just inside the cradle of the railway.

"I guess I took that as an omen, because here I am running my father's railway," she said.

Winegar's Railway is a living museum that shows the typical layout of how small railways grew along many creek banks on the Chesapeake. Although no longer in operation, a horse-drawn or hand-operated windlass used to haul boats is still where Cathy's father left it.

"I remember daddy talking about when his aunts would come down and turn the windlass to haul the boats," she said. "You see, most of the boats were small sailing bugeyes. They weren't big and heavy like boats with engines today.

"After the windlass, we got a one-cylinder make-and-break Lathrop and hooked it up to a belt system to haul the boats, and then we went to the four-cylinder Model A Ford engine. Believe it or not, we are still using the Model A engine."

When Cathy's father ran the business, the spring and warm weather months were set aside for railway work, but in the winter her father was always building a flat-bottom or deadrise skiff in the boatbuilding shed. Cathy remembers the shed wasn't very tight, and when it would snow she and her brother, Joe, would have to sweep snow off the unfinished boat.

Most railways, large and small, used their time in the winter to build a boat to sell in the spring. This helped to carry the workers through the winter when they did not have much work on the rails. If the boat was finished before spring, the Winegars used it to harvest oysters, and then sold it when a buyer came along.

"The old-time railway men are just about gone," said Cathy "There are very few good boat carpenters out there anymore. There is a house carpenter and a boat carpenter, and it is not the same thing. It is absolutely different. The mindset is different. With a house you are looking for squares. Nothing is square on a boat. You are looking at multi-curves and multi-bevels. You can't just say you are going to cut that piece of side out. You've got to cut a bevel here, here, and here."

David Winegar was typical of boatbuilders of that day, in that he had his own way of doing things. "One time, somebody wanted him to build a wheelhouse on a boat, and he proceeded to tell daddy the type he wanted.

"Daddy paused and then said, 'I ain't building no damn Guinea Neck wheelhouse on any boat. I'll build it my way and if you don't like it, build it yourself.'"

On any given day at Winegar's, Cathy can be found replacing a board on the bottom of a deadrise or refinishing a mahogany stern on a workboat. She turned out to be a good steward of her family's legacy.

Edward Diggs
Mathews County, Virginia

Mathews County is steeped in boatbuilding heritage and was a key area on the Chesapeake to contribute to the spread of deadrise construction throughout the bay region. Boatbuilders in communities such as Laban, Susan, and Peary in Mathews County probably turned out as many deadrise, cross-planked boats as any other area on the bay.

Part of the reason for the rise in Mathews County's role in building deadrise boats goes back to its heritage as a boatbuilding region. In the later part of the eighteenth century, at least three shipyards in the county were turning out large and small sailing craft. As early as 1835, one hundred vessels were built annually, from large ships to the smallest craft. By the time deadrise and cross-plank construction started on the bay in the 1880s, a boatbuilding infrastructure was well established in Mathews County.

Edward Diggs grew up among boatbuilders. He started as a boy, blowing sawdust off his father's saw mark. When he was sixteen, he went to work for his father, Edgar Diggs, and his father's partner, Ned Hudgins. Edgar and Ned had learned the craft under the tutelage of Ned's father, Theopholis Hudgins,

Edward Diggs (on left) stands by renowned Mathews County boatbuilder Alton Smith. Diggs grew up in the boatbuilding business and learned the trade from his father and uncle, Edgar Diggs and Ned Hudgins. Edward also worked for Alton Smith for many years. He received the supreme compliment when Smith said in a 1991 interview, "I don't know anyone who can build a boat as good as Edward Diggs." This came from a man whose father, Lennie, started building boats right at the beginning of the deadrise and cross-planked era, and who probably knew more boatbuilders than anyone alive at the time.

nicknamed Oph. When Oph got too old to build, Edgar and Ned teamed up and started building deadrise workboats for watermen in Edgar's backyard near Peary, Virginia.

"I started with my dad and Uncle Ned," said Edward. "I called him Uncle Ned because he was like an uncle to me, but he was not my real uncle. They built boats, but they also built houses in those days. That was in the 1930s, when you did whatever you could to make a dollar.

"When we would get an order for a boat, we built it in the yard. We didn't have any boat shed in those days. The biggest boats we built were around thirty-eight-foot long and we would have to get a trailer to haul it a quarter mile to water to launch, because we didn't live right on the water.

"The hardest part for us was flipping the bottom over in those days," said Edward. "We built the bottom upside down and then would flip it over to put sides and the house and everything else on. We would get a bunch of men in the neighborhood to come and help. We had a tree with a block and fall on to it. We would raise the bottom up, and we would put boards up against the tree and slide the bottom down, all the time tilting it. Then everybody would lift one end around and then lift the other end around until it was completely over."

Edgar and Ned built mostly round-stern and V-stern deadrise boats. "The old boats were all much narrower than what we build today, so it wasn't as hard to flip them over," said Edward.

They built boats at Peary together until 1953, when Edward got married and decided to build himself a house on Stutts Creek at Redart, and his father followed him up the road.

Edgar was tired of fighting the low land he owned around Peary. "My father always wanted to get out of Peary because the tide would make up in his yard any old time," said Edward. "He would get his garden going pretty good in the spring and summer and then there would be a high tide and ruin everything. So he decided to move up here, close to me."

The father and son then proceeded to build themselves two homes. "It was then that we got out of boatbuilding on our own. It wasn't because there wasn't any work," he said. "We wanted a job that would allow us enough time to build our homes."

It was about that time that renowned Chesapeake Bay boatbuilder Alton Smith, of Horn Harbor Marina, got a big job to put a bottom on a sixty-five-foot Chesapeake Bay deck boat. He was backed up with more work than he could manage, so he approached Edgar and Edward about working for him when he needed them. They did the job, and when they weren't busy at the yard, they worked on their homes.

It was at Horn Harbor that Edward Diggs became known as one of the best boatbuilders on the Chesapeake. He worked

The *Carolyn K* was brand new when owner Lowery Hudgins took her for a test run in 1984. She was built by Edward Diggs and finished off with mahogany trim and stern. Now retired, Diggs is considered one of the best deadrise boat builders on the Bay. The *Carolyn K* was alive and well in 2007, working in the Delaware Bay crab dredge fishery.

for Smith until Smith sold the yard, and then he worked for three other owners.

Smith had learned the craft working at his father's boatyard on Pepper Creek. His father, Lennie Smith, was a pioneer in the early years of the evolution of the Chesapeake Bay deadrise. He and others, like Gilbert White, of Lancaster County; John Wright, of Deltaville; and Perry Rogers, of Shady Side; passed on their knowledge to the next generation of builders.

By the time Edward Diggs was at retirement age, he had perfected the craft of building a deadrise boat. In a 1991 interview, Alton Smith gave him the ultimate compliment. "I'm going to tell you the truth now," said Smith. "I don't know anyone who can build a boat as good as Edward Diggs, and boy, I've known a lot of boatbuilders in my time. He does his best work on every project, whether it's caulking a boat or building a hull."

George M. Butler
A Third-generation Boatbuilder

About twenty years after Maine fisherman Elijah Reed struck gold on the Chesapeake Bay by establishing the bay's menhaden fishery near Reedville, Virginia, Isaac Bailey opened a little boatyard on Cockrell Creek, on the town's main street.

Deadrise and Cross-planked

George M. Butler stands by an 1890s "Josiah Ross" wood planer that his grandfather bought with the business in 1906. The planer originally ran off steam. George is the third generation of his family to run Reedville Marine Railway in Reedville, Virginia.

Reed ventured down the coast and into the Chesapeake Bay in 1867. By the 1890s Reedville was a small but growing community, and Bailey saw an opportunity to start a successful boatyard.

Bailey must have thought that it was a good location, being in town and on a creek with deep enough water to haul any size boat. Also, the region's economy centered on commercial fishing, and watermen required a variety of boats. All, of course, were made of wood, which was right up Bailey's alley.

There was plenty of work at Bailey's Boatyard. He hauled, maintained, and built boats of all kinds, but the menhaden

business kept him extra busy building striker boats. A striker boat is a small fore-and-aft planked skiff that was used in the menhaden fishery to direct the two purse boats in making a successful set.

Bailey's 1893 ledger states that he built and sold striker boats for $60, flat-bottom skiffs for $12, and an unidentified type of sailboat for $120. It may have been a deadrise style. We don't know for sure.

Being in such a good location, it's no wonder that when Bailey decided to hang up the broadax and foot adz, someone took over the yard.

Most folks living in Reedville today don't recall the name Isaac Bailey, but you mention Butler and they associate it with Reedville Marine Railway. In 1906, Bailey sold his railway to Samuel Butler and Joseph Davis. Davis got out of the business sometime in the mid-1920s, and since then the yard has been exclusively owned and operated by the Butler family.

Today, George M. Butler runs and operates Reedville Marine Railway. The 1890 Josiah Ross planer and band saw that his grandfather bought with the business are still in use, and God only knows how many boats have been built on that site.

"My grandfather built boats ranging from twelve-foot skiffs to thirty-foot crab boats for the crab trotline business," said George. "In those days everybody had a rowboat. Some families couldn't afford to buy bicycles for their children, but even the poorest families had a skiff to get around in.

"I heard my daddy [George P. Butler] say he and my grandfather would build these rowboats and they were named Bailey skiffs. They were modeled after some Mr. Bailey built," said George. "They would build them in their spare time and hoist them up in the ceiling at the shop until someone came along who wanted to buy one.

"Daddy said the worse burn he ever had was when he went to hoist one down and it got away from him and the rope burned his arm up.

"My father got into the business the day he was born, and one of his first jobs as a boy was to fire up the boiler to the steam engine that powered the planer and band saw. The saw and planer worked off a jack shaft from the ceiling," said George.

Samuel died in 1933, leaving the business to George's father. He ran the business for seven years, and then closed it in 1940 and moved to Baltimore to work at a Coast Guard Station.

"Dad moved back after World War II and started building boats again," he said. "I started hanging around the yard when I was a child, and by the mid-1960s I'd spend my summers scraping bottoms of boats and helping my father build boats.

"I won't say he purposely taught me how to build boats," said George. "I started out holding a board. Then he'd let me drive a nail. Then he'd let me cut a board. I learned from observing more than from him trying to teach me."

George's father built boats ranging from twelve-foot skiffs to fifty-foot head boats, and whether he was trying to teach George or not about boatbuilding, he did. When George's father died in 1976, George took over.

His yard has also been a godsend to the Reedville Fisherman's Museum in Reedville. The museum has been a forerunner in saving wooden boats, and the railway has played a major role in their project.

Today, George builds flat-bottom skiffs for the Potomac River pound net fishery and a variety of different sizes and style of deadrise boats. Unlike most Maryland and Virginia deadrise builders, George builds his larger boats right side up, because his boatshed does not have enough height for him to hoist and flip the hull. Most builders complete the bottom upside down and then flip it to finish the decking and

house. The right-side-up method eliminates flipping the hull, while the upside-down method makes it more comfortable on the builder, who does not have to hold a board and nail it at the same time overhead. George said it is much easier to build a hull upside down, but he builds his thirty-five footers and larger right side up the entire way. "It was simply a matter of space," said George. "When we stopped building outdoors and went inside into a boatbuilding shed, we didn't have enough height in the shed to flip the hull over. So, we started building right side up the entire way. My father did it that way too."

In 2003, George built a deadrise boat named the *Iris Marie*, a 39' 6" x 12' 4 1/2" x 4' 6" gillnet and recreational fishing boat powered by a 225-horsepower John Deere diesel engine. It was built for Hudnell H. Haynie Jr., of Fleeton, Virginia.

The *Iris Marie* has the classic traditional Chesapeake Bay deadrise hull that George regularly builds. All planking on the staved cross-planked bottom and strip-planked sides are made from 1 3/8" x 1 3/8" North Carolina white cedar. The strip-planked sides are fastened with nails, and seams are sealed with West System Epoxy. He also edge nails the side planks to the frames.

The sheer and bilge clamps run the length of the boat and are made from 1 1/2" x 6" pressure-treated wood. Frames are cut from 2" x 4" pressure-treated pine timbers. The horn timber is made from a 10" x 10" pressure-treated pine timber. For years, George used white oak for frames, horn timbers and other parts of the boat, but it takes a year for oak to cure. "I can buy white oak, and I do get some, but I've got to dress it and stack it and let it set for over a year before I can use it," he said. "The pressure treated is just as good and I can buy it and use it right then."

The sternpost and stem are white oak and shaped from 5" x 6" timbers. "Pine is not tough enough for a stem or stern post," said George. The cabin top is made of marine plywood, and the top and cockpit is covered in vinylester resin, used with two layers of fiberglass mat and woven roving. The wood is clear finished and bright all through the cabin and interior. This is made from a combination of white oak and white cedar. The transom is made of 1 1/4" mahogany and finished with four coats of Cetol sealer. The mahogany stern is a trademark of some Chesapeake Bay watermen as many wooden boats built now carry a bright stern. The fastenings are stainless steel nails and bolts.

Much of the interior house and deck design came about as the boat was being built. "Somebody would make a suggestion," said George, "and if we all thought it was a good one, we'd build it into the boat." One of the suggestions was a rod and reel holder on the underside of the pilothouse roof. George designed and built an attractive mahogany rod and reel holder, finished off in varnish. The rod holder holds six rods and reels.

White oak handrails are mounted along the pilothouse roof and also on the top of the house. The handrails are finished with several coats of varnish. Rod and reel holders are mounted along the deck to hold rods when trolling for stripers.

The *Iris Marie* has a V-berth and head up forward and a settee that can be folded down and converted into a bunk. Along the bottom of the settee, neatly arranged, are several drawers for storage.

"I wanted a comfortable place to sit down and eat or to rig fishing lines," said Haynie. "We've also left a little bit of space for a galley."

Butler and Haynie have used every square inch of space. The steps going into the house are hinged, so the step top lifts up to provide storage. There is also room under the seats of the settee and inside the bunks for storage of life jackets, rope, buoys, and other gear.

The *Iris Marie* represents generations of evolution of wooden boatbuilding on the Chesapeake, and George M. Butler's heritage goes back to the beginning of V-bottom boat construction on the bay.

Willard Norris
The Last One

Boatbuilder Willard Norris (on right) learned to build boats from uncles on two sides of the family, Alfred Norris and Lee Deagle. He is one of the last traditional deadrise builders and has a boatbuilding shop in Deltaville. Here he stands with his first cousin, Milton Ward. Norris is replacing a bottom on a boat his uncle, Alfred Norris, built in the 1960s. "We like to keep things in the family," he said.

Willard Norris can't recall the first time he wielded a foot adz, but he knows he was mighty young. In 1927, Willard was born to a boatbuilding family on Lovers Lane in Deltaville. In fact, he had boatwrights on both sides of his family.

His grandfather, Ed Deagle, built deadrise-style boats on the shoreline in front of his house on Jackson Creek where Willard was born. His uncle, Pete Deagle, repaired log canoes right next door.

"A many a time I've watched my Uncle Pete haul a log canoe up on the shore at high tide on two logs and put chunks [logs] in it," said Willard.

"I used to walk down the road when I was a child and watch John Wright build sixty-five-foot boats with nothing but hand tools—foot adz, hand planes, rip-saws, and that was it," he said.

"I can take you right down the street and tell you who built boats and where. John, Ladd, Tom and Lewis Wright, Rob Dudley, Hugh Norris, Edmond Harrow, Willie Marchant, and Alfred Norris, all built boats right here on Lover's Lane."

Willard first learned about boatbuilding by going over after school to help his uncle, Alfred Norris, work on a boat. When he was sixteen, he spent the summer working for his uncle, Lee Deagle, who owned Deagle's and Son Marine Railway on Fishing Bay.

"I learned to set up and build boats from my uncle Alfred, but I learned a great deal about working with wood at Uncle Lee's," said Willard. "There were so many woodworkers there in those days, and they were all willing to give you a tip on this and that."

Willard got married when he was eighteen, and the first thing he did was build himself a round-stern boat to go patent-tonging for oysters. "I started the boat in my backyard with no shed or nothing, he said. "John Wright was old then, and his wife Blanche was my wife's aunt, so he'd come by every morning and help me out.

"I laid it out the way I was taught, but didn't think the stern looked just right, so I asked Mr. Wright what he thought," said Willard.

"John Wright said, 'Let me tell you something. You do it the way you think it is right, and if you need to change something you can do it on the next one. But if you let everybody tell you how to build that boat, it's going to be a damn mess.'"

Sometime in the 1960s, Willard went to work for the Virginia Marine Resources Commission, but kept building boats at night. He built a closed-in pole boatbuilding shed behind his house and turned out more than a hundred boats there.

Twenty years ago, Willard was diagnoised with pancreatic cancer and doctors gave him only months to live. Even when he was sick, he went to the boatshed and started building a skiff.

"I couldn't stop building boats, and then, when I beat the cancer, I kept building skiffs."

He had watched as one boatbuilder after another got old and ended their careers as skiff builders. "It's the life cycle of a wooden boatbuilder," said Willard. "You start life out learning to build skiffs and work up to the big stuff. When you get old, you go back to building skiffs. That's where I am."

Willard's boatshed is the last active backyard boatbuilding facility in Deltaville. Inside his shop, he has old hand wood-working tools that he has picked up at yard sales, and others he has gotten from older builders in retirement. A block and tackle is attached to the rafters for hoisting and flipping hulls, and out back is the community boat trailer.

When boatbuilding was flourishing, several builders got together and had a trailer built to haul finished boats down to the creek. It is complete with a vee cut into a wooden brace across the front axle to slip the deadrise bow into.

"When I needed the trailer, I'd go to the last builder who used it and bring it to my place, haul my boat, and then store it behind my shed until somebody else needed it. Nobody comes for the trailer anymore and it's all fallen apart."

In 2003, Willard decided he had enough strength to build one more Deltaville deadrise, so he turned out a thirty-two footer that he named *The Last One*.

Francis Smith
Guinea Neck Boatbuilder

Francis Smith, of Bena, Virginia, has been building boats since he was thirteen, and before that he helped tote boat lumber for his father and grandfather.

Deadrise and Cross-planked

Francis Smith was still building boats in Guinea Neck in Gloucester County, Virginia in 2000.

Francis is a fourth-generation boatbuilder from an area known as Guinea Neck in Gloucester County, Virginia, where the men of that area make their livings mainly from the water.

His grandfather and great-grandfather specialized in building Chesapeake Bay log canoes for area watermen. Francis's grandfather, James "Big Jim" Smith, built boats in his backyard on the Perrin River, and had four sons, Little Jim, Sidney, Jack, and Frank, who he taught to build boats. Big Jim and his sons built several of the bay's more famous deadrise buyboats, the most noted being the *Little Muriel Eileen* (1926) and *Big Muriel Eileen* (1928).

Francis's father, Frank, taught him the trade. "My grandfather and great-grandfather built mostly log canoes, and daddy built a few, but when I came along he had gone to plank boats," said Francis. "I do remember the last log canoe daddy built.

A fellow down the road cut his own logs and brought them to the house. I was small but I remember. I guess that was the last log canoe built in Guinea Neck."

Smith's grandfather and great-grandfather built mostly for area watermen, but his father's boats and reputation went much further. "Daddy got out of building traditional deadrise workboats and went into building [wooden] trawlers for fishermen working off-shore in Ocean City, Atlantic City, and Cape May, and Long Island."

Francis built his first boat for a crabber in Mathews County. It was a sixteen-foot skiff that was used for poling along the shore for peeler crabs.

"As far as I know, she's still going," he said.

He worked with his father and his two brothers building boats for many years before going into business for himself. Since then, he has built traditional workboats that have gone all over the bay and East Coast.

Smith has built large skiffs for working the bay, to fifty-foot trawlers for Atlantic Ocean fisheries. The largest he built was an eighty-seven-foot trawler that his father, brothers, and he built in the 1950s.

In 2000, Francis was constructing one of the sturdiest deadrise boats ever built. He had a 51' x 15' 8" x 46" underway in his shop for a watermen who planned to conch pot in her offshore in the Atlantic Ocean. Like his father before him, Smith was always looking for a better way to do things. He was one of the first traditional commercial boatbuilders in Virginia to use the Gougeon Brothers' West Epoxy products in the construction of wooden workboats, and he was one of the first to go away from traditional single-board cross-planked bottoms.

The bottom on his boat was triple planked and the sides were double planked, all laminated. "It's the first time I've ever triple planked a boat," he said. "I'm installing four bulkheads in her, but it don't need it."

Smith said the tripled-planked juniper (also called Carolina white cedar) bottom and double-planked juniper sides, sealed together with West Epoxy products, make the hull sturdier than a traditional deadrise with bulkheads.

The building method in the bottom was not a stripped-plank style, but rather Smith used 4"-wide-x-15/16"-thick juniper planks—two rows of planks installed diagonally and a third row installed fore and aft. Smith said no seams were left uncovered and it gave the vessel extraordinary strength. It was glued together and screwed with silicone bronze screws.

Juniper was used throughout construction, except in the outer layer of the stern and the inner stem post. The double-layered stern was made of a layer of 7/8"-thick juniper and a layer of 7/8"-thick mahogany, while the inner stem post was made from a 7" x 8" piece of Georgia pine.

Since juniper is a soft wood, Smith said he covered the bottom and sides with three coats of epoxy primer, which provided a hard cover over the wood.

The three-foot-thick keel was laminated out of eight pieces of 2"-thick-x-14"-wide juniper planks on the inside and 10 pieces on the outside. Smith sank 3/4"

Francis Smith came from a long line of deadrise boatbuilders. His grandfather, James "Big Jim" Smith, built this double decker buyboat *Big Muriel Eileen* in 1928. Francis's three uncles, Little Jim, Sidney, and Jack, all built boats, and his father, Frank, is believed to have been the first boatbuilder to use a solid-piece S-shaped horn timber, an innovation that replaced pieced horn timbers that were leak prone. (Courtesy of William C. Hight Collection.)

stainless steel bolts through the keel. The bolts helped hold the outside keel and skeg to the boat.

The 3 1/2" x 3" timbers were on 16" centers, with 56 in total. The timbers were cut from solid pieces of juniper. Two layers of juniper 5" wide x 15/16" thick were attached to the timbers and compose the sides. The outer stem post was cut from a 6" x 8" piece of juniper.

Eight sister keelsons attached to the inside bottom gave strength to the vessel. Four sister keelsons were on each side of the keel, all made from juniper. Four of the sister keelsons were laminated to bend with the flow of the bottom, while the other four were cut from a solid piece of juniper.

Smith says he has been laminating his boats for years and he believes it makes for a stronger boat, but strength wasn't the only reason he went to lamination.

"I used to keep $7,000 to $10,000 worth of lumber on hand all the time for boatbuilding," he said. "It got so good boat lumber was hard to find in the way of big pieces."

When local pine and oak were no longer attainable, Smith, like other local builders, went to West Coast fir for the big pieces, such as 12" x 12" keel beams. He contends the fir has not held up well in boats. "I wouldn't use a piece of fir now if someone were to give it to me. Lamination is the only way to go," he said.

Francis has been willing to change with the times and has incorporated new methods of construction into building the V-bottom boat.

"My daddy taught me that there is always a better way to do something, and I've learned that to be true," he said.

Alvin Sibley
Traveling Boatbuilder

Alvin Sibley owned his own boatyard and built nearly one hundred boats. Today, he travels from yard to yard working on wooden boats.

Alvin Sibley married into a Deltaville boatbuilding family in 1950, and learned the wooden boat trade from some of Virginia's most noted wooden boatbuilders. During a long career, he built ninety-five wooden boats in the forty- to fifty-eight-foot range, owned boatyards and boatbuilding facilities at three different locations in the Deltaville area, and would be building boats still if he had not been forced to confront three bouts of cancer.

Today, he and his son Chris work from a Toyota pickup truck and travel from yard to yard repairing wooden boats.

In 1989 Sibley battled lung cancer, and after winning that fight, discovered in 1995 that he had cancer of the prostrate. He thought he had that licked, but it reoccurred in 1998. Most anyone else would have given up the daily hard work of repairing wooden boats, but not Sibley.

Today, the telephone rings frequently for him, just like it did when he had his boatbuilding business. Every weekday morning, bright and early, Alvin and his son, Chris, get into his truck and head to work. He works on wooden boats for watermen, head boat captains, and recreational boaters at yards on the James, York, Rappahannock, and Potomac rivers.

Years of experience that Alvin received working with his father-in-law Johnny (Crab) Weston and with well-known boatbuilders, such as Lee Deagle and Ed Norton, have earned him a reputation as a man who knows wooden boats.

"I started when I was fifteen years old, working on boats at Southside Marine in Urbanna, Virginia," said Alvin, at his home in nearby Saluda. Southside Marine was one of the largest wooden boat service yards on the Rappahannock River in the 1940s and '50s.

"I was just a boy, but I must have been pretty good, because I was getting paid seventy-five cents an hour and other boys like me working there and in sawmills and on farms were getting forty-five cents and fifty cents an hour. I think it was because I wasn't lazy and I didn't mind working."

When Alvin married his wife, Barbara, he went to work for his father-in-law. One of the first boats Alvin and Johnny Crab built together was a forty-foot round-stern deadrise boat that they used to dredge and patent-tong for oysters in the winter. During the warm weather months, they built boats.

"When I was with Johnny Crab we built deadrise workboats, and the biggest one we built was a fifty-five-foot buyboat for York River Oyster Company," he said. "I learned to weld when I was in the Navy and people started to come around from other yards wanting me to do some metal work, and that's how I moved on to other yards."

In 1959, Alvin and Barbara opened their own yard and boat-building facility on Broad Creek in Deltaville. He built traditional Chesapeake Bay deadrise workboats there until 1979, when he moved to a smaller facility.

"I learned that I could make more money building a couple boats at a time with a two- to three-man crew than I could building five and six boats at a time with a five- and six-man crew," he said. "Social security, insurance, and benefits for those other men just ate up my profits."

Over the years, Alvin built boats for commercial fishermen, charter boat fishermen, and recreational fishermen up and down the East Coast. His ninety-five boats included one for a lobsterman in Connecticut; charter boats in Florida; and commercial fishing boats in Virginia, Maryland, North Carolina, New Jersey, and Delaware.

Alvin's struggle with cancer is a testimony to the courage and strength of the human spirit. "I never really stopped doing boat work, even when my lung was removed. I slowed up, but when I got enough strength I went to work and worked for fifteen minutes that first day. The next day I stayed for a half-hour and kept going until I could work a couple hours a day. I kept going until I was able to work a full day.

"I think that is part of the reason I'm alive today," he said. "All I've ever known all my life is hard work. There are some things you can't do anything about when you are sick, but I tried to keep my mind on positive things and boats and work have been my life."

Alvin moved to Saluda in 1998, when he had a third bout with cancer. He sold his boatbuilding shop in Deltaville and moved twenty miles down the road.

"It wasn't far enough," he said. "The phone started ringing the day after I got home from having my prostate removed and it hasn't stopped yet.

"The main difference from the way it used to be with me is that when I feel bad I stay home and no one questions it," he said. "Everybody knows I'm a lucky man to still be here. Every day I think of how fortunate I am to be doing what I love to do.

"When I was young, there were a lot of men around working on wooden boats, but there aren't many anymore," he said. "There's plenty of work and not enough good craftsman around who can do it. I guess that's good for me."

Alvin doesn't build new boats anymore, but every once in a while he'll get a call from someone to set a new boat up. "I got a call from a man on the Northern Neck about setting a boat up for him. I wound up doing most of the woodwork and he did just enough to make it look like a corncob. Then he told everybody I built it."

Glenwood Sampson
Waterman / Boatbuilder

In 1972, Glenwood Sampson built *Sam*, a 38' x 12' deadrise boat in his backyard at his home in Milo, Virginia. He built the boat for himself to work in the oyster fishery and to pound net on the Great Wicomico River. Glenwood is a World War

Watermen often built their own boats with the help of professional boatbuilders. Glenwood Sampson, of Milo, Virginia, got George P. Butler of Reedville to help him with some particulars, and then Glenwood built a deadrise boat. He named the boat *Sam*, after the nickname he acquired in World War II.

II veteran. During the war someone nicknamed him Sam, so he decided to name his boat *Sam*.

Many talented watermen build their own boats, but, like Glenwood, most are close enough to a boatbuilder to get advice when needed. Milo is in Northumberland County and not far from Reedville and Reedville Marine Railway. George P. Butler, then owner of the railway, provided invaluable help to get Glenwood started on his boat.

Glenwood, born in 1918, worked early in life in the peeler crab fishery in skiffs, and he built his own flat-bottom crab skiffs. His father had taught him how to build skiffs.

"My daddy told me that when I learned to swim, he would build me a skiff. I learned to swim when I was six years old and he built me my first skiff."

In the winter that Glenwood turned sixteen, he went to tonging oysters in a twenty-eight-foot log canoe powered by a five-horsepower Regal engine.

"It didn't push her very fast, but the boats weren't built to go fast," said Glenwood. "We didn't have to go very far in those days to catch oysters."

Charlie Mothershead of Wicomico Church built Glenwood's first V-deadrise boat. Glenwood and his partner, Cleveland Dameron, helped, and they owned the boat together. Glenwood and Cleveland worked together for more than fifty years.

"We helped Charlie Mothershead on that first boat, but he was the boss and he laid off everything on that boat. He was an old-time boatbuilder with an old-time railway. He had a windlass that we had to turn by hand to get boats up and down in the water. I got my lumber for that boat from my father-in-law, Ernest Cockrell. He was running a sawmill then.

"On *Sam*, I worked on it on Saturdays in the wintertime and I had a fellow who I paid to help me some," he said. "It took me a couple years. The hardest part was getting the staving for the deadrise in the bow just right. I had never done that before. The man working for me was a house carpenter and he couldn't figure it out. I had watched Charlie [Mothershead] do it years before, so I had some idea of how it went and I got it done. I had also built a skiff and put a little deadrise in the bow."

George P. Butler got him started by writing up the amount and size of lumber needed for the boat. Glenwood took Butler's notes to Meade M. Hinton of Brownstore, Virginia. Hinton cut the lumber to size and delivered it to Glenwood's house in the spring and summer of 1971.

He then stacked it for air drying. All of the wood was cut from spruce pine. The total cost of lumber for everything on the boat was $488.60. The Monel nails for the boat cost $324. "I just about paid as much for the nails as I did the wood," said Glenwood. He also had the wood dressed by Butler, which cost him an additional $217.

Glenwood used *Sam* to dredge for oysters on private oyster grounds and hand tong on public grounds. He installed a used 110-horsepower diesel engine.

"I was a couple years building it. I didn't work on it in the summertime because I was crabbing and it was hot out there," he said. "I did most of the work in the winter months. I built it myself to save money, but also because I knew I could do it. It might not be the prettiest or the best, but I knew it would take me out and bring me home. That's all any boat is supposed to do.

"I had two brothers who worked the water and they had the *Silver Star* built by Odis Cockrell for haul seining," he said. "Odis was a good builder and, of course, his son Tiffany is a master builder of wooden boats." Tiffany Yachts is located on the same site that Odis built deadrise workboats at Glebe Point on the Great Wicomico River.

"George Butler helped me a lot, but I can't build boats the way he builds them and I think his son does it the same way," said Glenwood. "They build the bottom and the entire boat right side up. I built mine upside down because I couldn't hold my arms up long enough to build it that way. It's harder. You've got to hold your boards while you nail. When it's upside down, the board is laid flat down in place while you nail."

"I did get George to cut and shape the 34' x 10" x 12" keel, and I floated it home from Reedville and dragged it up into my yard," said Glenwood. "I cut my own horn timber, which added four more feet on the boat. I installed the engine. I had a tree out in the yard and after I turned the boat over, I put it underneath the tree and I used a block and tackle to hoist the engine into the boat."

When the boat was launched, Glenwood nailed pound net poles he found around the shore to it and dragged it to the creek with a tractor. "When I dragged it down the road, the state police came to keep the road clear until I got it down to the creek," he said. "Everybody in the neighborhood came out to see the launch. It was the biggest thing to happen in Milo in years."

Glenwood worked the boat until the early 1990s, when oystering played out. He sold *Sam* a few years ago and doesn't know if she is still alive. "I didn't want to get rid of her, but she got to be a dead expense. I could fish my peeler traps in a skiff. I just didn't have any work for her to do."

Glenwood retired from the water in 2005 at the age of eighty-seven. "The government made it so hard," he said. "Now, you got to have a license for everything and you've got to report everything. They took the freedom out of working the water. That's the main reason I did it was because I loved the freedom. You had to work hard but I liked the challenge."

Billy Williams
Haul Seiner / Boatbuilder

Some watermen had boatbuilders build half their boat and then they finished the rest. In 1972, Billy Williams, of Horse Point on the Piankatank River, had Earl Weston, of Deltaville, build most of the hull on his wooden deadrise *Gwen Marie*.

Billy purchased all the materials to build the boat and he finished off the decks and house.

"I didn't know anything about boatbuilding, so I got Earl Weston to build the bottom and I finished off the rest," he said.

"Earl and his father, Big Johnny Weston, had built my other boat in 1934. I paid $455 for it and it was a good boat, so I went to Earl and told him I wanted another one.

"I used my first boat for haul seining in the 1930s and 1940s, when you could make some money fishing," said Billy. "In 1943, we got into a mess of croaker for about five weeks and my share of one catch was $5,500. We did that for about five weeks when the weather allowed us to work and I made enough money to buy my land, build my house, and buy a new car and a new truck. I paid for it all with cash. I thought I was going to be a millionaire. It didn't last, but it gave me a good start in life."

The *Gwen Marie* was built in one of Westons' boatsheds on Broad Creek in Deltaville. "I had all the lumber cut and milled locally," said Billy. "The bottom boards and keel are spruce pine and it came from Mathews County."

The sides, house, and pilothouse are made of cypress. "I got my cypress out of the Dragon Run at the headwaters of the Piankatank River."

The sides and bottom on the *Gwen Marie* are built out of 1 1/2"-thick lumber. "Most boats are built out of 1 1/4" lumber, but I wanted my boat to have thick sides and bottom," said Billy. "I dressed the lumber myself, staked it, and let it dry for a year before we started building the boat."

The handrails and trim were made of walnut and stained brown. The stem was made of a piece of cherry. "I bet I'm the only one around here who has got a stem made out of cherry wood," he said.

Billy fastened his boat with Monel nails and galvanized bolts. He said he wished he had used stainless steel bolts.

"You can see some rust places on her side and that's from those bolts," he said. "I should have used stainless steel.

Watermen Billy Williams had Deltaville boatbuilder Earl Weston set the boat up for him and build the bottom, then Billy did the rest of the work himself.

"I paid Earl $900 for what he did. He set the boat up and he pretty much built the bottom. When we turned it over, I did the rest. I sealed every seam on the boat with a sealant compound and made sure she was nailed right."

Billy built the boat to go bottom fishing and oystering. He installed wide washboards for oystering, but never has oystered in the boat. "I made sure I could use it for oystering just in case oysters come back," he said. "But they really never have, not like they were when I was young."

five
BATEAUX

Sail- and pole-powered bateaux were forerunners of the modern engine-powered Chesapeake Bay deadrise workboat. Throughout most of the bay region, vee- or cone-shaped bow boats were called bateaux.

Bateau is French for boat. One of the earliest types of bateau in the New World was mentioned in Thomas Jefferson's account book, dated April 19, 1775. The book noted that Jefferson had purchased one of the vessels. The third president of the United States was speaking of the James River bateau, which was used to transport tobacco and freight.

It was most certainly only related in name to the nineteenth- and twentieth-century V-bottom deadrise, but it shows how far back the word goes in American maritime history.

These styles of bateaux were used on the James River between Lynchburg and Richmond, a tobacco port and center of commerce. The width of the boat, six to eight feet, was to accommodate forty-eight-inch by thirty-inch tobacco hogsheads (large barrels full of tobacco leafs). The length varied but the most popular size was around fifty-eight feet. The boats were fore-and-aft planked, powered by poles, and had a pointed "nose cone" bow that was attached separately.

The 1680 Assembly Act of Jamestown established port towns. These ports had customhouses to monitor and regulate tobacco shipments, which generated tax dollars for the colony. Some type of bateaux or scows was used on most rivers in Virginia to haul and carry tobacco and freight to ports of call.

The common scow was perhaps the most popular vessel used to haul hogsheads from shore to ships bound for England. However, boats with sides were needed for longer trips down river. Several types of boats evolved out of this need.

As the business of growing and selling tobacco began to wane, harvesting seafood became more important to the bay region's economy, and the bateaux took on a new role and new shape. V-bottom deadrise vessels were called bateaux long before the name deadrise surfaced.

The three main vessels in the twelve- to forty-foot range used by bay watermen before engine power were sail- or oar-powered log canoes, skiffs, and bateaux. Though skipjacks and sailing crab-scraping boats (barcats) had their own distinct names, the common name for all V-bottom and cross-planked boats was bateaux. Log canoes were not considered bateaux and were often just referred to as cunoes.

Generic names for styles of boats were not always the same throughout the bay region. In some areas, planked bugeyes were called canoes. Isaac Davis of Solomon & Son and Davis, of Solomons, Maryland, in 1877 referred to planked bugeyes in his logbook as canoes.

Traditionally, bugeyes were built of logs, but planked construction began around 1877. Some builders continued to call the new style of planked bugeyes, canoes. These vessels and others with fore-and-aft planking were also called planked boats.

In some areas, large hull styles, such as deadrise buyboats, were called bateaux. A. Bennett Wilson wrote in a newspaper column in the *Southside Sentinel* in Urbanna, Virginia, that in 1936 his grandfather referred to his 65' x 22' buyboat as a bateau.

Chapelle's booklet, *Notes on Chesapeake Bay Skipjacks,* confirms that most builders referred to V-bottom boats as bateaux. "The type name for all deadrise (or V-bottom) hulls above the size of a skiff is bateau; whether the hull is powered or sail-powered," wrote Chapelle. He also referred to single-mast skipjacks as a "one-sail bateaux," two-masters as "two-sail bateaux," and three masters as "three-sail bateaux."

Since the 1880s, when V-bottom construction arrived on the Chesapeake, the term bateau was used longer and more widely throughout the region than the term deadrise. It appears that the word deadrise is fairly recent. It also is not unusual for names of styles of Chesapeake Bay boats to change over time. The James River bateau of the late 1700s was certainly not the same style boat as the skipjack. Yet, the boats were both called bateaux.

Short bow sprits on this John Wright-built bateau were standard. The bow sprit extended the length of the boat to accommodate rigging.

This small bateau has a centerboard trunk inside the boat. The centerboard took up work and payload space inside the boat, so some oystermen opted for space and did not put centerboards in their boat.

These two small sailing bateaux were built by Deltaville boatbuilder John Wright. The deadrise and cross-planked hulls on the two boats are similar to the style on larger sailing bateaux used in the oyster and finfish fisheries.

This photo of a seaside bateau on the Eastern Shore of Virginia shows the tuck stern and other features of these boats that were used in the seaside to oyster and fish. (Courtesy of the Cape Charles Museum and John S. McMath Jr.)

The French word bateau, meaning boat, was used for a variety of styles of Bay boats. The seaside bateau, also called the Sinepuxent skiff by Howard Chapelle, was a style of sailing skiff used on the seaside of the Eastern Shore of Maryland and Virginia. (Courtesy of Craig O'Donnell.)

This seaside bateau was alive in the late 1980s, and owned by Joe Conboy, who grew up on the Eastern Shore of Virginia.

Another style of bateau is the two-masted seaside bateau, referred to by Chapelle as the Sinepuxent skiff. Joe Conboy, an Eastern Shore native who owned a seaside bateau for many years, said the bottom on these boats was much harder to build than a standard deadrise-style vessel. "It's a V-bottom boat, but a different technique is used for the bottom planking. It is harder to build than most deadrise boats. It takes a very proficient carpenter to build a seaside bateau."

Conboy said there were two popular sizes. A sixteen-footer was used to go out to larger thirty-foot bateaux that were moored out from shore. The four- and five-foot rise and fall

in tides kept the larger boats from coming close to the shore. Watermen used larger bateaux to fish in the ocean.

Chapelle states in *American Small Sailing Craft*, "The V-bottom hull was used on the Atlantic Coast side of the Virginia Eastern Shore in a small sailing skiff of distinctive form and rig.

"The boats built at Chincoteague Island were half-decked, V-bottom, marked by very great flare in the sides, light construction, and their rigs."

Chapelle said that he was told that some as large as forty feet were built on the shore. He also wrote that most of the sterns were square, but some were round, and the square "staved" sterns were built similar to sterns on the New Haven sharpie and very early Tangier Island V-bottom skiffs.

The seaside bateau is another example of the use of the word bateau for a V-bottom boat. Most certainly there were other forms and styles of bateaux in the bay region.

Remembering Nineteenth-Century Life and a Rappahannock River Sailing Bateau

Richard Smith was born in 1883 to an Essex County, Virginia oysterman and farmer. When Smith was born, the Civil War had been over for just eighteen years.

His father owned a sail-powered bateau, and on Richard's hundredth birthday in 1983, he spoke of his life as an African-American child growing up less than two decades after slavery, and the role his father's boat and the river played in the family's survival. His interview is a unique look at the use of the bateau right before gasoline engines were introduced into boats.

"It seems like a long time ago since I was a boy," said Smith about his childhood days.

Throughout the bay region, the main vessel of choice of most Tidewater families before gasoline engines was sail-powered log canoes. The Richard Smith family, however, owned a sail-powered bateaux.

He recalled attending a one-room schoolhouse in Essex. "I didn't go to school much. My mamma was sick a lot and I had to help around the place, but I can read and write," he said with pride. "Everybody didn't have the same opportunities back then like they do now. I had to do what my parents said and if they didn't want me to go to school, I didn't go."

Richard's school served twenty-five to thirty students and hot meals were not available. "You'd take your lunch or you wouldn't get one. We took it in a tin bucket and we'd have a cup for water and an apple or maybe a rare turnip for lunch. We didn't have much.

"Our drinking water came from a spring that was a quarter-mile away from the school and the children would tote buckets of water to the school. It was mighty good water and

it was cool at the spring, but on hot days the water was too warm to drink by the time we got back to school."

Richard was the oldest of six brothers and six sisters. By the time he was seven years old, his father had him culling oysters in the winter on his boat.

"My school days didn't last long, and, like most boys, white and black in those days, I started helping my father doing man's work when I wasn't ten years old," he said. "I worked on the farm and on my father's bateau."

Richard's father owned a thirty-foot sail-powered bateau that they used to tong and to plant oysters on the Rappahannock River and to buy shad from James River fishermen.

"Oysters were plentiful back then and you did better at that than anything else. I don't know what we would have done if it wasn't for the oyster," he said. "When the season started, my daddy and other ole-timers called it opening the smokehouse door and some said opening the bank. Just before the season opened mid-September, they'd be talking around a potbellied stove down at the store and one of the boys would say 'the smokehouse door opens next week' or 'the bank opens next week.'

"During the oyster season, it was the time of the year we all had money and everyone felt better because we could look after ourselves and our families and that was a good feeling.

"Sometimes oyster buyers were paying fifty and sixty cents for a bushel of oysters and we would catch fifteen to twenty bushels a day.

"My daddy's boat was a thirty-foot-long open bateau. There was no house or pilothouse on it," he said. "When it rained or snowed, we got wet and cold. The boat had a mast and sail, a centerboard, and a hand rudder."

Smith remembers having to saw the vessel out of the ice in the Great Freeze of 1917–18, when the Chesapeake Bay froze solid for fifty-two days.

"The ice was twelve-inches thick and we would beat on the ice until we punched a hole wide enough to get a sawblade down through it. Boy, that was a job, keeping the ice from around the boat."

In the spring, when the herring and shad spawned in the James River, the Smiths would sail from the Rappahannock to the mouth of the James in the bateau and buy a boatload of fish from pound netters. Richard said they paid $2 for a hundred fish. They brought the fish back to the farm, salted the fish down in tubs and tins, and sold salt-fish year round to people living in the neighborhood.

"If there was good wind, we'd sail to the James River in a day, buy our fish, and get back the next evening," he said. "We'd sleep right on the boat under the stars. The worst part was cleaning all those fish and salting them down. We started cleaning and salting the fish in the boat coming home, but we always had to finish up when we got home. We didn't have enough room in the boat for all the fish and tubs too."

One of the family treasures was two acres of oyster ground leased by Richard's father on the Rappahannock River. They used the bateau to plant seed oysters and harvest market-size oysters from these grounds. The boat was equipped with oars and oarlocks.

"When the wind was gone, I've rowed out a many a time in that bateau to scatter seed oysters on the beds and then had to row back," he said.

"Today, people want big boats like forty- and fifty-feet, but our bateau was all right for rowing and sculling back to shore. There might be wind when you start the day, but there might not be any when the day is done. It's much easier to row a thirty-foot boat home than a fifty footer."

When Richard was eighteen, he hopped a steamboat to Baltimore and eventually ended up in Philadelphia, where he became a butler for a millionaire sugar dealer. "I made $17 a week working for him. That don't sound like much now, but things were cheap back then. You could buy more for $17 then than you can buy with $50 now."

He said life was good to him and he enjoyed every aspect.

"It seems like it has been a long, long time from when my daddy and I worked aboard that old bateau, and I guess it was," he said.

A Fleet of Sailing Bateaux

This rare photo of sail-powered bateaux at Bowlers Wharf in Essex County, Virginia, shows the layout and sail configuration of these early boats. The photo was taken around the turn of the twentieth century. (Courtesy of Wit Garrett.)

Wit Garrett's grandfather, C. P. Garrett, owned and operated Garrett and Hunt Oyster Co. from the 1880s until his death in 1918. The oyster house was located on the steamboat dock at Bowlers Wharf, near Center Cross, Virginia.

Wit recalled that his grandfather had a fleet of sail-powered bateaux to harvest and plant oysters on the family oyster grounds in the Rappahannock River.

Usually boatbuilders worked out of their own backyard or boatbuilding shed, but, Wit said, his grandfather and partner, Ivy Hunt, had local boatbuilders come to Bowlers to build and repair their boats, and Garrett and Hunt supplied all the materials. Wit recalled that some of the wood was selected and cut from the forest nearby, and nails, some wood, and other supplies were purchased in Baltimore, Maryland.

The oyster house was built on the steamboat dock at Bowlers and Garrett and Hunt had easy access to Baltimore and its lucrative oyster market via the steamboat that came weekly.

Oystermen from around the community came each year during oyster season and worked for Wit's grandfather. Garrett supplied the boats and hand tongs. Oystermen were paid "piecemeal"—so much per bushel that they caught on the company's private oyster grounds.

This is different from the more typical situation where independent watermen owned their own boat, worked their own tongs, and sold their catch to the buyer with the best price. Virginia's private oyster ground policy, which allowed growers to lease oyster grounds and plant and harvest their own oysters, resulted in this system where the oyster grower controlled almost every aspect of the business.

"I wasn't born when this happened, but my father told me this," said Wit. "We had some oystermen working our bateaux who lived in Ino in King and Queen County. They would get up in the morning and light a lantern and walk from Ino to Bowlers, work all day in the river until after dark, and light a lantern to walk home at night." Ino to Bowlers is a distance of about seven miles, one way.

Wit said that when oysters were harvested, some were brought back to the shucking house and others were sold to buyboats that came from Carters Creek in Lancaster County, Virginia. When oysters were sold to buyboats, Ivy Hunt would go by boat out to the buyboat and keep tally, along with the buyboat captain, as to how many oysters were offloaded from each bateau. Once oysters were offloaded from each boat, Hunt was paid so much per bushel for the oysters by the buyboat captain, and each oystermen was given a ticket as to how much they caught that day. At the end of the week they were paid ten or fifteen cents for every bushel they caught.

"These oystermen lived around the community," said Wit. "They owned a little farm that was three or four acres. In the summertime, they'd raise tomatoes, black-eye peas, or something like that, and would carry them to the canning factory. That was their living. In the wintertime, they'd catch oysters.

The *Michelle Dawn,* out of Glass, Virginia, 2006. She is loaded down with James River oysters going to Deep Creek in Newport News, Virginia. Today, the *Michelle Dawn* is considered a Chesapeake Bay deadrise, but well into the 1940s, she would have been called a bateau. In the 1940s and before, watermen and others used "bateau" to identify the style of boat in general terms. This distinguished it from a log canoe hull. At some point in time, deadrise became the main term used to identify a V-bottom, cross-planked, bay-built boat.

Deadrise and Cross-planked

"My grandfather's bateaux were about twenty-four-feet long and had a six-foot beam. There was no centerboard. The boats had keelsons and the bottoms were planked and they were sail powered," said Wit.

"We had some grounds over near Jones Point that was real shallow and we had to use the bateaux to plant oysters there," he said.

Ordinarily, a buyboat would bring seed oysters from the James River and the seed would be scattered over grounds right from the deck of the buyboat. Men would take shovels full of oysters and throw seed over the oyster beds. However, when oyster beds were in shallow water, seed oysters had to be offloaded onto the bateaux and hand scattered from smaller boats.

"When we did this, we pulled the mast out of the boats and towed the bateaux to the grounds behind a power boat," said Wit. "It's an art to scattering oysters too with a shovel. You take the shovel and flick it so the oysters will spread out over the grounds. It's hard work.

"Our bateaux were built out of rosemary pine, which is a long leaf pine and has more heart wood than Virginia or spruce pine," said Wit. "Rosemary pine is more like Georgia pine, which is good for building boats.

"My daddy and grandfather always wanted rosemary pine and would search the wood around home to find it, and if they couldn't get what they wanted they'd buy pine boards in Baltimore.

"Daddy would go to Baltimore and hand pick boards because he wanted sideboards long enough to go the full-length of the boat, and he didn't want any knots in the boards. His bateaux were built mostly out of rosemary and Georgia pine and locally cut white oak.

"Spruce or Virginia pine was used too. Captain Johnny Ward of Deltaville had his buyboat *Iva W.* built out of spruce pine and he liked it better than rosemary pine," said Wit.

"Later, when my daddy got in the oyster business, he had rowboats built for the oyster business. We had oyster grounds in real shallow water and would load the skiffs up with seed from a buyboat and scatter it out of the skiff onto the beds. Those skiffs were made of cypress wood from the Dismal Swamp. Daddy knew of a mill down that way, and he'd get in the truck and go and buy a load. It was short stuff, but long enough for the sides to reach from stem to stern on a sixteen-foot skiff.

"We had a man at Capahosic in Gloucester County on the York River who built all our skiffs," he said.

"For bigger boats, there was a man in Church View [Virginia] that had a carriage on his mill that would saw long stuff for my grandfather and father," he said. "We'd cut the trees and haul them to the mill and he'd saw it into planks. We'd take planks home and stack it to air dry. It stayed stacked around the place for months.

"I remember other sailing bateaux. There were tongers who owned their own boats and they moored at Layton Landing. They would tong on the public oyster rocks. The boats were twenty- to twenty-five-feet long and they were the same kind as my grandfather had," he said.

Motor-powered Bateaux

Wit Garrett's grandfather died in 1918, and his father, Fred Garrett Sr., continued in the oyster business. He switched to motor-powered bateaux and used the boats to tow skiffs made of cypress to his oyster grounds. Oystermen would tong from the skiffs.

"Daddy got Cole Brizendine, a boatbuilder from Center Cross, Virginia, to build him a powered bateau. By that time, oystermen worked out of large flat-bottom skiffs and we towed them most everywhere," Wit said. "There were sculling paddles and oars in the boats if they needed to get to shore. We named our new bateau *Lindy* after Lindbergh because it was built in 1927, the year Lindbergh made the first solo flight across the Atlantic in the *Spirit of St. Louis.*

"I went with daddy to Norfolk to buy a Palmer engine for the new bateau. John Hughs Curtis had the agency and we went to talk with him. Somehow he was involved in the Lindbergh kidnapping and his phone was ringing off the hook.

"We decided to get away from there and we left, but daddy got a one-cylinder Palmer engine. He could tow three or four skiffs with the *Lindy*.

"Man, we thought we had died and gone to heaven when motors came along," said Wit. "I don't know when they started calling the bateau a deadrise, but it hasn't been that long ago.

"When I was a boy, deadrise boats were all called bateaux, and now most of the time it's called a deadrise boat," he said. "It was not much difference in hulls of sail and motor-powered V-bottom boats except we started building the boats wider for motors.

"The style was just right for what we were doing with it and that's what made it so popular all over the bay," he said.

Wit Garrett's family watched the evolution of the deadrise as it went from sail to power and from bateau to being called deadrise.

six
SKIPJACKS—
DEADRISE SAILING VESSELS

The skipjack *Claud W. Somers* has a deadrise and cross-planked hull, which evolved in the 1890s. The skipjack became the main vessel of choice in the oyster dredge fishery because its shallow draft allowed it to work in waters that other large sailing craft could not approach. The Reedville Fisherman's Museum in Reedville, Virginia has beautifully restored the *Claud W. Somers*.

Skipjack hulls, which are deadrise and V-bottom, were one of the first large cross-planked, sail-powered hull types to evolve on the bay. However, not all skipjacks were cross-planked, and numerous variations of hull and deck styles occurred throughout the bay region.

The one thing that seems to distinguish a skipjack from other sail-powered boats and variations of skipjack hull styles is that the rigging is pretty much the same. The skipjack is a centerboard craft that has a raking mast, jib, and leg-of-mutton mainsail.

Robert Burgess in his book, *This Was the Chesapeake Bay*, wrote that in certain sections of the Eastern Shore of Maryland the term skipjack refers only to the rig, rather than the type of craft. Yet, he also noted that watermen on the lower James River called skipjacks Crisfield flatties or sharpies, and did not recognize a craft by the name skipjack unless its bottom was planked fore-and-aft, instead of cross-planked.

Deck layouts were different on many boats too. All of the later built skipjacks carry a cabin aft, but early styles had the cabin forward. Some were decked over and others were open boats.

This is typical of the evolution of most hull styles where historically the starting point has been lost to time or there was no starting point. The final model of a craft is often pieced together by many different boatbuilders in many areas through trial and error. When there is a study of a craft, often no one can remember who started what.

Burgess also wrote, "The ancestry of the skipjack, as with all the bay's commercial sailing craft, is interesting. It is presumed that the type developed in the early 1890s from the earlier enlarged types of flat-bottom or V-bottom skiffs once so common on the lower Eastern Shore of Maryland."

M. V. Brewington wrote in *Chesapeake Bay—A Pictorial Maritime History*, "The skipjack was sired by the V-bottom skiff commonly used in sailing along the crab trotlines in the shoal waters of the lower Eastern Shore."

We do know that skipjacks around today, with the exception of the sloop *Rebecca T. Ruark*, have V-deadrise hulls and the bottoms are cross- or herringbone planked.

Skipjack Fleet and Its Origin

The Maryland oyster dredge skipjack fleet is still active and the last commercial sail-powered fleet in North America. The surviving skipjack fleet is a national treasure. In 1985, Maryland's state legislature named the deadrise skipjack the official boat of the state.

A relic of the past, the heritage and culture that surrounds the fleet is as interesting as the boats, and is a reminder that sail power was used on the bay much longer than steam or engine power has been around. The skipjack is proof that the deadrise/cross-planked hull style was built first in the days of sail and adopted to motor-powered engines.

Although the skipjack was not introduced on the bay until around the 1890s, its creation came from events that happened nearly a century before. New England oyster beds were depleted in the late 1700s and early 1800s and Yankee oystermen came to the Chesapeake to harvest and buy seed and market-size oysters. The New Englanders came in schooners and sloops, and brought with them a gear form called the dredge. The dredge had originated in England to harvest oysters in the English Channel.

Mark Kurlansky in his book, *The Big Oyster,* wrote, "As early as 1816, Chesapeake Bay oysters were being sold in New York. In the spring of 1825, Chesapeake spats for the first time were brought up by schooner and planted in Princess Bay, Staten Island.

"Numerous schooners with a captain and a four-man crew began doing the same thing from Princess Bay, and from the New Jersey side out of Keyport and Perth Amboy.

"These crews could import hundreds of thousands of seed oysters each year. It took thirty-five to forty hours for a schooner to sail from Raritan Bay to the rivers of the lower Chesapeake. In two days, they could load between 2,500 and 3,500 bushels of seed."

Yanks came to the Chesapeake prior to 1816 because in 1810 the Virginia legislature had passed laws prohibiting the use of the dredge, and northern oystermen were on the bay by 1808. As Yankee oystermen moved north on the bay, Maryland followed Virginia in 1820 and passed a law prohibiting the use of the dredge and transporting oysters out of state.

Even though it was illegal, Virginia and Maryland oystermen began to use the dredge. This forced Maryland legislature to pass another law prohibiting its use in 1833. In 1854, oystermen in Somerset County, Maryland, persuaded the Maryland legislature to allow watermen to use a small dredge. The success of the dredge in Somerset prompted watermen in other areas to lobby for statewide use of the dredge in fifteen feet of water and deeper. In 1865, the legislatures approved a law to allow the use of dredge in Maryland's deeper waters, under sail power only. Steam power was specifically prohibited. Having to work in the deeper waters under sail created the need for larger sailboats.

Virginia held fast to its prohibition of the dredge, but when motor power came along at the turn of the twentieth century, the state agreed to allow the use of dredge under motor power on private oyster grounds.

These laws set the stage for the evolution of several styles of dredge boats. In Maryland, logged brogans, coasting canoes, and bugeyes (logged and planked) were built and used in the dredge fishery. These boats were not deadrise or cross-planked.

In the 1890s, the V-bottom, cross-planked skipjack came on the scene. In Virginia, when motors became large enough to push a fifty-foot and longer hull, the deadrise, cross-planked buyboat-style vessel became the main platform for dredging oysters.

Pat Vojtech wrote in her book, *Chesapeake Bay Skipjacks,* that J. L. Harrison of Tilghman Island, Maryland, was one of the first boatbuilders to experiment with the cheaper V-bottom/cross-planked-style vessel. In 1883, he built two forty-five-foot sail bateaux.

These early boats were considered variations of skipjacks. The first known skipjack was the *Ruby G. Ford,* built in Fairmount, Maryland, in 1891 by William Smith. The late Captain Edward Harrison of Ewell on Smith Island, Maryland, was captain of *Ruby G. Ford* in the 1930s–50s. In a 1989 interview at his home on the island, Captain Harrison said, "The boat I loved the most was the *Ruby G. Ford.* She had a bateau hull, but was skipjack rigged. My brother and I paid $600 for her in the late 1930s, and the first year we worked her we dredged seed [oysters] for a nickel a bushel. That same

year we got twenty and a quarter cents for a bushel of oysters to the shucking house. Now, boy, I tell ya, things were tight.

"One of the best times we ever had a-oystering was the third year we had the *Ruby G. Ford*," said Captain Harrison. "We caught 1,803 bushels in Tangier Sound in one week. That was nothing, though, compared to those big schooners. I'll tell ya, I've seen the [schooner] *Mattie F. Dean* catch a thousand bushels in a day. I know it sounds unbelievable, but it's the truth. That was one great sailor—now she could solid sail."

The *Mattie F. Dean* measured 68' x 25' x 5.8' and was built in 1885 at Madison, Maryland, while the *Ruby G. Ford* measured 45' x 15.6' x 2' 6".

Captain Harrison oystered aboard skipjacks, schooners, sloops and pungies. He said the advantage of the skipjack (bateau hull) over pungies, schooners, and sloops was that the skipjack had a shallower draft, which allowed oystermen to work in close to shore. Also, the small skipjack could make a closer turn. When it crossed an oyster bar, the vessel could nearly "turn on a dime" to start back across the bar for another "lick." Sloops and pungies needed more water to make a turn and their rigging needed more wind.

These advantages, coupled with the fact the deadrise and cross-planked skipjack was less expensive to build and had less sail and rigging, which meant smaller crews, marked the end of sloops, pungies, and schooners as the vessels of choice for Maryland oystermen.

The heyday of skipjack construction occurred between 1896 and 1915. The island communities of Deal, Taylor, Hooper, Watts, Smith, Holland, Tilghman, and Crab Islands were centers of skipjack construction.

Many variations of the cross-planked skipjack were built around the bay. Some were nearly completely flat-bottom, while others were shaped like a vee from stem to stern.

Another interesting variation built around Pocomoke City, Maryland, was a round-bottomed and longitudinally planked style named Pocomoke round-bottom.

The skipjack has a rich, colorful culture and heritage that comes from the lives of those who work the vessels in Maryland's winter dredge season. Part of that culture is experienced each year with the annual Deal Island Skipjack Race.

September 4, 1995
Deal Island Skipjack Race

About half of the bay's surviving skipjacks were on hand to hoist sails for the race. As a sign of the changing times on the bay, where there were once thousands of sailing vessels, only nine were on the starting line.

The Night Before

Perhaps it was an omen, but late Sunday night, as a group of skipjack captains, crew members, and groupies stood along the docks speculating on who would win the race the next day, Captain Wade Murphy made a prediction that was to come true.

Murphy, captain and owner of the *Rebecca T. Ruark*, had won the race seven years in a row, and the sloop (round and for-and-aft planked) hull *Rebecca* was the runaway favorite to win it again.

The oldest dredge boat still working on the bay, the *Rebecca T. Ruark* was built and rigged as a sloop on Taylor Island, Maryland, in 1886. She is the last sloop hull style still working on the bay. Some years back, her rigging was converted to sharp-headed skipjack rigging, but her round sloop hull style has given the boat a definite edge in races where conditions provide steady wind and deep water. She draws five feet six

inches, whereas the rest of the field draws only about three feet. For seven years the wind has favored the *Rebecca*.

"I can't get over the *Thomas Clyde*," said a thirty-five-year-old Deal Island woman with a crusty voice. She was standing amongst a group of men observing the boats. The *Thomas Clyde* had recently been overhauled and painted and had a spit-shine look. She also was a Deal Island boat, whereas the *Rebecca* hailed from Tilghman Island.

"I've never seen her look that good. Somebody must have died and left him [the captain] some money. She's looking good bo - y," she said with an Eastern Shore accent.

"She's sitting up higher than I've ever seen her," said Charles Abbott III, whose grandfather had owned and captained the vessel for many years.

"If there's a breeze tomorrow she'll give you a run for your money, Wade boy," said the woman.

"Is that right? Is that right?" said Wade with authority. "We'll find out! The *Clyde* is the least of my worries. I'm more worried about Art Daniels and Dickie Webster."

"Dickie ain't railwayed his boat [the skipjack *Caleb Jones*] all year," the woman said. "She's been tied to the damn dock gathering barnacles and Art Daniels is damn near eighty years old."

"Art Daniels has forgotten more about sailing then I'll ever know," said Wade. "Art Daniels is good."

"I believe ya!" said the woman.

"I'm just as good as Dickie Webster," continued Wade.

"You're better," said the woman.

"No, I'm not! But I'm just as good. The one that bothers me is Art Daniels."

This stern photo of three skipjacks shows the beauty of the boats under sail. It is no wonder that past maritime historians of the bay hated to see the great sailboats of the Chesapeake fade into memory. The patches in the sails only enhance the picture. Skipjack racing is a Maryland cultural experience at its best. (Photo by Hannah Chowning.)

Art Daniels was one of the oldest captains in the Maryland skipjack fleet. He was captain and owner of the *City of Crisfield*, a traditional-style skipjack. A local favorite, he moored his vessel at Wenona, Maryland, on Deal Island. Wade said about once every ten years Art pulled off a major upset.

Captain Wade knew that on certain days if there was light air and the wind had a tendency to start and stop and gust here and there, it gave him trouble. If air blew in areas where there was plenty of water, the *Rebecca* would have the advantage, but if not, and the air was moving close to shore, Art Daniels, with all his experience, would surely recognize this advantage and use it to his benefit.

The Race Aboard the *Rebecca*

Sunday morning at 8:00 a.m. all the captains, crews, and spectators gathered at the docks for the annual blessing of the fleet. The local Methodist minister gave a Chesapeake-flavored prayer and at the conclusion there was a resounding, "Amen."

Starting rules were explained to the captains and the boats made their way into Tangier Sound, where the three-mile race would be held. A new rule this year was that the race would end at 12:00 noon, finished or not.

The year before, Wade had stormed across the finish line in forty-five minutes. He paid little attention to the new rule.

The race is not just a fun time and a cultural event. A $1,000 purse goes to the winner and the boats get sponsors that help pay expenses. For instance, Wade's sponsor paid him $1,000 and allowed six paying customers to go along for the ride. Each customer paid $300 for that privilege.

The money is an incentive to race, says Wade. "Win, lose or draw, I'll have $2,800, and that's not a bad days work," he said.

Some boats were towed to the starting line, while others used their push boats to shove them out. Wade used his push boat and then hoisted it back to the davits when he reached the starting line.

In 1967, Maryland law was modified to allow the use of push boats to power skipjacks on Monday and Tuesday. Recently the law was modified to allow the use of push boats two days a week, with watermen picking their days.

While racing, most captains do not carry the push boat to the davits because they feel it slows them down. "I always have my push boat to the davits, but if they beat me this year I might have to rethink that," Wade said.

A red flag waved and a cannon sounded to start the race. Small boats carrying spectators darted out to get a better view of the sailing skipjacks.

From the start Wade yelled orders to the crew. "Flat her down a bit," he hollered. "Ride the jib up a bit. Pull the jib a windward."

Art Daniels in the *City of Crisfield* came up on the starboard.

"He's trying to block what wind we got," said Wade. "Seems like the wind is a hair to the westward. Do we got plenty of water ahead of us?"

A member of the crew checked the depth finder and told Wade there was plenty of water.

With the faster *Rebecca*, Wade was able to get out from under the sails of the *City of Crisfield* and take the lead.

"We are ahead right now," said "Mad Bob" Reddington of Bayhead, New Jersey. Reddington has crewed aboard the skipjacks in the annual Maryland races for more than twenty years, and sailed with Wade the past five years. "Unless something happens, when Wady gets out in front, he usually stays there."

"Look out for the landmines," yelled Wade.

Tangier Sound is loaded with crab pots, and the captain was referring to snagging one of them. On occasion, the *Rebecca* would run over a pot, and Wade was concerned that a line might get snagged on the bottom of the *Rebecca* and slow him down. Every time the boat went over a crab pot buoy, someone on the stern would watch to see if it came out from under the boat.

"Wade is his own sailor," Reddington said. "You don't tell him nothing. He always says, 'I'm here to win! If I lose, I lose on my own!'"

As the *Rebecca* cruised toward the turn home (half-way mark) at about five to six knots, the *City of Crisfield* edged into shallower water. Suddenly, as if a door closed and shut the wind out, the boat stalled.

"I knew it was going to happen sooner or later," said Wade out loud, but to himself. "We got a calm spot here and he has got a little bit of air over there."

The *City of Crisfield* darted on ahead and made the turn towards home ten minutes before the *Rebecca*.

"I don't know who to blame this bad luck on," said Wade jokingly. "We got a lot of newcomers on this boat and somebody brought us bad luck.

"Art has got this race buddy. He's a good sailor."

The next problem was Captain Ed Farley in the *H. (Herman) M. Krentz* from Royal Oak, Maryland. He also had slipped by the *Rebecca*.

"I think I can get Ed," Wade said.

The *Krentz* missed the turn on the first tack.

"If I can make this turn on one tack, we got him," said Wade.

The *Rebecca* made the turn on the first tack and passed the *Krentz*, but not before the noon cut-off time. As the *Rebecca* cruised past the *Krentz*, Farley raised his arms in victory.

"That's a happy boy there," said Wade. "First time Ed has beaten us. It's just the breaks you get, boys, and these guys are good too. They do it for a living. Every one of these captains is an expert, and the older they are, the better they are.

"When you're running light air and it's coming down and changing all around, the fastest boat doesn't always win. A lot of times, it's the luckiest boat that wins.

"Art was in the right place at the right time," he said. "I told you last night, Art Daniels has forgotten more about sailing than I'll ever know."

The *City of Crisfield* took home the $1,000 purse. The *H. M. Krentz* was second and the *Rebecca* finished third.

Labor Day 2001

In 2001, several Deal Island boats entered the Deal Island Skipjack Race and one was the *Fannie L. Daugherty*, a 42' x 15' 6" x 4', (60' long with bow sprit) skipjack, owned and captained by Captain Delmar Benton.

The *Fannie L. Daugherty* was built in 1904 at Crisfield, Maryland, and has been in the Benton family since 1969. Delmar bought it from his father in 1989.

To get ready for the race, Delmar took the boat to the railway and had the bottom cleaned. He left his push boat, which is normally to the davits, at home. His sails were the same that he used for dredging, but, he said, sails were not used much these days.

"I'd like to have gotten new sails, but most of us don't use sails much because we don't catch enough oysters to work on sail days," he remarked.

The Race Aboard the *Fannie L. Daughterty*

There was a slight breeze in the air as captains, crews, and spectators lined up on the docks at Deal Island Village for the annual skipjack race in Tangier Sound. The *Fannie L. Daugherty, Caleb W. Jones, Martha Lewis, Ida Mae, Nathan of Dorchester,* and *Somerset*, boats and names that have been known for nearly a century or more around the bay, were all rafted alongside the docks.

The Blessing of the Fleet and a captains' meeting kicked off the annual event. A good race is as much a part of the Chesapeake Bay culture and heritage as the boats participating. Pride and love of one's boat brings out the emotion in men and women.

"Ya see that stern," said a woman in the crowd, pointing to the *Ida Mae*. "You will be seeing it all day!"

These two Chesapeake Bay skipjacks are participating in the age-old tradition of racing. Years ago, sailors raced out to the oyster grounds and raced back when the day was done. Sailors took great pride in who had the fastest boat. Maryland's skipjack fleet is the last commercial sailing fleet in North America and the Deal Island Skipjack race is a colorful part of that tradition. (Photo by Hannah Chowning.)

Between the sail and bowsprit of the skipjack *Caleb W. Jones* can be seen a classic wooden deadrise motor-powered boat. The hull of the skipjack and the hull of that deadrise both evolved from an 1890s, V-bottom-style Eastern Shore crab skiff. (Photo by Hannah Chowning.)

"Yeah, we'll see about that!" said a mate aboard the *Somerset*.

Everyone in the group of captains, mates, and fans laughed as they made their way to their boats.

Each boat and captain has its fans, who have the same passion for the boats as NASCAR fans have for their cars. Several people on shore lamented the absence of the *City of Crisfield* and the dean of the skipjack captains, Art Daniels. The more than eighty-year-old Deal Island skipper had his boat on the rails at the Chesapeake Bay Maritime Museum yard, where the State of Maryland had set aside $50,000 for repairs.

The state had finally appeared to be seeing these boats for what they are—a national treasure. Maryland had pledged $150,000 for skipjack fleet repairs. The first $50,000 had gone to a Deal Island boat, and the second $50,000 would go to a Tilghman Island skipjack, and back and forth until the funds run out.

Delmar had the *Chelsea Nicole*, a deadrise workboat, tow the *Fannie L. Daugherty* into Tangier Sound. A good start can make or break a race, as Delmar was about to experience. The race was to start at 9:00 a.m. Each boat had to be behind the starting line without going over when the starting canon fired. To get an advantage, Delmar wanted to make the first turn before everyone else.

With Delmar at the helm, a crewmember stood beside him with a watch sounding the minutes to the canon fire. Another crewmember stood near the bow watching for "land mines," and every time one would come close he snagged the crab pot line with a boat hook and carried it aft until it was past the stern. This happened a dozen or more times in the race.

The *Fannie L. Daugherty* had a good start and was ahead, but the tide caused Delmar to hit the bell buoy turn at a bad angle and he could not get around it. He had to turn around, go back, and make the turn again on the starboard side. The rest of the fleet jumped way ahead.

Throughout the morning race, Delmar kept saying, "Eliminate that bell buoy and I'd be in the race."

After rounding the bell buoy, there was a three-mile straight stretch of water until the last turn. The wind died and this seemed to help Delmar.

"We ain't doing nothing but drifting," said Delmar.

Someone else aboard said, "We must be the fastest drifter, because we are catching some of the other boats."

Everyone laughed but it was the truth. The skipjack passed two vessels on the straightaway.

"I think they are anchored," said someone else. "Maybe a crab pot got them."

"It's that clean bottom. Some of those boys didn't go to the railway," said Delmar. He then jokingly added, "Everyone get up front and start blowing."

The rules call for the event to be finished at 12:00 noon, over the finish line or not. The 2000 race was over in an hour and a half. There have been years when it finished in forty-five minutes, but it was apparent that it would take the full amount of time this year, and only one boat made it to the finish line before noon.

The *Martha Lewis* made the final turn for home first, and the long straightaway to the finish required tacking. Several boats tacked toward shore, while Delmar tacked toward the channel.

"I hope they don't catch a breeze up close to shore because I can't get up in there," he said. The *Fannie L. Daugherty* has a "plug" rudder submerged under the stern, while most skipjacks have the "tiller across the stern" outboard sailboat-style rudder, which is traditional. The plug rudder requires at least four feet of water, whereas the traditional style allows for three feet draft.

Deadrise and Cross-planked

The wind began to pick up and Delmar made several long tacks before the race was called. When time expired, Delmar lowered his sails and was towed back to Deal Island Village.

The *Martha Lewis* ran away from the field and took the first-place $1,000 prize. The *Ida Mae* was second and won $500. The *Nathan of Dorchester* took third, but did not qualify for the winnings because it did not hold a commercial oyster dredge license. Next in line was the *Fannie L. Daugherty* and Delmar, who picked up $250.

"If I hadn't messed up on that first bell buoy, we'd have been in the big money," said Delmar, still lamenting the start of the race. "But what the heck, we got next year."

Skipjacks provide the last living hint of how life used to be when sail was the main power for craft on the Chesapeake and throughout the United States. The vessel is deadrise and cross-planked and is a wonderful example of how the V-bottom boat excelled under both motor and sail power.

The skipjack *Caleb W. Jones* has a traditional sailing outboard-style rudder, while some skipjacks have a plug rudder submerged under the stern. The advantage of an outboard rudder is that it requires less draft. A plug rudder requires about four feet of water to operate, while the outboard style requires about three feet. (Photo by Hannah Chowning.)

In the 2001 Deal Island Skipjack Race, these two skipjacks appear to be running into one another, but one has made the turn for home and the other is approaching the halfway buoy. (Photo by Hannah Chowning.)

seven
CHESAPEAKE BAY BUYBOATS

"The gasoline boat *Crescent,* owned by Messrs. Clarkson, Garrett and Hunt, of Bowlers, is on Chowning's railway having her bottom coppered. Young Mr. Garrett is overseeing the job." *Southside Sentinel,* December 15, 1905.

A gasoline boat the size of the *Crescent* made the social pages of the 1905 Urbanna *Southside Sentinel* because it was news for a gasoline-powered boat to be on the rails. In 1905, the era of internal-combustion engines was in its infancy, and little did folks know that the combination of V-bottom construction and motor power was ushering in a new day on the bay.

With the introduction of the gasoline engine, it did not take long for bay sailors to realize a good motor mounted in a good boat could cut out several days of waiting for a fair wind to blow. The old saying "time is money" came into play, and the days of commercial sailboats hauling freight and oysters gradually came to an end.

The bottoms on these new large gasoline boats were built deadrise and cross-planked, fore-and-aft planked, and logged. The *Crescent* appears to have been a fore-and-aft planked vessel with a very interesting round stern. Over time, the deadrise and cross-planked bottom boats became the popular style.

At first the large gasoline-powered freight boats were called gasoline boats, but later became known as buyboats, deck boats, run boats, runners, mast boats, bay freighters, bay boats, and freight boats.

The *Wm. B. Tennison* is the last surviving buyboat converted from sail still operating on the Chesapeake. She is a nine-logged bugeye built in 1899 by Frank Laird, of Crabb Island, Maryland. Large logged and planked sailing vessels were forerunners to the large deadrise and cross-planked boats used to buy seafood from commercial fishermen and haul it back to processing houses on the shore. The *Wm. B. Tennison* is owned by the Calvert Marine Museum in Solomons, Maryland.

The *Dillard,* built in Whealton, Virginia, in 1905, was an early motor-powered deck boat. The large hulls of the Chesapeake Bay buyboats made great platforms for church picnics and other social events of the day. (Courtesy of Wit Garrett.)

Deadrise and Cross-planked

The boats got the name buyboat from being used to go out to the fishing grounds to buy oysters, crabs, and fish from independent commercial watermen, and then hauling the produce back to the seafood-processing houses onshore. When a seafood dealer or oyster planter who was working his own grounds used the vessel to carry oysters back to his own processing house, the boat was referred to as a run boat or runner. These terms were a carryover from the days of sail, when sail-powered boats were used for the same thing.

The boats often were called deck boats because decks were installed around the outside of the house and forward to the bow, with an open hold at amidship for storing payload, and another opening aft for the engine. A booby hatch with decks all around it usually was installed forward to enter the forepeak. Deck boat was a very common name for boats that were not used to buy seafood, but deck boats usually were the same style and shape as buyboats.

The term mast boat comes from the crab dredge fishery to distinguish between those boats with masts and the smaller deadrise boats without masts. The terms freight boat and bay freighter was used for boats used to haul freight, which could

Captain Perry Rogers, of Shady Side, Maryland, is standing on the bow of the *Princess*, a semi-deck boat built in 1904. The *Princess* is an example of an early style deck boat. The evolution was not to the point that the house was raised up on deck as on modern buyboats, but the *Princess* is decked everywhere else. (Courtesy of Betty Lou Leatherbury Senesi and the Captain Salem Avery Museum.)

be anything from live hogs hauled to Smithfield, Virginia, to fine linens brought from Baltimore, Maryland. The term also was a carryover from when sail-powered schooners and bugeyes were around. The era of motor-powered freight boats ended as highways improved and trucks took over the business of hauling goods.

Boats powered by gasoline and diesel engines were part of major technological advancement of that era, and the Cadillac of bay motor-powered wooden boats was the Chesapeake Bay buyboat. It was the largest hull style built for power. On the social spectrum of those working the water, a captain of a buyboat was at the top of the ladder.

The boats ranged from forty feet in length to nearly one hundred feet. The largest deadrise and cross-planked style deck boat built was the ninety-eight-foot *Marydel,* built in 1927 by Linwood Price of Deltaville for W. E. Valliant & Co. of Delaware. It was used to haul fertilizer.

The second largest one built was the ninety-three-foot *Chesapeake,* built by Lepron Johnson, of Crittenden, Virginia, in 1936, for J. H. Miles & Co., of Norfolk, Virginia, one of the largest oyster growers in the state. The *Chesapeake* was a fore-and-aft planked, round-bilge boat. Johnson and his yard foreman, Clifton Haughwout, were well versed in the skills involved in lofting and the use of half-models, and specialized in fore-and-aft planked vessels.

Most deadrise and cross-planked boats were not lofted, but built from "rack of eye." Linwood Price and his son, Milford, built the last two large deck boats on the bay for Miles in 1946 and 1949, and the boats were cross-planked.

The reason Miles went with the cross-planked style was because Johnson's fore-and-aft planked *Chesapeake* was limited where she could go on the bay due to her seven-foot draft. The twenty-five-foot beam on the *Chesapeake* was just right in width, but Miles needed boats to travel and work the shallow oyster grounds on Mobjack Bay and elsewhere. They needed boats that had the beam of the *Chesapeake,* but a draft of around five feet. They could get the draft from a cross-planked boat, but the beam was a problem.

Linwood and Milford Price, of Deltaville, Virginia, built the *Mobjack* for Rufus Miles, of Norfolk, in 1946. The seventy-three-foot vessel was designed by naval architect Carl T. Forsberg, of Freeport, Long Island, to provide a 24' beam with a 5.5' draft. Miles needed a boat that could carry large amounts of oysters in shallow waters. Forsberg took the time-tested deadrise hull and designed the *Mobjack,* *Ocean View* (1949), and *Marie* (1952), which Price built in his yard on Broad Creek. The *Marie* was built for Eddie Abbott, of Water View, Virginia.

Miles and Price hired naval architect Carl Forsberg, of Freeport, Long Island, to work on the hull designs of the *Mobjack* and *Ocean View*. Forsberg took the time-tested Chesapeake Bay cross-planked hull and restructured it to accommodate twenty-five-feet of beam and a five-and-half-foot draft.

The old master builder Linwood Price had started building boats around 1910. He had learned how to build with foot adz and broadax, and probably built more cross-planked deck boats than anyone else on the bay. Who better to go to than Price and his son? They took Forsberg's plans and built to perfection the 73'x24' *Mobjack* in 1946, and the 72'x24' *Ocean View* in 1949 on Broad Creek in Deltaville. These were the last more than seventy-foot-long buyboats built on the

bay and, some said, the dreamboats of the buyboat era.

All of the best attributes that had evolved from years of trial and error were built into the hulls and decks of the *Mobjack* and *Ocean View*. They also had the finishing touch of a naval architect. The boats were part of a dream shared by many after World War II, that the oyster industry would flourish on the bay. Unfortunately, that was not to be. Several buyboat-style boats were built in the 1950s and 1960s, but the era peaked with the *Mobjack* and *Ocean View*.

Price and his son built their last buyboat in 1952, when they constructed the 59.5'x18.5'x6.3' *Marie* for Eddie Abbott, of Water View, Virginia. Forsberg helped with the design of that hull also.

Linwood Price died May 14, 1957, ending a golden era of wooden boatbuilding on the Chesapeake.

Sail and Motor Buyboats

Even though motor boats replaced sail-powered boats, the Chesapeake Bay buyboat in the early years used sail for auxiliary power and steadying the boat while it was underway. When engines became powerful enough to push a fifty-foot hull, the era of sail and motor together came to an end.

It was, however, an interesting sight to see a motor-powered buyboat underway with sail, high and catching a fair wind. Stuart Edwards, ninety-two years old in 2007, of Gwynn's Island, Virginia, recalls that his father, Emmett Edwards, had a 40'x10' five-log canoe (buyboat) built in 1912 in Poquoson, Virginia, by Andrew and Akana Moore. She was built for power, had a two-cylinder, sixteen-horsepower Lathrope engine, and carried a sail.

The boat was named *Rescue,* and Emmett and Stuart used the boat to haul seine, pound net, and to buy fish from local watermen. They hauled the fish to Cape Charles, Virginia, and sold to a buyer who loaded the fish on the railroad train and shipped it to a fish house in Baltimore.

"The first time I ever saw a train was on the other side of the dock where we sold our fish," said Stuart. "The dock was high. We'd load the fish onto the dock and they'd carry the boxes fifteen feet and load it on to a train car.

"My daddy had a mast installed and a house mounted aft on his boat," said Stuart. "We'd take the house off when we were hauling pound poles, but we had it on when we were buying and hauling fish to Cape Charles.

"Daddy had a sail canoe with a centerboard before he had the *Rescue* built. The *Rescue* didn't have a centerboard," he said. "Daddy knew how to sail and he liked to use the sail and motor together. When the wind was nor' east, daddy would put that big sail up and, boy, would we move. It was a nice rig. He would slow the engine down and let that big sail take us. When it was real rough, it would help steady the boat."

Buyboat Captain Talks about the Boats

Neil Groom, ninety-five years old in 2006, was captain and mate aboard several buyboats. He spent twenty-five years aboard the boats before landing at Shady Side, Maryland, in 1937, where he put down roots and lives today.

At the turn of the twentieth century there was not much future in areas like Hell's Neck, near Wake, Virginia, where Neil was born and raised. So when the opportunity came to mate aboard a little three-hundred-bushel canoe named the

Bruiser, Neil jumped at the opportunity. She was a freight boat and he started out making a dollar a day.

"I was fourteen years old and my uncle, Winnie Revere, and I went down to Mobjack Bay to go hard crabbing," said Neil. "Winnie had a little round-stern boat that John Wright had built for him. It had a seven-horsepower Palmer engine in her for power.

James "Big Jim" Smith built the *Little Muriel Eileen* in Bena, Virginia, in 1926, for R. E. Roberts of Baltimore. He named the boat for his two daughters. He had a second boat built in 1928 by Smith and named it *Muriel Eileen*. When the first *Muriel Eileen* was sold it became known as the *Little Muriel Eileen,* and Roberts's bigger boat, a double-decker, became known as the *Big Muriel Eileen*. In 2007, the *Little Muriel Eileen* is owned by David Cantera, of New Castle, Delaware, and is kept in first-class condition. She was also one of many buyboats owned by the legendary Captain Johnny Ward of Deltaville.

"We were selling crabs to Captain Johnny Ward on the buyboat *Lagonia,* and my first cousin was on the boat working for Captain Johnny. He asked me if I wanted to go with them to Crisfield to see where they took the crabs," said Neil. "I remember asking Captain Johnny, 'What are you going to have for breakfast?'

"He said, 'Spuds and codfish.' That sounded good to me, so I told my uncle I was going to make the trip. I told him to tell my mamma I was going and that hopefully I could find a job over there."

The *Lagonia* was a log canoe built in 1913 by Jas. H. Moore in Poquoson, Virginia. She was 44.3' x 11.7' x 4.4' and had a twenty-five-horsepower two-cylinder Palmer engine.

"Johnny Ward was a buyboat legend," said Neil. "He was the hardest driver on the bay when it came to buyboats. Johnny's father, Henry Ward, of Crisfield, owned the sailing bugeye named the *Louise Travers*. Johnny first came over to the Western Shore of the bay in a small motor-powered canoe, and the story goes he and his daddy got to arguing over what was the fastest, gasoline engines or sails. So, Johnny took off with his father trailing. Johnny got right far ahead when his rudder came unhooked, and when Henry got up to him Johnny was hanging overboard trying to get it hooked. Henry laughed and laughed, but it wasn't too long after that Henry had the *Louise Travers* converted to power."

James T. Marsh of Solomons, Maryland built *Louise Travers* as a sailing bugeye in 1896. She was originally 58' x 18' 6" x 4' 4", but was later enlarged to 70' x 19' 5" x 5' 7".

"I already knew a lot about buyboats because Lawrence and Russell Parker built boats close to where I lived. Lawrence also sold Regal engines, and when Russell built the *Juanita*, a sixty-foot buyboat in 1926, he put a fifty-horsepower Regal engine in her. That was a big engine in those days.

"Russell Parker could build a boat and you could steer her, but those buyboats built over there on Fishing Bay by Lee Deagle and Lin Price, you couldn't steer them with two rudders," he said, and laughed.

"When I got to Crisfield, we were standing on the dock and this little boat came in there loaded with peanuts. Syd Conley, captain of the *Bruiser* came up and asked us if any of us boys wanted to mate aboard his boat. I figured it was a job and I didn't have much else.

Russell Parker, of Wake, Virginia, built the sixty-foot *Inez* in 1936. Captain Neil Wake, who worked aboard many of the boats, said jokingly that Captain Parker's boats steered extremely well, whereas the boats of such master builders as Linwood Price and Lee Deagle would take two rudders to steer the vessel. The *Inez* is loaded down with oysters. (Courtesy of David Rollins.)

"My first trip on the *Bruiser* was to Gywnn's Island to buy fish that we took to a cutting house in Fredericksburg. They would put the fish in a big vat and they'd salt it down. We also bought oysters right there at Mill Creek on the Rappahannock and took them to Morattico to a shucking house. The *Bruiser* had a sixteen-horsepower Lathrope without a clutch. I was on her for about two years.

"One day we were in Crisfield, and Captain Joe Carter of the *Miss Holland* came up to me and asked me if I wanted a job. I told him I'd give it a try," said Neil. "I knew there wasn't much future on the *Bruiser,* because the boat was owned by Syd Conley's father-in-law and all I'd ever be was a mate.

"We left Crisfield on the *Miss Holland* and went to Battery Park on the James River and got a load of oysters," he said. "On the way back, I'd asked him to carry me home so I could pick up some clothes. Well, when we got to the Piankatank River, I told him, 'If you give me five dollars, I can buy a pair of pants at Crisfield and I can make it until September.' That way we wouldn't have to stop, and that's what he did."

The *Elsie Louise* was used to haul freight for Lord Mott Co., of Baltimore, Maryland and Urbanna, Virginia. J. Wood Tull built her in Irvington, Virginia in 1914. (Courtesy of Selden Richardson.)

Neil was sixteen when he went aboard the *Miss Holland*. He became captain at nineteen. Robert G. Neale owned the *Miss Holland* and most of Bowler's Wharf, which was a steamboat dock composed of an oyster house, store, tomato canning factory, and a hotel on the shore. He had bought the *Miss Holland* from Nonie Holland of Crisfield, Maryland. She was an eighty-ton boat and was sixty-five feet long x twenty feet wide.

"John and Tom Wright of Deltaville built the *Miss Holland,* and she was a mighty fine boat," said Neil. "When Nonie sold the *Miss Holland* to Mr. Neale, Nonie had another boat built on the Eastern Shore and named it *Miss Dorothy*.

"By law, we had to have a skiff and water barrel on the boat," he said. "Now you can get by with a life raft. We had a little short skiff on the *Miss Holland* that we'd throw up on the stern and we always carried a barrel of water. The Wright Brothers in Deltaville built the skiff for the *Miss Holland*. When I got to be captain, we'd haul the *Miss Holland* out and work on her bottom twice a year. We would take her over to Humphrey's Railway in Weems or to Captain Dick Hudson's railway in Irvington. There weren't too many big railways in those days.

"I ran everything under the sun in the *Miss Holland*," said Neil, "but in the spring I mostly ran fertilizer to Baltimore from Bowler's Wharf, and I'd pick up empty cans for Mr. Neale's canning factory on the return trip. I ran lumber to Norfolk and I'd pick up coal on the return trip for the boiler in the tomato factory. I liked soft coal because you could bank a good fire in the stove on the boat and it would last all night. I'd stash soft coal away for real cold nights.

"I ran oysters in the winter from the James River. I would take oysters to New Jersey sometimes. We'd go up to New Jersey through the Chesapeake/Delaware Canal. I also ran cans of tomatoes and black-eye peas to Norfolk and Baltimore from Bowlers

"I was on the *Miss Holland* when the August Storm of 1933 hit," said Neil. "We had been in Baltimore and gotten a load of fertilizer and had left. When we got out on the bay, the sky just didn't look right. Irvin Callis was with me and I told him, 'Irvin, this just don't look right. Something is getting ready to happen.' There was plenty of wind and sea. I turned her around and went back to Baltimore.

"The tide came up in the harbor and I didn't think it was going to stop. The next day when the tide went out, Baltimore Harbor was loaded with lumber and cord wood that had floated up during the high water," he said.

"The wood wasn't there long because the next day there were entire families, little children, and old people carrying the planks away. I guess to burn in their wood cook stoves.

"I left the *Miss Holland* and went to work on the *Thomas F. Jubb* in the fall of 1937," said Neil. *Thomas F. Jubb* was built in Weems, Virginia in 1909. It was 65' 8" x 20' 9" x 6' 8." The *Jubb's* homeport for many years was Shady Side, Maryland.

"The biggest boat I ever worked on was the *Lula M. Phillips*," said Neil. "She belonged to Willie Ward of Deltaville and I mated on her. She was a schooner boat."

The *Lula M. Phillips* was originally the sailing schooner, *Annie M. Leonard*, built in 1877 by William Benson of Oxford, Maryland. She was 77' 5" x 22' x 5' 6" and she was converted to power in the 1920s.

"I had a chance to buy a boat once," he said. "I was in Crisfield and Shad Crockett came in there in the *Nellie Crockett*. I was standing on the dock and he walked right up to me and said 'Neil, I want to sell you the *Nellie Crockett*.'

"I said, 'Shad, how much do you want for her?'

"He said, '$6,000.'

"I told him, 'Christ! I ain't got six cents.'"

In 2007, the *Nellie Crockett* was alive and well and listed on the National Historic Landmarks Program. She was built in 1925 by Charles A. Dana of Crisfield and is 61.7' x 20.4' x 6.5'.

At Shady Side, Neil worked for an oyster company and was captain for a while of the motor-powered bugeye the Edna D. Lightheiser. She was originally built as a sail-powered bugeye in 1900 by C. C. Durm & Son at Baltimore, and was 68' x 18' 9" x 5' 1". The vessel spent much of her life in Shady Side, and was owned by Bertha A. Woodfield, and later by Esther F. Hallock. Oftentimes, boat ownership was given to the wife and the husband was captain. This enabled both husband and wife to use the Merchant's Marine Hospital in Norfolk through the registration of the boat.

"I ran the *Lightheiser* and *Jubb* until World War II started," said Neil. "By then I had already made Shady Side my home. I tried

The *Ellen Marie* was built by Lennie and Alton Smith, of Mathews County, Virginia, in 1926. Until several years ago, she was used in the Virginia crab dredge fishery. She still carries the dredge post and other gear related to dredging. The last commercial fishing use for deck boats was in the Virginia crab dredge fishery. When watermen started using double dredges on sterns of standard deadrise workboats, the larger and more costly to operate buyboats were out of a job. In 2006, only one boat of this style was being used on the bay as a commercial crab dredging boat.

to go fight in the war, but they said I was too old for active duty, so I got a defense job. After that I stayed on land and never went back on the boats.

"I loved running the boats, but it didn't lend itself well to family life and I could tell things were changing on the bay. I watched the schooners and bugeyes pass, so I knew the same thing could happen to the buyboats.

"Some of my fondest memories now are of those days when I was on the boats."

Oyster Business and the Boats

In 1958, Ivy Hunt of Littleton, Colorado, wrote down his Chesapeake Bay memories of working in the oyster business in the late 1800s and early 1900s at Bowler's Wharf in Essex County, Virginia. Hunt was part owner of the *Crescent*, mentioned earlier in this chapter, and captain of a sailing schooner *Garland*, which was an oyster buyboat. The term buyboat goes back to the very early 1800s when Yankee schooners came down from Long Island and started buying oysters from bay hand tongers. When the tradition of buying oysters from boats continued into the era of internal combustion engines, so did the name buyboats.

Fred Ward built the *Crescent* in 1904 in Urbanna, Virginia. This photo is one of the earliest pictures in existence of a Virginia motor-powered Chesapeake Bay buyboat. Note the rounded pilothouse that sits atop an engine room house, with windows mounted low in the sides for ventilation. The boat appears to have a fore-and-aft planked bottom with a interesting round stern. The photo was taken around 1905 at C. P. Garrett and Ivy Hunt's oyster house on Bowler's Steamboat Wharf in Essex County, Virginia. (Courtesy of Wit Garrett.)

Hunt and his father-in-law, C. P. Garrett, ran a very successful oyster business at Bowler's Wharf, and owned the *Garland* with a Mr. Julian.

In his writings, Hunt gives some interesting insight into the buying and selling of oysters and the use of a buyboat. Hunt recalled that in 1897, "We made some money freighting that summer (in the *Garland*) . . . and with my contact, with captains and oyster vessels while in Baltimore Harbor, I learned that there was an unusually good strike of seed oysters in the James River that spring.

"I reported this to Mr. Garrett and Mr. Julian [owners of the *Garland*]. There had been no planting of seed oyster in the upper Rappahannock River since the year 1888, the year of the Johnstown [Pennsylvania] flood, when so much fresh water came down into the Rappahannock that all oysters were killed as far down as Morattico Bar.

"This disaster was the cause of Mr. Julian discontinuing the oyster business and going into the mercantile business, at Center Cross. The report of there being an exceptional strike of seed oysters gave rise to a renewed anxiety on the part of both Mr. Garrett and Mr. Julian to get back into the planting of seed oysters.

"I went to the James on September 1 at the opening of the oyster season to get a load, which Mr. Garrett and myself would plant as our own and particularly to get a first-hand knowledge of the conditions of the reported big strike of seed oysters.

"I was in the James River … and loaded in one day with the most wonderful quality of seed stock they had ever seen, at a price of ten cents a bushel. Mr. Julian almost had a fit when he saw what was to be had when on the third day of the season I was anchored off Garrett's landing with the evidence.

"So enthused was Mr. Garrett, that I immediately went back for another load for us. When I returned with that load Mr. Julian had decided to chance one load for himself to plant on his grounds. So I went back for the third load. Mr. Julian had not forgotten the loss he sustained in 1888, and wanted to get oyster ground further down the river, where the chance for another freshet would not be as dangerous as at Garrett's Landing."

The three men were able to obtain grounds further down river and entered into a three-way partnership.

"Everyone was so excited that they proposed to furnish the capital and I give my time in taking care of the buying, planting, and the supervision of selling (market-size) oysters to … Baltimore markets.

"We owned the boat so that meant it would cost us less than two cents a bushel of seed (to transport the seed), whereas if we had chartered a vessel it would cost us five cents a bushel freight. Also, if I did the buying myself, I (being part owner) naturally would be interested in getting the best planting stock, while others would be interested only in their five cents freight per bushel and there is always a chance of getting an unscrupulous or dishonest captain who could pad or claim he had bought more bushels than he really did buy.

"We started planting in March [1897] and at the end of the season had over ten thousand bushels of good quality seed stock planted on the beds," he wrote. "This process of buying and planting seed went on each season for three years before the first planting was ready for market."

Although Hunt's writings do not speak totally to the conditions of the life of buying oysters in the late 1800s on the James, he most certainly was buying oysters from independent oystermen working out of sail, oar, or sculling paddle-powered canoes and bateaux.

Wit Garrett of Center Cross, Virginia, contacted me shortly after *Chesapeake Bay Buyboats* was published in early 2004, and introduced me to Ivy Hunt's memoirs. Hunt was Garrett's uncle and his grandfather was C. P. Garrett, the Mr. Garrett in Hunt's writings.

Wit also introduced me to Neil Groom, of Shady Side, Maryland. In one of several interviews with Wit, he asked me if I had ever heard of Claude Chowning of Urbanna. I informed him that Claude was my father's first cousin, but had died before I had any memory of him.

"You know, Claude was real good friends with my father [Fred Garrett Sr.], and every time we'd go to Urbanna he would look Claude up and they would have the best time talking. I wonder how they knew one another?" he asked me.

"I have no idea Wit," was my answer.

At the end of that same interview, Wit provided me the wonderful old photo of the *Crescent,* and informed me this was his grandfather's buyboat.

In 2007, Jean Dunn of Gloucester County brought a December 16, 1905 issue of the *Southside Sentinel* into the *Sentinel* office. Her husband J. W. Dunn had recently died. J. W. was grandson to Julian Brown, owner of the *Sentinel* for more than fifty years, and Jean had found the old paper in some of his things.

As I was looking at the worn and tattered issue of the *Sentinel,* I realized I could now answer Wit's question about his father's relationship with Claude Chowning.

The Chowning's Railway mentioned in the social notice of the 1905 Urbanna paper belonged to my great-uncle, George S. Chowning. His son Claude, a young man then about the age of Wit's father, worked at the railway. The young Mr. Garrett in the notice was Fred Garrett Sr., Wit's father, and the mystery was solved. Their introduction most certainly came about because of the motor-powered *Crescent*.

Even more interesting was that in January 2007, Wit came across papers in some of his grandfather's things that spoke to the history of the *Crescent*. One of the papers was written by Ivy Hunt in an effort to sell the boat. It is a wonderful description of an early dredge boat/buyboat and, as it turns out, the *Crescent* was built in Urbanna at my great-uncle's railway.

Hunt wrote, "The oyster dredge boat *Crescent,* was built for the present owners by Fred W. Ward (in Urbanna, Virginia) in 1904. Her bottom, sides, deck beam, and decks are of all heart seasoned Georgia pine. Timbers, stem, keel, keelson, bilge keelsons, clamps, and ceiling are all of selected white oak. The boat is thoroughly bolted throughout with galvanized iron bolts. The boat was especially designed and built for a dredging boat, having round bottom, round stern, and sharp bow, with pilothouse aft. She is 45'3"x13'9"x4' and has a draft of about 42" of water when light. Will carry handily 400 bushels oysters on deck and trim. She is equipped with a 25 h.p. two cylinders Automatic gasoline engine of the 1908 type. It has athwart ship hoisters made by the Automatic Marine Co. all of which are in first class condition. Engine and hoisters are controlled from pilothouse by one man."

The round-bottom *Crescent* was the forerunner to the modern deadrise and cross-planked V-bottom deck boat. The *Crescent* was built in 1904, the same year Perry Rogers built the *Princess*. The *Crescent* and *Princess* are two of the earliest motor-powered buyboats built on the bay.

The *East Hampton* on its way to buyboat rendezvous in Rock Hall, Maryland, in 2004. Only a few of these large deadrise buyboats are alive today on the Bay and most have been converted to pleasure craft. Freeman Hudgins and Napoleon Bonaparte (Bony) Diggs built the *East Hampton* in Mathews County, Virginia, in 1925. She originally was an open boat with a V-stern. Here she sports a traditional round stern.

eight
POTOMAC RIVER DORIES

The north bank of the Potomac River was one of the most interesting boatbuilding regions on the bay and home to the Potomac River dory.

The dory boat was a fore-and-aft planked vessel built primarily in the seventh district of St. Mary's County, Maryland, along the creeks of the Potomac River. It was a competitor of the deadrise, cross-planked boat, used in the same fisheries and mostly for the same purposes. It is also a deadrise style with an extremely high chine line.

The history of the dory and cross-planked deadrise parallel one another in that they came along about the same time

This 1904 photo off Nomini, Virginia, in the Potomac River, shows the layout of sail-powered Potomac River dories. The mast layout is similar to the style used on the seaside bateaux, a deadrise and cross-planked vessel used on the seaside of the Eastern Shore. (Frederick Tilp Collection and Calvert Marine Museum.)

period in the 1880s. The forerunner to the dory was a flat-bottom sailing craft called a black "nancy." It was used on the Potomac as far back as the colonial period.

Edwin W. Beitzell in his book, *Life on the Potomac River*, described the nancy. "The nancy was usually painted black (with tar from pitch pine trees) and its length ranged from 18 to 27 feet," he wrote. "The sides were usually of single pine boards, about 2 1/2 feet high, topped by wide washboards. The stern was square and undercut at an obtuse angle. The larger boats were ribbed. The keel was 2 feet x 6 inches and the planking ran lengthwise. They had a centerboard and could be sailed against the wind."

Perhaps the most significant thing about the nancy was that the planking ran lengthwise, and this style carried over to the dory boats. Also, the area around Solomons Island, Maryland, in Calvert County, right next door to St. Mary's County, was where fore-and-aft planked bugeyes evolved in the 1880s. James T. Marsh of Solomons is credited with building the first one. When the first dory boat was built, the region already had a strong heritage in fore-and-aft plank construction.

Many developmental issues that arose on cross-planked boats were also issues on dory boats. V-bottom deadrise boats and dories evolved from the days of sail. The tuck, or shield, stern was the main style used on sailing dories. The tuck stern was also used on some early cross-planked sail-powered vessels. This style stern was later transferred to both motor-powered

Deadrise and Cross-planked

dories and deadrise boats with limited success. Squat-boards had to be used on both styles and, square, round, and duck-tail (similar to draketail) sterns evolved on engine-powered dories, just as they had on cross-planked boats. The decks, wide washboards and house/pilothouse all evolved on both styles in similar ways.

Most areas throughout the bay region started out building fore-and-aft planked bottoms but switched to the cross-planked style. There were fewer construction complications in building a cross-planked boat in the back yard than having to deal with steam-bending bottom planks and shaping long stem-to-stern planks on the dory. The steaming of bottom planks is one of the few instances on the Chesapeake Bay where this practice could be found in small craft construction. It was not, however, the only place on the bay. Lepron Johnson in Crittenden, Virginia, built the second-largest deadrise buyboat ever built, the *Chesapeake*, with fore-and-aft planking and the bottom planks were steam bent. He built most of his boats this way, large and small. Whether or not Johnson's method was passed down from earlier builders in that area is not known. His boatbuilding techniques were advanced for the time. He lofted and used half-models in his building methods.

These oystermen were working in motor-powered Potomac River dories on the Potomac River in 1936. Note the shield, tuck stern, outside rudder, and tiller stick on the dory in the foreground. This shield-shaped stern was found mostly on dories, yet similar styles of tuck sterns were common on deadrise and cross-planked boats. The use of the sailboat style outside rudder and tiller on gasoline engine-powered dories was also found on early deadrise boats. (Courtesy of Library of Congress, LC-USF34-5433 and Calvert Marine Museum.)

Oystermen in these sail-powered Potomac River dories are selling their catch to buyers on a Chesapeake Bay schooner. Before gasoline engines, sail-powered schooners and bugeyes were used as buyboats. The photo was taken in 1904 off Lower Machodoc, on the Potomac River. (Courtesy of Frederick Tilp Collection and the Calvert Marine Museum.)

The *Sea Mist III* is a Potomac River dory and shows off the classic high, rising dory chine line.

The *Jeanne S.* and the *Lillian B.* are two workboats converted to pleasure craft. The *Jeanne S.* is a classic deadrise and cross-planked hull with a low chine line. The *Lillian B.* is a Potomac River dory with fore-and-aft planking and a very high chine line, as shown in the photo. (Courtesy of Gary Thimsen.)

It is known that Johnson employed Clifton Haughwout as his yard foreman. Haughwout's relatives were in the New York oyster business and came to Virginia before the Civil War. This type of Yankee influence could explain many northern innovations found in Chesapeake Bay boats.

Dory builders, however, were, for the most part, rack-of-eye builders. Richard J. Dodds, Curator of Calvert Marine Museum's Maritime History, wrote in a 1996 article on dories in *Woodenboat Magazine* that, "Dory builders were mostly self-taught or learned by working under other

These two photos, at about the same angle, compare frame construction techniques of the fore-and-aft planked dory and the cross-planked deadrise. The dory in the left photo has framing that extends across the bottom, so longitudinal planking can be attached and stiffened. The right photo shows a traditional deadrise and cross-planked boat with two stringers giving stiffness to the bottom. Note that framing does not extend across the bottom. (The deadrise photo is courtesy of Joe Conboy.)

builders. They worked without formal plans or half models, and in most cases the boatyards were small and power tools were few, if any."

In just about every region on the bay, builders made the switch from lengthwise to cross planking fairly early in the evolution of deadrise boats. So why didn't the Maryland builders on the north bank of the Potomac switch to cross-planked boats?

This question was proposed to Dodds. "This has puzzled me as well," he wrote. "I think that one explanation is that they went from building larger fore-and-aft sailing craft (such as planked bugeyes) to the small workboats of the same construction with no period of cross-planked boats along the way.

"Until 1931 oyster dredging on the Potomac had to be under sail, which probably continued the longevity of hulls built for sail," wrote Dodds. "When dredging was banned in 1931, the dory evolved in shape more suited to power but still kept the same style of construction.

"I think watermen of this region were just used to this style and the preference was passed through a number of generations," he wrote. "The dory was held in high regard and still is today."

The history of the region may also have played a role in the continuation of the fore-and-aft planked dory. Strong attitudes towards the dory may have been fueled by conflicts between Maryland and Virginia watermen. The Potomac is unique in that its waters and bottom lie in State of Maryland and tributaries on the south bank belong to the state of Virginia.

Historically this has created conflicts that go back to the beginning of our country. Virginians got the right to work the Potomac under the Compact of 1785, which provided that, in return for free entry of Maryland ships through the Virginia Capes, Maryland would give Virginia full and equal fishing rights in the Potomac.

Maryland had laws that Virginia would not obey, and, to make matters worse, the Compact of 1785 dictated that if a Virginian broke a Maryland law he was to be tried in Virginia. Consequently, very few Virginians were convicted of anything, and illegal oystering flourished on the Potomac. This created bad blood between the two sides.

Perhaps the dory, along with its very stable platform, became symbolic of St. Mary's County watermen. Dodds also wrote concerning Maryland watermen's loyalty to the dory, "I think, too, there was a strong prejudice against cross-planked boats because of the opinion (rightly or wrongly) they were not as safe."

The museum interviewed a Potomac River boatbuilder who specialized in building fore-and-aft planked boats. He had strong opinions about cross-planked boats. "They're trash. They'll kill ya ass and they are built by men who don't know how to fit a plank," he said.

It is an age-old debate. Virginia boatbuilders counter this by saying that dories require more caulking than cross-planked boats and that a fore-and-aft planked boat has a tendency to lose caulking in extremely heavy seas. Maryland builders contend that a cross-planked boat can lose a plank easier than a fore-and-aft planked vessel.

Dories were built on both sides of the Potomac, but cross-planked boats were the vessel of choice on the Virginia side. Lester Boothe of Lewisette, on the Virginia side of the river, was born there in 1921. "I never knew of any amount of dories built on the Virginia side of the Potomac, but some were built here," he said.

"When I was a boy, Captain Buck Web 'planked' some. Planked boats are what we called the dory-style boat. I hung out around Captain Buck's boatyard because he would always give me a penny or nickel or something for helping out.

"He built whatever you wanted—dories or deadrise cross-planked boats," said Boothe. "He did it all by hand. He never had a band-saw and I don't reckon he ever saw one."

Virginia Potomac River boatbuilder Francis Haynie built one dory in his long career of boatbuilding on Cod Creek near Heathsville, Virginia. "Dory builders on the other side of the river used black gum wood for keels," he said. "I know because I repaired a many a one. If black gum stays wet or dry, it will never rot. It's the best wood in the world for a keel. They also used cypress for bottom planking and longleaf yellow pine for side planking.

"When I worked at the railway, I worked on a lot of dories," said Haynie. "I'll tell you this, the men who built them were for the most part very good boatbuilders. I learned a lot just from working on those boats, but I stuck mostly with cross planking because that's what my customers wanted. I did build one fore-and-aft boat for an oysterman and it worked out fine."

Dory Builders

One of the finest bay maritime books written on any region of the Chesapeake Bay is Beitzell's *Life on the Potomac River*. Beitzell saved for posterity some wonderful history and culture surrounding the dory and the business of building boats in St. Mary's County, Maryland.

He wrote of the sailing dory, "The dory was deadrise and something of a small edition of the Chesapeake Bay bugeye, which was developed after the Civil War to dredge oysters.

The sides of the dory were steamed, twisted, and curved to form a rounded surface forward with moderate sloping bottom, resembling a wide V. The stern was undercut, sloping upward and rounded, somewhat resembling a shield." (This is a style of a tuck stern.)

Potomac River dory builder Garner Gibson, of Avenue, Maryland, built this square stern dory, *Nancy B* in 1969. It is believed that Gibson installed the first square stern on a dory boat in 1928. In 2005, the *Nancy B* was still working the Potomac in the river's pound net fishery. "She has been a great boat for what I use her for," said owner Robert T. Brown. "As long as you look after a wooden boat, she will take you out and get you back."

"The boat was reinforced with ribs from bow to stern, the planking ran lengthwise and warped both fore and aft. The earlier models ranged from 25 to 30 feet in length, though in later years they were built up to 42 feet. Generally the width was about one-third of the length. The boat was equipped with a center well and two slightly raked masts, and she was an excellent sailor, very fast and easy to maneuver."

As is often the case, there are questions as to who actually built and designed the first dory. Beitzell wrote that Captain Charles Huseman and his son Zach, of St. Patrick's Creek, built his grandfather's boat in 1882. "Some say they were the designers of this new model, but others say that this honor belongs to Captain Kelly Cheseldine of White's Neck. Still others say that Rome Thompson and his son, Willie, built the first dory boat. However, most believe that Captain Kelly was the designer of the dory and this writer believes this to be correct," Beitzell wrote.

However, Dodds wrote in the *Woodenboat* article that Garnett Arnold told Ed Beitzell in 1969 that Grason Thompson and

Charles G. Huseman, both of St. Patrick's Creek, built the first Potomac River dory in 1875.

Interestingly, the styles of sterns on the dories developed similarly to sterns on cross-planked boats. John Cheseldine built a dory with a ducktail stern, which is similar to the Hooper Island draketail. He built the ducktail style into sail- and motor-powered dories. Beitzell wrote that Captain Willie Thompson built round-stern dories and Garner Gibson is credited with designing the first square-stern dory for motor-power in 1928.

Dodds wrote that Garner's brother, John, said in a 1983 interview that his brother, Sidney Gibson, built the first square-stern dory, and his other brother, Garner, built the second.

The box-stern dories were built until World War II, with the traditional high chine and plumb stem, but with a flat, vertical stern replacing the tuck, shield stern. These dories were built specifically for engines, he wrote.

Dodds also wrote that there are no active dory builders today. David Lawrence and Herman (Bill) Dixon were two of the last builders of dories in St. Mary's County. Dixon's boats came to be known as "Potomac River Sliders" for their ability to slide across the water. His last boat in this design was a forty-one footer, built in 1981.

One of the things that is interesting about the boatbuilders of St. Mary's County, Maryland is that so many father and sons were in the business. This seems to be the main ingredient of successful boatbuilding communities throughout the bay.

The Wrights, Greens, Prices, Waldens, Nortons, and Westons were all Deltaville family boatbuilders who passed their skills to the next generation. Virginia's log canoe capital in Poquoson had the Moore and Smith families, who kept the business going for several generations there.

Deadrise and Cross-planked

St. Mary's County had the Cheseldine, Gibsons, Beitzells, Goddards, and Palmer families who kept the tradition alive in that area. These families contributed greatly to the success and longevity of the dory boats on the Potomac.

For Maryland's Potomac River watermen, the dory boat was a symbol of life on their side of the river. It was their river and their boat, and as far as they were concerned the dory provided the best working platform on the bay.

nine
DELTAVILLE DEADRISE

Just as areas around the bay became known as centers of log canoe and fore-and-aft planked boatbuilding, Deltaville, Virginia, emerged as a center of deadrise cross-planked construction in the twentieth century. The term "Deltaville Deadrise" was known all over the Chesapeake Bay region and in its heyday, Deltaville builders built boats for customers up and down the East Coast.

Several things happened that contributed to Deltaville's rise as a wooden boatbuilding center on the bay. In the 1890s, the watermen of Sandy Bottom, as Deltaville was known then, like most other communities on the bay, used the log canoe hull as the main craft. Men scattered here and yonder on different creeks built and maintained the local canoe fleet.

Brothers Edward and Pete Deagle were on Jackson Creek and maintained the canoe fleet in that area. The Hacketts, an African-American family, located in what is called Pace's Neck, just down the road from Sandy Bottom, looked after canoes on Moore Creek on the Piankatank River.

In the era of log canoes, nothing was very unusual about Deltaville boatbuilding. Just a few miles away by water, Mathews County had a boatbuilding heritage that went back to colonial days. When the V-bottom boat came along, Mathews boatbuilders picked right up on it. Plenty of evidence indicates that Mathews played a strong influence in the rise to prominence of V-bottom construction on Virginia's Western Shore.

Grover Lee Owens, of Deltaville, built the *Jamie Lynn* and *Virginia Lynne*. By the time Owens got into the boatbuilding business in the 1960s, most of the evolution of deadrise construction had taken place and Grover Lee built what are considered some of the prettiest deadrise boats on the bay.

V-bottom and cross-planked boatbuilding pioneer Gilbert White was born and raised in Mathews and started out building canoes there. He later moved to Palmer on the north bank of the Rappahannock River in Lancaster County, Virginia, and became known up and down the bay for his skills in deadrise construction. He passed on those skills to boatbuilders like O. W. Payne and others in that area.

Other early pioneers were the Smith family in Mathews. Lennie and his son, Alton Smith, of Susan, Virginia, nearly filled up the bay with early style deadrise craft. Lennie built a fleet of sail and motorized deadrise-style vessels with sailboat-style tuck sterns and tillers and outside rudders for steering.

Boatbuilders from the Smith family ended up in Guinea Neck in Gloucester County and in Dare in York County and brought V-bottom deadrise construction to those areas.

113

Deadrise and Cross-planked

So, what made Deltaville rise to prominence in the business? There are several theories. Deltaville men had an uncanny knack for marrying Mathews girls and there is speculation that skills of Mathews County boatbuilders followed their daughters to Deltaville.

Also, strong evidence indicates that two Yankee boatbuilders, Basilee Cornelius and Ike Thomas, were the fathers of modern boatbuilding in Deltaville and contributed greatly to the rise of the business.

Joyce Green recalls that her father-in-law, early Deltaville boatbuilder P. S. Green Sr., said, "Mr. Cornelius and Mr. Thomas started building boats and everything gravitated towards them, and the men on Lovers Lane developed an uncanny interest in boatbuilding."

Around 1900, Cornelius and Thomas were building small yawl (push) boats for sail-powered schooners and striker boats for the menhaden fishery.

In numerous interviews with old-timers, they speak of Cornelius and Thomas as having come from up north. There is evidence that Cornelius moved to Sandy Bottom from the Northern Neck, the home of Virginia's menhaden fishery. He could have been one of many who followed the menhaden fishery south from Maine and other northern states, or he could have been a Yank who came down after the Civil War.

This would account for the fact that old-timers refer to Cornelius's and Thomas's boats as "frame boats," meaning they were round bilge and fore-and-aft planked, a style used extensively up north. Unlike the skills used in building log canoes, the techniques used to build a frame boat could be transferred easily to building a cross-planked deadrise vessel.

Cornelius and Thomas were building boats while men such as John Wright and his younger brothers, Tom, Ladd, and Tollie, and Edward W. Deagle and his brother, Pete, were living right down the lane. All of these men went on to become well-

Alfred Norris was one of many boatbuilders who built wooden deadrise boats in his backyard shed on Lovers Lane in Deltaville, Virginia. Around 1900, Ike Thomas and Basilee Cornelius started building fore-and-aft planked yawl and striker boats there. Shortly afterward, men in the neighborhoood began learning to build boats and backyard boatbuilding sheds were up and down Lovers Lane. By the 1920s, Deltaville had grown into a major wooden boatbuilding center. (Courtesy of Joe Conboy.)

John Wright was considered by many the patriarch of wooden boatbuilding in Deltaville. He built all kinds of wooden boats, from sixty-five-foot Chesapeake Bay buyboats to round-stern bateaux. In the last years of his life, Captain John, as he was affectionately called, built small deadrise sailing bateaux and flat-bottom rowing skiffs. He built some of the better-known buyboats on the bay, including the *Blanche, Iva W.* and *Miss Holland*. (Courtesy of Bob Walker.)

known boatbuilders in Deltaville. It is believed they learned much of their early skills from Cornelius and Thomas.

Strong physical evidence supports this theory, as the *Blanche*, built in 1912 by John Wright, and the *C. E. Wright*, built by Ladd Wright in 1918, were frame built and fore-and-aft planked, which was Cornelius's and Thomas's style. Also, Ed Deagle, born in 1875, made the switch from log canoes to frame boats about the time Cornelius and Thomas were building.

John Wright was the oldest of the Wright brothers, born in 1876, and he and his brothers built boats together in their back yards and worked the water. John and Tom became more boatbuilders than watermen, and Ladd and Tollie became more watermen then boatbuilders, but they all helped one another when the need arose. When they needed more help, they called upon others in the neighborhood to help build boats. From this, boatbuilding skills spread and back yard boatbuilding shops began to spring up all along Lovers Lane. There is no way of knowing when or how the deadrise and cross-planked style came to Deltaville, but it was certainly there around 1915.

By the 1920s, Deltaville, Virginia, had emerged as a baywide center for the construction of deadrise and cross-planked boats. In its heyday, John Wright's back yard on Jackson Creek was filled with boats under construction. The Wright brothers, John, Tom, and Ladd, were instrumental in teaching others in the neighborhood the art of boatbuilding. There are still a few wooden boats built in Deltaville, but the business waned in the 1980s. (Courtesy of Bob Walker.)

Probably someone saw an Eastern Shore V-style, cross-planked boat from Tangier Island and copied the style, or maybe it came from builders in Mathews, or maybe one of Perry Rogers's boats came down from Shady Side. Whatever happened, it did not take long for Deltaville builders to realize that cross-planked boats lent themselves to one-off back-yard construction and the business took off.

In Deltaville, John Wright became a well-known back yard boatbuilder. In 1927, John, Tom, and other members of the Wright family built the deck boat *Iva W.* for Captain Johnny Ward. Ward was originally from Crisfield, Maryland, and married Iva Deagle Ward of Deltaville. He and his boats were known all over the Chesapeake Bay. He had a reputation for working a boat hard. When Ward got the Wrights to build him the deadrise and cross-planked *Iva W.*, it gave their talents great credibility and helped spread the word that good boats could be built in Deltaville.

Linwood Price was born in 1888, John C. (Big Johnny) Weston in 1885, and Paul S. Green in 1889. All three of these men went on to become major boatbuilders in Deltaville. Big Johnny Weston learned to build boats from John Wright, and Paul Green learned to build from Big Johnny. In a 2002 interview, James Crittenden, who worked for Linwood Price, said that Price learned to build boats from Ike Thomas. Linwood Price and his son, Milford, became major players in bringing East Coast and baywide attention to Deltaville as a wooden boatbuilding center.

"The first boat Mr. Price built was for my father. It was a thirty-foot-long oyster boat," said Crittenden. "He built a few more small oyster boats, and then Captain Al Ruark brought him a frame-built buyboat named *Virginia* to be enlarged. Captain Ruark talked to Mr. Price about cutting it in half and making it larger. He agreed to do it and he built a railway on the shore there on Moore Creek to haul the *Virginia*.

"Mr. Price changed from John Wright and all the others and started using a large filler block [bilge clamp] to connect the sides and bottom at the chine," said Crittenden. "The other builders had the sides come down on two-foot frames, like they do on small deadrise boats. When Mr. Price started building larger boats, he let the frame come down to the bottom. He bolted the board to the frame on the outside with a three-and-a-half-inch chunk [bilge clamp] so he would have five and a half inches to bolt the bottom and sides to."

Moore Creek, however, presented a problem in that it was shallow, and in 1923 Price moved to Fishing Bay to what is today Deagles and Son Marine Railway. Just as John Wright would get his big break with the *Iva W.*, Price got his in 1926 when W. E. Valliant Company of Wilmington, Delaware, placed orders for a seventy-four-foot deadrise vessel named the *Del-Mar-Va,* and the ninety-seven-foot *Marydel*. The *Marydel* was the largest deadrise, cross-planked hull ever built. This brought more attention to Deltaville.

Price's move to Fishing Bay was a major shift from building one-off deadrise boats in the back yard to using a railway and hauling large boats. Price's business began to grow and he started building open boats ranging from forty-two to forty-five feet for Mathews and Gloucester counties' pound net fishermen. He also got steady orders and requests for enlarging powerboats and converting schooners and bugeyes from sail to motor-powered boats.

Price's Railway grew in size and more local craftsmen started working there, fueling the back yard boatbuilding business in two ways. More potential builders were learning the trade and some were stepping out on their own. In the 1920s, business was so good that Price needed workers daily and would hire on the spot. If Big Johnny Weston had a lull in his back yard boatbuilding business, he had the option of working on the water or for Mr. Price until orders picked up. This kept builders in the Deltaville area from going out of

business when orders fluctuated. This happened in Mathews with Lennie Smith's boatyard, in Crisfield with Howard & Smith Railway, and in other areas up and down the bay where there was a fairly large railway. The locations without a large boatyard to provide work in slack times often lost their local boatbuilder to steady shipyard jobs in Norfolk, Baltimore, or Portsmouth.

Another factor for the rise of Deltaville was the low cost of building a boat there. Deltaville is located in Middlesex County, Virginia. After the Civil War, the county and the rest of Tidewater Virginia suffered an economic depression. There was very little money, as most southern families had converted their currency to Confederate dollars, which were worthless after the war. In the Tidewater region, people bartered for chickens and hogs, raised big gardens, and caught crabs, fish, and oysters to eat. There was plenty to eat, but not much money, and this kept wages low. By the early 1920s, the nation had experienced an economic revival. It was around that time that northerners like W. E. Valliant of Delaware recognized that they could get a mighty fine boat built in Deltaville for less money than anywhere up north. This fueled an already growing boatbuilding business.

In a 2005 interview, boatbuilder and waterman Billy Joe Groom of Shady Side, Maryland, said that in 1969 he had Deltaville boatbuilder Virgil Miller build him a wooden deadrise boat.

"'You are a boatbuilder. Why did you go to Deltaville to have your boat built?' he was asked.

"Well, I couldn't get good boat lumber and Virgil could build it cheaper than I could buy what lumber I could get," said Billy Joe. "Virgil called me up right after we agreed to build the boat, and he said the only place he could get a forty-foot long, 12" x 12" fir keelson was from Oregon and he wasn't going to pay the freight for that.

"So I told him I'd pay the freight. I figured it was going to cost me a $1,000 for the freight, but it was only $112," he said. "They brought it in on a freight car and Virgil picked it up in Norfolk. Virgil built that boat for me and I couldn't have bought the lumber for what he charged me for the completed boat."

Another factor was Deltaville builders had a local, reliable, reasonably priced supply of quality boat lumber. From 1905 until the 1970s, Bernard L. Wood's Sawmill in Hartfield was about ten miles down the road from Deltaville, and Wesley Enos's sawmill was in Church View, about twenty miles away. Wood and Eno's custom-cut boat lumber and were the lifeblood of the Deltaville boatbuilding industry. Also, Moses White had a lumberyard in the Dismal Swamp, and Deltaville builders purchased top-quality boat lumber of juniper and cypress from him.

Later, Bernard Wood's sons took over his business and fueled the Deltaville boatbuilding business more by custom cutting timbers for keels, frames, and planks. While other boatbuilders throughout the bay suffered with trying to find and purchase good lumber at a reasonable price, Deltaville builders could build boats with good wood and keep their prices competitive. Wood Brothers was right down the road, and depended heavily on the boatbuilding business. The sawmill and boatbuilding industry had a vested interest in one another, as Wood Brothers catered to that end of the business. When they closed in the late 1970s, builders faced the same dilemma of finding good wood as boatbuilders everywhere.

Interestingly, the Great Depression had both a positive and negative effect on boatbuilding in Deltaville. The Depression played a major role in Price losing his boatyard on Fishing Bay. It was auctioned off in 1934. But the Depression also fueled the back yard boatbuilding business, because craftsmen who had left Deltaville for higher wages at shipyards in Portsmouth, Norfolk, and Baltimore came home. There was not much money at home, but, just like after the Civil War, they could eat from the big garden and creek out back. Paul S. Green never would have left Portsmouth and his housing construction business except for the effect the Great Depression had on him and his family. He came home broke and homeless, but he knew he could survive in Deltaville better than in Portsmouth. He, his sons, and grandson became Deltaville boatbuilders, and have carried on the wooden boat building tradition to this day.

After the Depression, boatbuilding knowledge and the manpower for Deltaville to become a major player in the bay's boatbuilding business were in place. Lee Deagle, son of canoe and early deadrise builder Edward Deagle, bought Price's railway on Fishing Bay and hired Lin Price to share his knowledge of boatbuilding with Deagle and William Emerson Wright, son of Ladd Wright. Lee Deagle was a machinist, and Wright learned his back yard boatbuilding skills from his father. Price taught them skills in building large deadrise boats. Deagle and Son Marine Railway became a center for converting sailing schooners and bugeyes to powerboats.

After helping Deagle get on his feet, Lin Price and his son, Milford, established a railway and boatbuilding facility on Broad Creek. They built and sold hundreds of deadrise boats that went to New York, New Jersey, and Delaware. Whereas back yard builders built by rack of eye, Price went on to work with naval architects, such as Carl Forsberg of Freeport, Long Island, New York; and Harry Bulifant of Newport News, Virginia. Through Price and others, the Deltaville deadrise spread far and wide. Linwood Price died in 1957, and Milford carried on the tradition until he sold the yard to Virgil Miller. Miller and his son Brian continued to build wooden- and steel-hull boats for Chesapeake Bay and New England buyers, until they closed in the early 1990s. Brian built a steel-hull New England lobster boat in 1985, named the *William Bowe*, for the late Bob Brown, who gained national attention as the owner of the fishing vessel *Andrea Gail*, which was lost at sea in *The Perfect Storm.*

Just days before he died, at eighty-seven years old in 1963, John Wright was still going out in his back yard, working on a skiff. In some ways, Wright was the patriarch of boatbuilding in Deltaville. He certainly could be considered the father of back yard boatbuilding, as he spread his talents as much as anyone to others in the community.

Perhaps the most important ingredient to why boatbuilding thrived in Deltaville had to do with family. At a very early age, sons and daughters went out back to see what daddy and granddaddy were doing. While there, the builders needed their help to hold a board or pass a bolt. This led to fastening boards, cutting bolts, and eventually to building boats on their own.

Green Family

Paul S. Green's family is a good example of how Deltaville boatbuilding progressed from days of no electricity to modern times. Paul was born in Lancaster County in 1889. His father, James Franklin Green, was a Presbyterian minister, house carpenter, and boatbuilder. James built his own log canoe on Taylor Creek on the north bank of the Rappahannock River and used it to travel his circuit to spread the word of the Lord throughout the region.

Unfortunately, James Franklin drowned in an unsuccessful attempt to save his oldest son, who fell out of a skiff into Taylor Creek. Paul S. was a little boy and watched the horror of his father and brother's deaths with the rest of the family from the creek bank.

In a 2003 interview, Joyce Green, wife of Paul's son, Paul S. Green Jr., gave some history as to how the family got to Deltaville.

"On August 7, 1901, twelve-year-old Robert Franklin, with his father, left their wharf in the family skiff. In the middle of the creek, Robert Franklin fell overboard and his father went in after him. Hindered by heavy boots, both father and son drowned, as the other children, Victoria, John, and Paul watched.

"Their mother had died earlier, so now with their father gone, they were orphaned. Soon thereafter, Victoria married Samuel

Paul S. Green Sr., pictured here, passed the skills of building wooden deadrise boats on to his three sons, Bobby, Paul, and Maylon. The key to Deltaville's rise in the wooden boatbuilding business in the early part of the twentieth century was that the skills were passed to the next generation, which resulted in five generations of wooden boatbuilders in that area. (Courtesy of Paul and Joyce Green.)

The round stern *Sherry-Sue* was a Paul S. Green boat, built in 1949 for Melvin Dize, of Urbanna. Here she is getting her bottom painted in June of 1959, at Southside Marine in Urbanna, Virginia. (Courtesy of Ben Williams.)

Christopher and moved with both her brothers to his home at Sandy Bottom in Middlesex County."

When John and Paul grew up, they married cousins and moved to Portsmouth, where the brothers opened a home construction business. In 1933, the Depression killed their business, so Paul and his wife, Clementine Lydith (Callis) Green, moved back to Deltaville. The couple had four children, Elizabeth, Robert (Bobby) Franklin, Maylon, and Paul Jr.

When the family came home to Deltaville, Paul Sr.'s uncle, Johnny C. (Big Johnny) Weston, was building boats and asked Paul to give him a hand. It wasn't long before Paul was building boats on his own. He was able to get enough money together to buy land right next to Big Johnny's on Broad Creek, and the two boatyards worked side by side. Sons Bobby, Maylon, and Paul Jr. worked at the yard with their father. Paul Jr. recalls that in 1947, when he went to work full-time at his father's yard, his father ordered him a new foot adz. In 1956, the Greens had a staggering fifteen boat orders.

"I was helping with the books that year," said Joyce. "Bobby owned a piece of land right next to Mr. Green, so that year they split the business. Bobby took eight orders, and Mr. Green, Maylon, and Paul Jr. kept seven. So, there were three boatyards right next to one another. Big Johnny, Mr. Green, and Bobby were all side by side.

"It was a good situation with three builders side by side because we built the hulls upside down and then had to flip them over to finish it off. When a boat needed to be flipped, everyone in all three yards came to help.

"Daddy was something, he could work all week in the same pants and shirts and not get a drop of paint or anything on him," said Paul.

Joyce laughed and said, "Yeah, Mr. Green always had a toothpick in his mouth and he'd grumble and growl about the boys. When he'd get really disgruntled, he'd put his hands in his pockets and shake his coins together making a loud noise. One time he said, 'In all the years I've been building boats, I've never seen two men [Paul Jr. and Maylon] tear up more clothes and waste more paint by getting it all over themselves. It takes twice as much paint to paint a boat when you two are around.'"

In 1966, Paul Jr. opened Amburg Boat Craft at his home in Deltaville. He built hundreds of boats. Once, Newport News Shipyard ordered a skiff from him.

"That was something, driving up to the gate of one of the biggest shipyards in the country and telling the gatekeepers I had a wooden skiff to deliver, but they gave us a hard hat, let us in, and we made the delivery."

Passing on the tradition of building boats in the family is what kept the boat-building business alive in Deltaville for so long. Paul S. Green's grandson, Robert Green, built the *Gloria J* that was being commercially fished in the James River in 2006. Robert is the third generation of his family to build boats in Deltaville

Robert (Bobby) Franklin Green had a son, Robert, who picked up the trade. After Bobby stopped building boats, Robert took over the business and built boats on Broad Creek until about 1995, when he sold out, but he can still be found working occasionally for Deagle and Son Railway on Fishing Bay.

"When granddaddy started, he didn't have any electricity and had to cut everything out with hand tools," Robert said. "He used a hand plane, foot adz, and drawing knives to shape his boats."

As a boy, Robert would work in his father' shop sweeping floors; painting, sanding, and filling nail holes. As he grew older, his father taught him how to lay out a boat and passed on his building techniques to his son.

The Greens advanced from building skiffs and small deadrise boats to fifty-foot and over-ocean charter boats. Like the Prices, they built boats for markets in New Jersey, New York, Delaware, and elsewhere. By the 1950s, Deltaville was well established as a center of boatbuilding on the Chesapeake.

Robert was one of the last Deltaville boatbuilders. He excelled in strip-planking the sides, which gives his boats lots of flare in the bow and sides.

Walden Brothers

The Sputnik II, built by Moody and Alvin Walden, being worked in the Rappahannock River oyster fishery in 2006. The brothers built boats in Deltaville from the late 1940s until they retired in the 1980s.

Raymond, Moody, and Alvin Walden were the Walden Brothers, and right after World War II, the brothers brought Walden's Marina and boatyard from Johnny (Crab) Weston. The boys were two boatbuilding generations behind John Wright and Edward Deagle, and capitalized on the strong boatbuilding heritage that had been established in Deltaville over the years.

Raymond passed away in 1972, and this interview was conducted in January 2007 with Moody and Alvin.

"Our daddy was a clammer and we started out our lives on the water patent tonging with him for clams," said Alvin. "Lennie Smith from Mathews County built my daddy's boat, and she was a deadrise cross-planked boat, but she had a sailboat stern [tuck stern] with an outside rudder and hand tiller. She was a real early style deadrise made out of 2 1/2"-thick lumber.

"Right after the Depression, when we were coming along, a boy either had to go work on a farm or work the water. My daddy was a watermen so the three of us naturally went to work on the water."

This photo at Walden Brothers' boatyard in Deltaville, taken around 1950, shows the hull of the deadrise and cross-planked buyboat *Rebecca Ann,* which has been turned over and topside work is underway. The *Rebecca Ann* was named after Alvin Walden's wife, and the brothers used the boat in the bay crab dredging fishery for a few years before selling her. The *Rebecca Ann* measured 45.6' x 13.6' x 4.6', and was one of the last buyboats built in Deltaville. Note the other boats in the water. They show from start to finish the evolution of the house on these boats. There is an open deadrise without a house, one with a just a trunk cabin, and another with the house/pilothouse configuration. (Courtesy of Arthur Lee Walden.)

"It won't much money to be made anywhere," said Moody. "You could go work the water and make a little bit or not make any somewhere else."

"In those days, everybody had a boat," said Alvin. "Around here farmers did a lot of oystering, because they needed to make money over the winter to pay their spring fertilizer bills, so they all had boats. It won't just watermen.

"When we were fairly young we got into the boatbuilding business. I had built a few skiffs as a boy and everybody was doing it down here.

"I told my Daddy I wanted to learn how to build a deadrise so Raymond, Moody, and I could build our own boat and go work the water," said Alvin. "My father knew Paul Green Sr. real well, and he asked Paul if he'd show us boys how to lay a deadrise boat out.

"Mr. Green was very helpful. He let us build our first boat in a shed he wasn't using there on his property, and he was right there to help us out when we needed help.

"He even sold us the lumber for our first boat," said Alvin. "He'd gotten right much lumber from Baltimore and had a lot around. When we had questions he'd stop what he was doing and come over and help us. He showed us how to lay the boat off and showed us how to put the staving on and stuff like that. We worked the boat for a while and then we sold it and built another one. That's how we learned."

Right after the war in 1947, Raymond, Moody, and Alvin's luck changed. They were down at Little Johnny (Crab) Weston's boatyard on Broad Creek when a chance of a lifetime came along.

"Raymond, Moody, and I had gone to Richmond and bought a snub-nose Ford truck and an old dump body from Brownie Wood," said Alvin. "We were going to go in the hauling business, and we were down at Little Johnny's place in a shed putting the dump body on the truck, when he came up to us. It was near about twelve o'clock, and he said to us, 'Boys, let me sell you this place.'"

The land was located right at the mouth of Broad Creek and was an ideal place for a commercial waterfront business.

"Yeah, it was near about twelve o'clock," said Moody, "because we had stopped to eat a sandwich. I said, 'How much do you want for it?' I said it just like we had money to buy it," Moody said with a laugh.

"Yeah, we didn't have money enough to buy the paper the deed was on," Alvin said.

"Little Johnny said he wanted $3,000 for it, and he said he was going outside to let us talk it over," said Moody.

"Raymond said to me, 'What do you think?' I said, 'Raymond, we ain't got hardly any money,'" said Moody. "'We got some things we can sell. I got a car in A-one shape that's worth about $1,000, and we got this dump body that's worth something.' So Raymond went out and offered Little Johnny $2,500."

"Little Johnny said he would go home for lunch and talk it over with his wife, Molly, and when he came back they had agreed to take $2,500," said Moody.

"We got a note for $100 down and the rest had to be paid in thirty days," said Moody. "Well, in thirty days we had sold the car, the dump body, and a few other things to get enough money together."

"We kept the truck so we had someway to get around, and right from the start things started jumping," said Alvin. "When people heard we had the place and the boatbuilding shed, all of a sudden we had five orders.

"We had also helped Ed Norton install his railway and cradle, so we knew how to do that too, and it wasn't long before we had our own railway and boatshed, and things were moving right along."

The Waldens expanded their property into a marina, boatbuilding, and boat repair facility and seafood buying business. Over the thirty-five years they owned the facility, Alvin said that he and his brothers built more than one hundred boats. Most were workboats and about a dozen were pleasure boats.

"We built deadrise boats ranging from thirty-five to fifty feet," said Alvin. "We would ask the man how much money he had and that would determine the length of the boat.

The boat they built that they remembered most was the *Rebecca Ann,* named after Alvin's wife. The brothers built her at their yard in 1949. They used her as a dredge boat until they decided to sell her.

Deadrise and Cross-planked

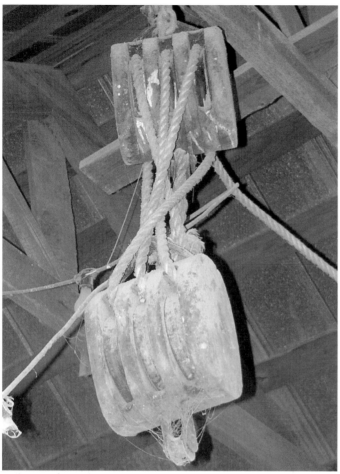

This block and tackle in the ceiling of Willard Norris's boatshed in Deltaville is a reminder that the community was once a boatbuilding center. When the bottom of a boat was completed upside down, the block and tackle was used to flip the hull over for the top work to be installed. When boats were ready to be turned over, the men in the neighborhood would come and help. The block and tackle takes the place of strong arms.

This trailer, used to haul deadrise boats down to the water in Deltaville, was of common ownership. The builders had it built and used it for launches. The trailer stayed at the shed of the builder who last used it, and was passed on as needed. It now rests behind Willard Norris's boatshed on Lovers Lane. Note the cut in the center of the wooden frames to accommodate the deadrise hull.

"We had an agreement between us that if two brothers made a business decision, then that was the way it was going to be," said Alvin. "When we built the *Rebecca Ann*, Raymond decided he was going to be captain and he started working her in the winter crab dredging.

"The best waterman of us all was Moody and I wanted him to captain the boat, but Raymond knew the water and I figured he would do all right," said Alvin.

"We all had our strong points," said Moody. "Raymond was a top-notch mechanic when it came to engines, Alvin was the boatbuilder, and I was the waterman.

"We dredged her for three years, but Raymond couldn't make any money in her, so one day he came in the creek on a Thursday in the boat and I told Moody, 'We need to sell that boat.' Moody agreed. So we did."

The *Rebecca Ann* was the only large dredge boat built by the Waldens. "We got some of the lumber for the *Rebecca Ann* from Wood Brothers, but we also bought right much from Happy South in Mathews County. He was cutting these old, big trees on Gwynn's Island and we got a lot of it from him. There was plenty of good, long lumber around right after World War II. We didn't have any trouble getting good wood then."

Below: Deltaville boatbuilder Willard Norris named the last large deadrise boat he built *Last One* because he felt it could be the last deadrise of its size built by a traditional boatbuilder in the community. Norris, eighty, is one of the last old-time deadrise builders in Deltaville. Grover Lee Owens and Robert Green are in the community and working on wooden boats, but no longer build boats.

Deadrise and Cross-planked

"Everybody talks about all the boats that John Wright and Lin Price built, and they built a lot of boats, but every boatbuilder in Deltaville was busy. I remember hearing Ernest Bryant say he built one hundred skiffs for one man. It was a man who owned a hotel and rented the skiffs to his customers and you don't hear much about Ernest. He was a good builder. There were a lot of guys building boats here.

This 1955 photo of the gas dock at Waldens Brothers' in Deltaville on Broad Creek was a scene found on just about every creek on the Chesapeake Bay. By then the gasoline engine was king. Johnny "Crab" Weston of Deltaville had recently built the boat at the dock. Right after Hurricane Hazel in 1954, the Virginia oyster strike soured, as did demand for new wooden boats. It was a busy time for boatbuilders in Deltaville. (Courtesy of Arthur Lee Walden.)

"Little Johnny Weston could build as pretty a boat as anyone around here. Deltaville got a name as a place where you could get a good boat built in a timely fashion. We had a lot of boatbuilders here, and if one was backed up with orders you could go down the road and find another good one."

"After World War II, there were plenty of oysters and plenty of sale for them. Everybody went oystering. Shoot, lawyers were out there oystering," Alvin said with a laugh.

Moody said customers came to them from Crisfield, Smith and Tangier Islands, Cape Charles, Baltimore, Norfolk, and all up and down the bay to have boats built.

"They liked that Deltaville deadrise style, but they also liked the price," said Moody. "You could get a boat built here for less money than most other places."

"We learned a lot about building boats because we installed a lot of engines and rudders and stuff in boats for other builders," said Alvin. "They would finish a boat and bring it to us to install the engine. By doing this, we got to see firsthand the different types of building [styles] and we tried to incorporate the best in our boats."

"I'm going to tell you something. Some of the heaviest built boats that we installed engines in came from down in Guinea Neck in Gloucester County," said Alvin. "There was a guy there named Smiley Jenkins who built V-stern boats and he put more lumber in his boats than anyone did in Deltaville."

The V-bottom boat experiment reached its peak in Deltaville, Virginia, and by the 1960s and 1970s the area was considered a major center of deadrise construction on the bay. With just cause, Deltaville became the self-proclaimed capital of deadrise boats on the bay.

ten
FAMILY BOATS

The lifestyles of eighteenth- and nineteenth-century Chesapeake Bay families varied from region to region and household to household, but no matter their status in life, wooden boats played a role in their lives.

Colonial river plantations were self-contained communities that depended on growing tobacco to provide the cash flow to keep things going. The rivers and bay helped feed those living on the plantations. As time passed, wars, slavery and its demise, the indentured servant system, immigration, primogeniture, and other social and economic factors changed the social dynamics of the bay region.

Early on, sweet Tidewater Virginia and Maryland tobacco was the money crop of the region. Growing tobacco and the colonial lifestyle were labor intensive. From this need, slavery and indentured servitude grew.

In Virginia, the indentured servant system, where a man could earn his freedom and the cost of passage across the ocean to America by being in servitude for so many years, created a class below plantation owners. When their indentured period was over, the former servants went out on their own, settling on small tracts of land or in small towns. They became artisans, storeowners, blacksmiths, boatbuilders, farmers, and watermen.

The old English custom of primogeniture, where the eldest son had the exclusive right to inherit the family's land and wealth, also added to the working class. As second and third sons left home, they ventured out on their own, moving to towns and cities.

When freedom came for slaves, they too had to fend for themselves or starve. Although a segregated social society evolved in Virginia, there was economic integration on the rivers and bay between the races.

Before the Civil War, expansion of the bay's oyster and finfish industries from Baltimore, Annapolis, Washington, and Norfolk sparked economic growth in the Tidewater region. During the war, the business stopped. After the war, the oyster and finfish fisheries quickly rebounded and helped stimulate the economy of a demoralized Virginia populace and a Maryland economy that was stagnant from the effect of the war.

Oysters and fish became the money crop of Tidewater Virginia and Maryland. Also, the crab fishery began to expand and grow in the 1880s. The seafood business helped to distribute wealth throughout the region. Families no longer had to own large tracts of land to improve their quality of life; what they needed was a good boat.

Any longtime Tidewater Maryland or Virginia family has a story that relates to using wooden boats. Mine is no different. There are many stories of boats passed down in my family, but boats on my mother's side played a definitive role in the economic success of the family. My grandfather's use of his deadrise boat speaks volumes to the importance of wooden boats to many post-Civil War families, particularly to those who followed the water to support their families.

My maternal grandfather, Raymond Blake, was born in 1898 in a log house at Nohead Bottom in Middlesex County, Virginia. His grandfather, Alfred Blake, was a Civil War veteran. His father, Jeter Blake, was an oysterman and farmer. The term waterman did not apply to the Blake family. They considered themselves oystermen above all and then farmers. Jeter and his family worked a twenty-eight-acre spread, but their main income came from oysters. They were not involved in harvesting finfish or crabs.

Raymond Blake stands inside his boat, shucking a mess of oysters on his culling board. As a small boy in 1904, Blake started working on his father's sail-powered canoe as a culling boy. He worked in the Rappahannock River oyster business until he retired in the 1980s. In 1940, he had a thirty-six-foot round-stern deadrise boat built by Lawrence Parker. He worked the boat for more than forty years.

When the oyster season was over, they grew tomatoes, cucumbers, peas, potatoes, and watermelons as cash crops. Much time was also spent growing corn and grain to feed the livestock. Two horses, two cows, four hogs, and chickens all had to be fed. They raised a large garden to provide food for the year. The hogs provided hams, middling, and sausage, and the family cows kept them in butter, cream, and milk. Chickens provided eggs and meat for the table.

Jeter owned a twenty-two foot, three-log canoe that was powered by sail. Raymond attended a one-room school until he quit in the fifth grade. As early as six years old, he was working with his father as an oyster-culling boy on the sailing canoe. It was not long before Raymond stepped up from culling oysters to hand tonging. In a 1987 interview, he recalled, "I learned how to tong oysters while daddy was eating his lunch. I was the culling boy, but whenever lunchtime rolled around I'd jump up on the washboard and try my hand at catching a mess. Well, on this one day, I tonged up fifteen oysters with one lick. Daddy stopped eatin' and came over and counted them out. He said then, 'I'm a putting a pair of tongs in here for you tomorrow.' From that day on, there were tongs in the boat for me."

During the oyster season, they moored the boat on Whiting Creek near Locust Hill, Virginia, not far from Drumming Ground, Temples Bay, and Hog House, all prime oyster grounds on the Rappahannock River. Each day, Jeter and Raymond walked a footpath through the woods from Nohead Bottom, about a mile and a half to the boat, to go hand tonging in the river.

The boat was not used except during the oyster season. At the end of the season, sails were well cared for and taken home to be stored in the loft of the barn. The fact they had a sail on their canoe showed they were serious oystermen.

In a 1992 interview, Morton Clark, who knew my grandfather and great-grandfather, said, "When I was a small boy, everybody in the neighborhood had canoes. There wasn't any need for a railway or a marina, because they'd get a bunch of boys and skid the canoes up onshore, flip them over, and leave them there for the summer. If they needed repair or work, they'd do it right on the beach.

"You see, a lot of the boys like Jeter and Raymond didn't use the canoes for anything but oystering. They'd farm or do something else in the warm weather months. The boats weren't very big either. Canoes would run twenty to twenty-five feet. Jeter had a twenty-two-foot canoe.

"I'll tell you something else. Most of the canoes in our neighborhood didn't have sails or even a mast in them. The boys around home would scull or paddle out to the oyster beds. Now, Jeter had a sail in his canoe and that helped him travel some when oysters were scarce close to home. He also had the advantage on a windy day of getting to the buyboat and selling his catch first. Then he could get home early so he could do other things. Most people think that all the canoes carried a sail. The truth is the harder-working oystermen had sails on their boats and the rest used paddles and oars. The Blakes were hardworking oystermen."

Around 1918, Jeter was able to buy a used canoe with a rebuilt one-cylinder Palmer engine in her. Charlie Lawson, who lived on Locklies Creek, rebuilt the engine for him. Lawson had a little shanty on the creek bank where he worked on Palmer and Lathrope engines.

The canoe was about thirty-two-feet long and had a small cabin. It stayed in the water year round. She was not real fast, but the powered canoe allowed Jeter and Raymond to sell to buyboats, as they had done in their sailboat, or to markets on shore. With a motor, they could work all day and know they would have enough time when they finished work to get to a buyer onshore. If buyboat prices for oysters were higher than the price at Burhans Steamboat Dock, they would sell to the buyboat. If dock prices were higher, they would sell to the buyer at the wharf.

Jeter died in 1937. By then Raymond had married Minnie Heath of Urbanna and was oystering on his own. He and Minnie went on to raise a family of eight—four girls and four boys. He had bought a small farm near Topping. His property backed up to Meachim Creek, just off the Rappahannock River. His first boat was a three-log canoe, which he moored on the creek and was powered by a Model A Ford engine.

Raymond Blakes's daughters Corrine (left) and Betty (right) are sitting on the house of the boat. A close look aft reveals the round stern. When the boat was built in 1940, Raymond, like many watermen, referred to his plank-on-frame deadrise as a round-stern canoe. This was carryback to just a few years back, when log canoes were the vessel of choice for bay watermen.

A Blake family outing on the boat shows off the bow style of the 1940-built deadrise.

In 1940, Raymond saved enough money to move from the log canoe era into the age of the deadrise bateau. Purchasing a new boat was professional advancement. When my grandfather could afford to have a new deadrise built it was a significant achievement for the family.

Raymond had boatbuilder Lawrence Parker of Regent, Virginia, build him a thirty-six-foot round-stern bateau. The boat cost $300. He had a Model A Ford four-cylinder engine installed, and later he installed a flat-head six-cylinder Ford engine. The boat was never named and had a house, but no pilothouse. She was nearly twelve-feet wide. As many watermen of his time did, Raymond referred to his boat as a "round-stern canoe."

When canoes began to go, and plank-on-frame boats began to take over, Parker began building round-stern canoes, or deadrise boats. Clark recalls that, "Mr. Parker lived up the road there and he would build boats back in the woods. He

built them by a wide stream that ran through a swamp. When he had the boat just about completed, he would wait for a real high tide and float it out into the Locklies Creek. He did everything by hand. He didn't have any electricity. He built mostly round-stern canoes, like your grandfather's boat."

Raymond moved his mooring from Meachim Creek to Locklies Creek, because Locklies had more water depth and was more accessible by land. A road came right down to the boat. This was certainly better than when he was a boy and had to walk a mile or so, toting a lunch and gear, to the boat. Now my grandfather could load his truck and drive right to the boat.

Like his father, Raymond used the boat for oystering in the winter, but it was more of a year-round boat. In the spring and summer, he installed a canopy and ran fishing parties on Saturdays. He also used the boat to haul and market his watermelons and tomatoes.

At the farm, he had a field he called Back Field, because it was back behind the house, where he raised watermelons. When the melons were ripe, he loaded his harvest onto a horse and wagon, rode to the water, and offloaded the melons into his bateau.

Raymond went across the Rappahannock to Carter Creek or Taft Menhaden Factory on the north bank of the Rappahannock River. At Carter Creek, he knew people because of the oyster business, and there was a dock where he tied the boat and sold the melons to locals. At the menhaden plant, workers took a break at lunchtime and came down to his boat to buy his melons. The watermelon season was a big part of the family's income, but nothing like oysters.

For several years, my grandfather grew enough watermelons to fill a buyboat. He took his load to Washington D. C. and sold watermelons to people coming to the dock.

His son, Melvin Blake, oystered on the round-stern canoe with Raymond for several years. "We would go out about 7:30 a.m. to oyster. It was after daddy milked the cow and fed the hogs," he said.

"We'd go out and catch twenty or thirty bushels, sometimes fifteen bushels. We'd get $2.75 or $3 a bushel," he said. "Daddy was a right good oysterman. He had been doing it since he was a kid. Luke Griffin, a black man who used to work on the boat with daddy, said he was one 'hard-driver.'

"Daddy was a small man, but he was tough. He would work like hell. He didn't have warm clothes or nothing on. He didn't have oilskins or anything like that. It could be freezing cold, but daddy never went in that cabin. He'd eat his lunch sitting on that motor box. I'd go in the cabin and try to get out of the wind and keep warm. He never had any fire on the boat to keep warm by. I remember old Dick Thornton would come down in the morning with his arms full of wood to heat the stove in his cabin. Daddy didn't have anything like that. He was old school. He grew up working on boats that didn't have cabins. He worked all day and never took a break except for lunch. Most of them out there didn't work like him.

"Oystering was good to daddy. I think there was more clear money in oystering than in farming. The boat was very important to the family, and daddy looked after the boat. He didn't seem to have a sentimental attachment to it, like some people get. He kept it in tiptop shape because it was our main way of making money.

"We painted the bottom twice a year at Morton Clarke's Railway," said Melvin. "The bottom was painted right before oyster season in September, and then we'd painted it again in the spring. He didn't want worms to get in her.

"Daddy also ran fishing parties in the summer. He'd get about $5 a trip. In those days $5 wasn't bad money. After oyster season, he would put an awning on the boat for the fishing party season, but he stopped running parties when the farming business got better.

"After 1934, tomatoes and vegetables were daddy's biggest land-based money crop," said Melvin. "In 1934, R. E. Roberts bought the Nelson Hotel property and old West Urbanna Steamboat Wharf, just outside of Urbanna. There he established a large vegetable canning factory. The factory was a branch of Lord Mott Corp. of Baltimore, Maryland. The local factory was called Lord Mott and it provided some economic rewards for my father."

Lord Mott had a truck that would come to the farm to pick up Raymond's tomatoes, peas, and string beans.

"It was around then that the vegetables started to play a bigger part in daddy's money situation," said Melvin.

Phyllis Bray, Raymond's oldest child, remembered that before Lord Mott came, her father would go to Burhans Wharf to sell his cucumbers to the pickle factory.

"I've been there a many a time with him," said Phyllis. "He would put the cucumbers in grass sacks, put them in the trunk of his car, and carry them to the factory.

"He raised Irish potatoes too. He would put them in barrels and ship the potatoes to Baltimore on the steamboat. He took a boat to Washington full of watermelons too. He paid the man who owned the buyboat to take them to the dock in Washington, and he would stand on the boat and sell them to people who came down and wanted a watermelon for ten cents. He did anything he could to make a penny.

"Before Lord Mott came, daddy took his tomatoes across the river in his boat to a factory on Carter Creek," she said. "He put the tomatoes in 5/8th bushel baskets, loaded the baskets on his horse and wagon, and carried them to his boat. Then, he'd load his boat and carry the tomatoes across

129

Deadrise and Cross-planked

No photos show the entire image of my grandfather's forty-foot round-stern deadrise boat, which he had built in 1940. What few photos there are were taken during special family moments. Here, Sharon Evans Bray, the first grandchild of Raymond and Minnie, is pictured sitting atop the house. The boat has a house configuration typical of the times, without a pilothouse atop the house. The family is probably returning from a Saturday fishing trip.

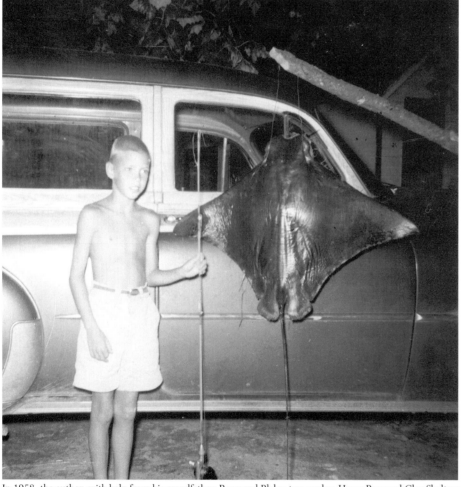

In 1958, the author, with help from his grandfather, Raymond Blake; two uncles, Harry Bray and Clay Shelton; and his father, Shep Chowning; pulled this ray in over the washboard of his grandfather's deadrise boat. Family fishing trips on the boat were special times.

the river to the factory over there. It was a job to load those baskets on the boat and then have to unload when he was across the river.

"The boat was a big part of our lives," she said. "Daddy used it to oyster, but he used it with the farming end too. We were lucky we lived on the water to be able to use it as a way to help make a living.

"Daddy raised a lot of corn, but I don't think he sold much. It was for the cows and chickens, and white corn was for cornmeal. He'd carry the white corn to the gristmill at Barrick's Mill Pond and have the corn ground into meal. Mamma made some of the best cornbread and corncakes in the world. She was a steady worker, who kept life at home going smooth so that daddy could go make a living.

"We usually had two cows. There were eight children, so if one cow went dry, he had the other to get milk from. Mamma made butter and was a great cook. Looking back, I don't see how she did all she did.

"Daddy's father put him to work on the boat full time when he was in the fifth grade of school," said Phyllis. "He learned the river young and he made a good living from it.

"There was a friend of the family who used to say about her husband, who was an oystermen, that he couldn't make enough on the river to pay for the salt to go in his bread.

"Daddy said to her, 'If you run up and down the river all day looking for a better lump of oysters, you waste too much time. I find a little lump and I work it until it's done, and then I move on somewhere else.'"

I remember vividly going on Saturday family fishing trips in the Rappahannock River as a child on granddaddy's round-stern canoe. Inside the cabin that never had a pilothouse, cork hand lines and lifejackets were stacked in the corner.

I had no idea then that my grandfather had seen so much change on the bay. I would have never known had I not asked him when I was working on *Harvesting the Chesapeake: Tools and Tradition* if he had ever worked the river in a sail-powered log canoe.

In the late 1970s, he sold his farm and his boat, and moved into a small home on Meachim Creek, hardly a stone's throw from Back Field, where he had raised watermelons and loaded tomatoes and melons on his boat so many years ago.

When I asked him about his round-stern canoe, he simply said, "She was a pretty good boat."

Oftentimes after death and some years have passed, questions are asked concerning someone's life. The memories of a life that may have spanned ninety years often come down to one or two sentences. "Oh, he fought in World War II," or "She made the best pumpkin pie the world," might be the only statement made. So, I guess when you ask about the life of a boat, my granddaddy's one comment, "She was a pretty good boat," was complimentary enough.

I doubt my grandfather shed any tears when he sold his boat. He was not that type. I bet, though, when he turned and walked away from her that last time, there came a sigh under his breath that meant "thank you" to a boat that made his life, and the lives of nine other family members, better.

eleven
DEADRISE BOATS—BASIC TO LIFE

Along with the internal combustion engine, the deadrise V-hull contributed greatly to a new era of transportation and communication on the bay.

The deadrise hull shape was just right to support and transport the bay wide economy that grew after the Civil War. Even after automobiles came on the scene, the road systems had not evolved to accommodate reliable transportation with any efficiency.

Although strides were made at the turn of the twentieth century in land transportation, it was not until after World War II that the modern road system came along and changed the way Americans travel.

In the 1920s, many localities on the Chesapeake had very few miles of paved roads. For instance, Middlesex County, on the south bank of the Rappahannock River, had only three miles of concrete road. Throughout the early days of the twentieth century, boats remained a necessary means of transportation for many families. The boat tied to the dock or anchored out in the creek meant the same to a family as today's car parked in the garage.

Deadrise boats and log canoes were used in about every manner that today's automobiles and trucks are used. The water highway followed deep water and commerce, and communities grew in locations where boats could access landings easily. These landings usually had winding dirt roads that ended at the water's edge. The deadrise boat energized a growing region. It was a platform for catching food, going to church, and visits from the family doctor. The deadrise hull carried the Chesapeake into modern life. The lives of Dr. William R. Gwathmey and Paul Feitig, and the tragic loss of Clarence Gray and Jeanette Dudley speak to how life was in the early years of V-bottom boats and gasoline engines.

Dr. William R. Gwathmey

A country doctor who lived in a good, accessible location on the water often had a thriving business, because the waterways and boats gave him the ability to reach many patients. One such doctor was Dr. William R. Gwathmey of Ruark, Virginia.

In the days before good roads, Dr. William R. Gwathmey used a log canoe from his office in Ruark, Virginia, to visit patients in neighboring counties. (Courtesy of Caroline Gwathmey Jones.)

Ruark was named for captains Al and Phil Ruark of Hooper Island, Maryland, who settled on Fishing Bay in the late 1800s. For centuries, Fishing Bay, right at the mouth of the Piankatank River, had been a haven for mariners coming and going on the bay. The long hook of land that reached out into the Chesapeake, known for three centuries as Store Point, and changed in the early twentieth century to Stove Point, was a natural barrier against wind and storm.

Captain Al and Captain Phil were seafaring men who moved up and down the bay. They knew about this place and sailed into Fishing Bay when storms came. Early in life they knew it as a good, safe harbor.

They eventually settled in homes there and capitalized on the boats going in and out of the harbor. In 1898, the community of Ruark had grown enough to support a post office and local doctor.

Captain Al became the postmaster, and in 1900 Dr. William R. Gwathney moved to Ruark and put out his shingle. Dr. Gwathmey came from King and Queen County to serve Ruark and surrounding areas, which included Gwynn's Island in Mathews County and Guinea Neck in Gloucester County. He wanted a community that needed a doctor, but also offered enough patients to support his practice.

In those days, country doctors spent most of their time making house calls. Dr. Gwathmey traveled by boat, horse, buggy, and car to visit his patients and neighbors, and patients would visit his office. When there was a problem, they would come by foot, skiff, log canoe, deadrise boat, or any means possible.

Dr. Gwathmey settled on Jackson Creek in a nice home with a nice office out in his yard, just down the road from Ruark. He always had a good horse and a good boat.

One of his first boats, the *W. A. Johns*, was a log canoe that has received some small fame on the Chesapeake. The boat is

Dr. William Gwathmey made house calls in this log canoe, and later had a deadrise and cross-planked vessel to visit patients in Middlesex, Mathews, and Gloucester counties. The *W. A. Johns*, used by Gwathmey, is on display at the Deltaville Maritime Museum.

featured in *A Heritage in Wood*, a book on boats owned and on display at the Chesapeake Maritime Museum in St. Michaels, Maryland. The boat is now on display at the Deltaville Maritime Museum in Deltaville, Virginia.

The *W. A. Johns* is a three-log canoe that measures 34' 9" x 7' 6". A two-cylinder Palmer engine powered it. Dr. Gwathmey used the boat to make house calls on Gwynn's Island and Guinea Neck. He later had a deadrise built down the road in Deltaville.

His niece, Caroline (Gwathmey) Jones, eighty-seven, still lives in the home place at Canterbury in King and Queen. She said that Dr. Gwathmey was born in 1870 in her family home in Canterbury, which is a couple miles from Walkerton in King and Queen County.

His early education was through his aunt, Miss Bet Ryland, who taught at a school on the grounds of Canterbury. He later attended Aberdeen Academy, a boy's school at St. Stephen's Church, and graduated from the Medical College of Virginia in Richmond.

"They had just started Medical College when he went there," said Mrs. Jones. "I think he moved to Ruark around 1900. I don't know why he moved there. I guess there must have been a need for a doctor."

Mrs. Jones knows Dr. Gwathmey was at Ruark in 1905 because that was the year her father contracted typhoid fever in New York State. He was being treated at a hospital there, when Dr. Gwathmey contacted him and told him to come to Ruark so he could take care of him.

"My daddy almost didn't go because he didn't think he was going to make the trip alive," she said, "but, he made the trip by steamboat and landed at North End Wharf on the Rappahannock River. It was really quite a miracle that he survived. That must have been a challenging case for a brother to look after a brother. He did a good job and my daddy lived."

Not long after he moved to Ruark, Dr. Gwathmey married Ora Vaughan of Middlesex. As a child, Mrs. Jones would visit them for several weeks during the summer.

"He was one of my favorite uncles. When I was real little, I wanted to be a doctor like him. When a chicken was sick, I tried to get the chicken well by practicing to become a doctor. My mother and father, however, said a lady doesn't become a doctor. You know, it was a different attitude towards women in those days.

"My mother told Uncle William about my hopes and he said, 'Let me have her one night and I'll get rid of those thoughts,'" said Mrs. Jones. "This must have been around 1925, and I was staying at his house in Ruark. I was born in 1917, so I

wasn't very old. Most every weekend the Guinea people in Gloucester County would get to fighting and Uncle William would have go down and stitch them up. They were pretty rough people in those days.

"Sure enough on this weekend, he got a call to go to Guinea and I went with him. He would go there by boat, and when he'd get to a landing there would be someone waiting there to take him to the house. He did the same thing on Gwynn's Island. Ruark is nowhere by water to Gwynn's Island.

"I don't remember too much about the Guinea trip, but I remember daddy asking him the next day when we got back, 'Did you cure her of wanting to be a doctor?' 'No, she didn't bat an eye,' he said. 'She handed me things and helped me sew up that man and he was ripped from his chest on down.'"

Mrs. Jones said, "Uncle William was very much beloved. He loved people, children, dogs, and horses," she said. "He had a horse named Ripple that he brought with him from Canterbury. Every generation at Canterbury had horses named Zephyr and Ripple. Zephyr means a gentle breeze. A gentle breeze makes a ripple on the water. So we always named the mother Zephyr and her offspring, Ripple.

"When Uncle William moved to Ruark from Canterbury, he took our Ripple with him," she said. The families at Canterbury had horses named Zephyr or Ripple into the 1980s. Mrs. Jones thinks the tradition may have gone as far back to the 1700s.

"Uncle William also loved to go swimming," she said. "He had a robust stomach and he loved to put me on his stomach and we'd float in the water."

Dr. Gwathmey had a reputation for serving wine to his patients in an area of strong Baptist faith that frowned on the partaking of spirits.

"I've heard that Uncle William would go down in his basement and get two glasses of wine—one for him and one for his patient," she said. "They would have a wonderful social period and then he would say, 'Now tell me again why you are here.'

"He was very dedicated to his patients," said Mrs. Jones. "He was supposed to have been best man at my father's wedding, but he didn't make it because he was involved in delivering a baby in Guinea and he spent the night there. I wouldn't be a bit surprised if the Guinea man we stitched up that night he had delivered as a baby.

"Also, he always had at least one well-trained bird dog and sometimes two."

William Brooke Gwathmey, Dr. Gwathmey's nephew, said the thing he remembered most about his uncle was his dog, Billy, and how well trained he was.

Dr. William W. Gwathmey's office in Ruark, Virginia, was located in his yard and positioned so the front door could be approached from either the road or Jackson Creek. At the turn of the twentieth century, Dr. Gathmey's office received just as many patients by boat as by land. Here, Dr. Gwathmey is feeding his hunting dogs, while a hand holds his horse and buggy. Gwathmey made house calls in a log canoe, horse and buggy, and automobile. (Courtesy of Caroline Gwathmey Jones.)

"Uncle William would bring the dog into his dining room and place a piece of bread on his nose. Billy would sit there until Uncle William called him by name, and then Billy would throw his head up and catch the bread as it came down and he would eat it.

"Uncle William was supposed to have been a great quail hunter. One time, my father was there and took Billy out by himself to kill some birds. Uncle William told him where to go and when daddy found a covey, he fired twice and missed. Billy just looked at him puzzled. He stood another covey and missed again. That time Billy just turned around and walked home. He wasn't used to that happening. Uncle William was an excellent shot.

"He cured all his own hams in a smokehouse and had a special recipe. I have his curing recipe at home written in his own hand writing," said Mrs. Jones. "He was known for his excellent hams."

Mrs. Jones recalls the day her uncle died. "Uncle William died in 1933, the same year of the August Storm that tore our area up. He had many dogs, but Billy [an English setter] was one of the most faithful. When he died, Uncle William's body was laid out in the reception room of his home and Billy got by that casket and wouldn't let anyone near it. He growled and barked whenever anyone got close. They didn't know what to do about him.

"Well, my father had stayed with Uncle William for about three months before he died," she said. "Daddy always remembered what he had done for him when he had typhoid. When he heard Uncle William was dying he went right on down," she said. "Every day daddy would go with Billy down the lane to get the morning paper in the paper box and it got to be a habit. Finally, someone told my daddy to tell Billy he was going for the paper and to see if he would come and move away from the casket. He did."

Part of the success of Dr. Gwathmey's business was having a good, dependable boat to get to his patients. He was an example of one of many Tidewater country physicians who used boats to attend to their patients. His office was located next to his house with easy access from Jackson Creek. In the early years, he had as many patients arrive by boat as he did from land. The front of the office faced the side of his house so it did not face either the water or the road. Footpaths leading to the front door of the office came from land and creek.

Paul Feitig

Throughout the Chesapeake region, the V-bottom deadrise hull is used in the oyster, finfish, and crab fisheries. The chapter on the family boat shows the evolution of the use of deadrise boats in the oyster fishery. The Blake family started with sail-powered log canoes and eventually moved up to a V-bottom boat. That same type of evolution occurred in the business of catching finfish and crabs. An area that is seldom discussed is the evolution of the boats in the charter boat business.

The business started as a spring and summer sideline for oystermen needing to generate money from their boat in the off-season. Usually, the boat was primarily built for oystering but worked great for a Saturday afternoon fishing party.

Interestingly, that sideline has grown to be a major industry today, and more wooden and fiberglass deadrise boats are built throughout the bay for charter boat fishing than any other fishery.

The charter boat business is a major player in the economy of Tidewater Virginia, but it had a very humble beginning. In 1990, I interviewed Paul Feitig for an article in the *Southside Sentinel* when he was named grand marshal of the Urbanna Oyster Festival. I would have never thought Paul would have had any connection to the river or bay. I had known him as a clerk behind the counter at Marshall's Drug Store, later as a supervisor of the processing plant at Barnhardt Duck Farm, and as mayor of the Town of Urbanna.

In the 1990 interview, he mentioned his connection with the charter boat business. I conducted a second interview

in 1995, when he was honored again for his many years of service as treasurer of the Middlesex County Volunteer Fire Department. I remembered from the earlier interview that he had told me a little about his early life on the water and decided to explore the matter further. Interestingly, Paul confirmed to me that there was some resistance to this new type of deadrise construction in wooden boats. The log canoe hull had worked well for centuries, and here was a new style that many felt was not as tough as a well-constructed log hull. Paul's father-in-law, Joe Eastman, always had log canoes, and when the 1933 August Storm hit the bay region, many planked bateaux were driven up on shore and broken in two. Mr. Eastman's log canoe survived and he made note of that to his neighbors. However, by the late 1930s, the advantages of motorized, planked deadrise boats had persuaded even Mr. Eastman to switch over. He moved to Urbanna and ran fishing parties out of a thirty-five-foot deadrise.

Paul Feitig, eighty-eight in 1995, was born in Richmond, Virginia. In the late 1920s, he married Louise Eastman Feitig from Christchurch, Virginia, located on the Rappahannock River. Paul had a job with the C & O Railroad in Richmond, but was laid off in 1931. Louise's father, Joe Eastman, persuaded Paul and his daughter to move to the country and to help him and his wife run a country-style boarding house. Along with the boarding house, Mr. Eastman and Paul, who was twenty-four years old at the time, ran fishing parties and tried their hands at oystering.

"I ran fishing parties with my father-in-law at Christchurch," he said. "We would take customers out for one dollar a head and we wouldn't take out any less than five (per trip).

"They could fish just as long as they wanted during the day for a dollar. If they wanted lunch, we would take them out in the morning, bring them in at lunchtime for one of Mrs. Eastman's meals, and then take them back out for more fishing.

"Mrs. Eastman was serving meals at the house for seventy-five cents and she never set a table that she didn't have fried chicken, ham, or roast beef. Seventy-five cents! A lot of people would drive from Richmond down there on Sunday just to get dinner.

"We had groups of people come down from Pennsylvania and spend whole weeks. It was a whole damn house full of them—seven or eight of them. Mr. and Mrs. Eastman would give them three meals a day, fishing and night lodging for fifteen dollars a week.

"In the fall of the year, she would serve oysters with dinner and supper. She didn't use any milk in her oyster stew, but she would take that oyster liquor and put the oysters in it and stew it in that liquor. Boy, you had something good there. Yes, sir!

"When we first moved in with the Eastmans, I'd ride around through the country and buy chickens for Mrs. Eastman," said Paul. "We would pay twenty-five cents apiece for a pound and a half to two pound leghorn rosters. I carried them home in a coop and killed and dressed them for when she needed them.

"We raised three hogs, but we had a friend in Richmond who would come down every other weekend to fish. He would bring down a twelve-pound sack of flour and a roast of beef. The next time he might bring a ham. Because he helped us, he would stay at the place and eat and fish for free. The house had eight rambling rooms," Paul said.

"Mr. Eastman taught me a whole lot about the water. One time, he wanted to get a bigger boat so he spoke to this fellow up on the top of the hill, Alfred Davis, about where we could get a new boat for running parties. He had always had canoes and wanted another one.

"Mr. Davis said he knew a fellow up on the Corrotoman [River] on the Northern Neck that had a twenty-eight-foot canoe that he would sell for $150.

"Mr. Eastman and I went over and looked at it. Of course, I didn't know a damn thing about it. Anyhow, the fellow who owned it said, 'Now, if she's not solid, I'll give you your money back.' Mr. Eastman said he couldn't tell much about it until we got it out the water.

"We pulled the boat out [of the water] the next day and Mr. Eastman went all around the bottom with his penknife trying to stick a hole in it, but he couldn't do it. 'Ain't no softwood in this boat' and he bought it," said Paul.

"The canoe turned out to be a good, sturdy boat. I can't say much for the engine though. It had a four-horsepower Regal engine in her," continued Paul. "I've cussed that thing and done everything to it when it wouldn't start.

"One summer, Mr. Eastman and myself didn't hardly stay a day at home. We had parties every day the sun shined. Most of the time, both of us would go out together. We would go right off from the house. Right near the channel was a deep [fishing] hole, and we'd go out and lower the anchor to sound the bottom and when we hit that hole we'd drop anchor and you'd catch fish every time.

"We didn't hardly know what a blood worm was back then. We supplied crabs for bait. That went with the dollar a day for fishing. The only bloodworms we saw were some that the fishermen brought with them.

"For bait, we would buy a bushel of hard crabs from a Mr. Fitchett. It cost us a dollar a bushel for hard crabs and we had a float down by the shore. We would put them in the float to keep them alive. Nowdays, everyone wants a peeler crab for bait, but we always did all right with just plain old hard crabs.

"Mr. Fitchett would bring me a bushel about three times a week. He was a waterman who lived on Robinson Creek and would catch his crabs on a trotline.

Before the 1930s, "Very, very few people from Richmond were coming down this way," said Paul. "Before, people came from all over the bay because of the steamboat, but not Richmond. The roads [by 1931] were better then and people had started owning automobiles and that's what brought them here.

"Sometimes when we didn't have any customers, Mr. Eastman and I would go over in shallow water off of Towles Point and troll along. It won't nothing to catch a boatload of six-, seven-, and eight-pound salmon [speckled] trout one right after another. Lord, was that fun.

"Funny, the people then that came down from the city didn't care about that. All they wanted to do was bottom fish," said Paul. "They liked catching croakers, flounders, and white perch. Those white perch would eat the bait up. Some people would bring their own lines, but we furnished hand lines and bait boards. I would take a piece of cork out of an old worn out life ring and wrap about thirty feet of cotton line around it, and put a No. 8 hook on it and a sinker. It made a good hand line.

"We didn't advertise. It was all word of mouth. Different ones would come down and then go back home and tell their friends, 'We went down to Joe Eastman's down at Christchurch and caught plenty of fish.' Word of mouth is the best advertising in the world.

"The only thing we did was stick a sign out at the end of the road, with an arrow on it to tell people which way to go. Boy, it was a hell of a rough road down in there.

"I'd clean all the fish for the people who came down from Pennsylvania and other places and they'd give me a tip," said Paul. "I would clean them and pack them down in crushed ice. They'd go up the road a ways and have to get more ice because what I put in there had melted. One time I got a $20 tip for cleaning fish. I thought I'd done all right.

"We weren't the only ones at Christchurch running party boats," said Paul. "Mr. [Delaware] Hibble had several boats and we were competitors. One time Mr. Eastman got to drinking a little bit and went down and was arguing with Mr. Hibble. They did that a lot. Lee, Mr. Hibble's daughter, came down and told them to stop arguing. Mr. Hibble, said, 'Go on in that house, girl, before I pick up a [pound net] trap stack and wear you out.

"We would laugh at Mr. Hibble because whenever he'd take a party out and they didn't catch many fish, he would say to the customers, 'Jesus Christ, man, you ought to have been here yesterday, fish were jumping in the boat.'"

"There were others at Christchurch besides Mr. Hibble who ran fishing parties. Most of the boats were used in the winter to oyster and to run parties in the summer.

"Dan Lockley and Daniel Jr. ran parties there at Christchurch too. They had two right nice canoes but one day the old man [Dan Lockley] decided they would switch from canoes to bateaux. He had right much money that he had gotten from somewhere. Just before the August Storm of 1933, Dan and Daniel Jr. went off and had two brand new thirty-three-foot round-stern canoes [V-bottom bateaux] built. That storm came and carried them up on our shore and broke them up. All they were good for then was stove wood and Mr. Eastman told them they should not have switched over," said Paul, shaking his head.

"During the storm, Mr. Eastman's boat broke loose and went up above Hibble's on that flat. He and I went out in the storm and waded with our boots on and dragged the boat out in deeper water. He started the motor up and be damn if it didn't start on the first crank and we come on down the river. It was still blowing a gale then. We were lucky. I don't ever remember it starting on the first crank but that one time in the middle of the August Storm.

"One year when fishing hadn't been too good, Mr. Eastman and myself decided we would go oystering. We got a patent tong rig that we would pull by hand. I would drop it and he would kind of feel the bottom to load it and I would pull it on up.

"One day we had a right good day. We caught about twenty bushels and we went up the river to sell to a buyboat. A man came out on the boat and said, I'll give you twenty-five cents a bushel.

"I told Mr. Eastman, don't sell those oysters for twenty-five cents a bushel as hard as we worked for them. We'll take them home and throw them overboard by the stake before we'll sell them for that.' We did that for several days—bring them in and throw them overboard by the stake—until we had right many oysters down there.

"I waded out, picked up a mess, and we got Lewis and Max Hibble's wives and Max's sister to shuck them. We started selling shucked oysters and it got to be a pretty good business. They shucked every Monday and I'd carry the oysters to Richmond on Tuesday and I'd get fifty cents a quart for them. It gave us some good winter money.

"My mother was living at that time in Richmond and she would call up different ones and ask if they wanted oysters and I would deliver them to their door," said Paul.

"On my way home, I'd always pick food up for Mrs. Eastman to fix and one day I bought a twenty-five-pound bag of prunes for one dollar. When I got home, Louise asked, what we were

going to do with all those prunes. 'What's wrong with you?' she asked.

"I said, 'I don't know, but it sounded like a good price to me. Have you ever heard of a prune pie?'

"She said, 'No, but I can make one'. We had prunes. We had prunes and we had prunes. I'll tell you something, prune pie ain't bad.

"One day Mr. Eastman and I were oystering in the fall of the year when it was right chilly. The wind was blowing southeast, and every time a spray would come up over the boat it would freeze on our clothes.

"I started pulling anchor. The old man asked, 'Where are we going now'?' I said, 'We're going home. Damn if we can't make it easier than this. We came in and pulled the tongs off the boat and that was the last time Mr. Eastman and I went oystering."

Some years later, the home at Christchurch burned down. The family moved to Urbanna where Joe Eastman continued to run fishing parties out of Urbanna Creek. He realized that to compete, he needed a better boat and better engine. He sold his canoe and bought a thirty-six-foot bateau with a four-cylinder Model A Ford engine for power, and Paul went to work behind the fountain at Marshall's Drug Store.

Clarence Gray and Jeanette Dudley

Gasoline engines were fairly new in boats in 1909. In those days, small launches were the thing for traveling here and there on rivers and creeks. In locations where there was no steamboat dock or creeks where steamboats only frequented occasionally, when there was enough trade to justify stopping, launches were used to offload people, supplies, and mail.

Deadrise and Cross-planked

This monument was erected in 1909 to honor Clarence Gray, who died trying to save Jeanette Dudley. Jeanette drowned when she jumped off a deadrise launch that caught fire in the Rappahannock River.

Left: The story of the 1909 tragedy of the deadrise launch named the Black Bird is etched in stone at Christ Church cemetery in Middlesex County, Virginia.

Below: This launch was used at Water View Steamboat Dock on the Rappahannock River to carry passengers and mail. It appears to have a deadrise hull. Some launches had V-bottoms and cross planks, while others were round bilge and had fore-and-aft planking. The *Black Bird* was an oyster boat converted to a launch. It most likely was a deadrise style. (Courtesy of Tommy Blake.)

Launches would meet the steamboat in the middle of the river. The boats were also used to carry groups to church meetings and other functions or take groups of people going to another town for a day of shopping and entertainment.

These boats often had seating accommodations, complete with a house that extended right far aft. Many launches were round hull, with stem-to-stern planking and very attractive spoon and round-shaped sterns. Bayside hotels often provided these boats to accommodate customers, and these launches were a bit fancy. There were also privately owned launches that had only basic accommodations. They were open boats with rough benches for seating that could be pulled out when the oyster season started in October. When the season opened, the launch became an oyster boat.

The *Black Bird* was a deadrise and cross-planked launch owned by a black man named Frank Banks. The story of the *Black Bird* is a tragic story of the times, but speaks to how boats were used before roads connected everything in a fashion of some convenience. The *Black Bird* caught fire in the Rappahannock with thirty-four young people from the Saluda, Virginia area, and two in the party drowned.

140

By now, all of those who were on the vessel on July 14, 1909 have passed. There are, however, two records of the happening. Urbanna's *Southside Sentinel* ran extensive eyewitness stories on the tragedy. Although *Sentinel* papers of those times have, for the most part, been lost, Flossie Bristow, a young survivor on the boat, saved copies of the newspapers in an old box that included many other treasures of her life. Her great-nephew, John M. (Buddy) Moore, found the family treasures and saved the stories for posterity.

The other physical reminder of the tragedy is a more permanent marker. A monument was erected by survivors of the *Black Bird* to honor Clarence Gray for his unsuccessful attempt to save the life of Jeanette Dudley. Gray also lost his life, and the monument was placed over his grave at Christ Church cemetery in Middlesex County, one of the oldest graveyards in America. The names of all those on the boat are etched in stone.

If ever there was fodder for a novel, it was the event and happenings that surround the day of July 14, 1909. The *Sentinel's* articles present the facts of the day, but between the lines youth, friendship, romance, fear, fire, and death at sea all ignite the imagination. In the July 23, 1909 issue of the *Sentinel*, survivors who were aboard the boat tell the account of what happened that fateful night.

"The young people of Saluda and vicinity had been planning for some time a trip to Irvington, so on Wednesday, July 14, most of the young people boarded the launch, *Black Bird*, at Oaks Landing (on Urbanna Creek) and expected to stop at Burtons Steamboat dock for others to come aboard."

Burtons Steamboat dock was located further toward the mouth of Urbanna Creek in the Town of Urbanna. Oaks Landing is located on Urbanna Creek, and in 1909 was a major water/land thoroughfare to Saluda, the county seat of Middlesex County.

At Burton's dock others were waiting to board, but a summer rainstorm came up quickly and forced all the people into a nearby warehouse for shelter, the article stated.

After the storm, several in the party did not wish to continue to Irvington, so they agreed to go to the head of Urbanna Creek, anchor *Black Bird*, and have a picnic lunch.

Typical of a summer storm, it left as quickly as it came and by the time the boat had reached the mouth of the creek, the sun was shining. Those onboard then agreed to continue their planned trip to Irvington.

"Finally, we all agreed to go on to Irvington and, after we reached the town, all seemed delighted. We ate lunch before leaving the boat and then proceeded to the skating ring to enjoy a merry party and I feel quite sure that no one regretted coming over.

"At 9:30 p.m. we left the rink and gave all of the skaters an opportunity to cool their bodies and rest, for all were tired from skating."

The group boarded *Black Bird* around 10:00 p.m. and headed across the Rappahannock in pitch dark. The group was scattered throughout the open boat sitting on benches, fish boxes, washboards, and up on the bow deck.

When they got out into the river and about ten minutes from Urbanna, the engine "stopped and positively refused to run." They were able to grab and tie to Towles Point buoy in the river. The problem was found in the fuel line as the gas line was plugged with something. Banks was working on the engine, with two boys holding kerosene lanterns for light.

"The owner of the boat, with one or two others, went forward to see if the trouble could be located and soon found it in a short piece of pipe that connected the fuel tank with the long pipe that led to the engine. He pushed a small piece of wire up through this short pipe, which removed the article that prevented the flow of gasoline. Of course, as soon as this was done the gasoline began to flow. He was in the act of connecting the two pipes when some of the gasoline spattered on the globes of two lanterns that was held near, and it seemed that in a second the entire front of the boat was in flames.

"This frightened all on board, but the boys soon regained themselves and in a short time had all the girls on the stern of the boat and told them to keep still, that the flames could be conquered. The girls threw their skirts and the boys their coats and dipping them in the water, fought heroically.

"There were only two small buckets on the boat and they were kept in constant use until the flames were under control. We realized that we could not quench the fire until the gasoline was burned, which was 20 odd gallons and our only hope was to keep the boat from getting too hot and burning, so we fought hard to keep the sides of the boat cool. This we succeeded in doing and in 15 or 20 minutes we had the fire quenched.

"The two young people holding the lanterns were badly burned, though not seriously, but the owner, Frank Banks, was seriously burned and we feared he will lose his sight. He worked heroically to save us and he has our sympathy in the affliction."

After the fire was put out, the group began looking around to make sure that everyone was aboard. During panic of fire and fear of explosion, Jeanette Dudley jumped overboard and Clarence Gray went in after her.

"As soon as we found out that the boat was not burned enough to leak any and assured all that there was no further danger, we inquired if anyone was overboard. Some one said: 'Jeanette Dudley said she had rather drown than burn, and in the excitement leaped overboard. Clarence Gray saw her go overboard and went over to rescue her.

"In the excitement, two oars, two planks and a bench that we had on board were thrown over. We had nothing to manage the boat with except a piece of board about five feet long, but we were helpful and unfastened our boat from Towles Point buoy, which we tied to keep from drifting down river.

"At the request all on board became quiet and some one called Clarence to see if we could locate him. We heard him answer, 'Save us!' or 'Save me!' we couldn't tell which, as we never knew whether he reached Miss Dudley or not. The tide was strong ebb and we tried with this five-foot plank to guide our boat in the direction of his voice, but the tide was carrying us down the river and carrying them down too, and we had no means of going faster than the tide. We called him once or twice more and heard him answer, but each time it seemed in a different direction. The last time we called him, we waited almost breathlessly, but did not hear him anymore and not knowing in what direction to go, we drifted along for a while and found we could not do anything more for our lost friends. We dropped anchor near the mouth of the Corrotoman River between one and two a.m. to await help.

"Finally morning came, and we saw, it seemed, boats all around us. We tried every way we knew to hail them, but of no avail. We could not get anyone to come to our rescue. About 7:30 or 8:00 a.m., we were so tired of the boat, some almost chilled through and all anxious about loved ones at home. We were determined to try and help ourselves to get ashore somewhere and get to our loved ones, and ask some one to go and look for those we had lost. We broke up two planks, and splitting them in half, made four oars about five- or six-feet long. We also arranged the engine so that with severe labor we could turn the main wheel and force the boat along. So with some one at each oar and two at the wheel we were making for Burhans Wharf. It was such severe labor that a good, strong man could only stand at the wheel or oar a short time. At last we saw a gasoline launch coming from a creek near Burhans Wharf and hailed them to come to our rescue and tow us to the wharf. He said that he was too busy to stop. He said he had a lot of men working with him, but we pleaded with him to come, so he finally said he would tow us there for two dollars. We told him to come on. We would give it to him. He towed us to the wharf and after paying him and giving him a short sketch of our trouble, he left and returned to his work.

The steamboat *Calvert*, leaving Urbanna Creek. Captain Archer Long, captain of the *Calvert*, carried the survivors from Burhans Wharf Steamboat Dock on the Rappahannock to Burton's Wharf in Urbanna. The log canoe in the fore water of the photo is an early style canoe, similar to the one used by Paul Feitig and his father-in-law in the 1920s as a party boat. Note the layout of the vessel. The engine is pushed as far aft as possible and a well-built house is constructed over the motor. A bow deck has been added for storage of ropes and gear. The center of the boat is left open for people to stand and fish with hand lines off the side. (Courtesy of Betty Burton.)

"We reached the wharf about 15 minutes before the Baltimore steamer, *Calvert*, reached there and as soon as she landed, that tenderhearted, loving gentleman, Captain Archer Long, came off the boat and we told him our trouble. He told us to go aboard his boat and he would take us to our homes, and further more, turned his boat around and went back towards Towles Point in search of our two friends, but of no avail.

"Some of our ladies were very nervous and Captain Long and his courteous officers were just as nice as they could be and extended their deepest sympathy and offered their assistance to help us in any way. Of course we appreciate this and shall never forget them. Captain Long would not accept one cent of recompense for bringing us to Urbanna. On reaching Urbanna [Burton's Wharf] with broken hearts and shattered nerves, we told of our distress. There were several lady passengers on the boat who were just as nice as they could be. There were also several gentlemen passengers, among them a young doctor, whose services can never be forgotten.

"Most of our party had to be taken up to Oaks' Landing and a young gentlemen Mr. George Van Wagenen Jr. in the launch *Mayflower* and Captain Billy Fitzhugh in the launch *Gentry* vol-

Captain Billy Fitzhugh, standing on the bow of his launch *Gentry*, used his launch to carry the young people from Burton's Wharf to Oak's Landing on Urbanna Creek to meet their families after the disastrous night on the Rappahannock in 1909. The *Gentry*, a round bilge launch, was used at the Rose House, a boarding house in town owned by Fizthugh. (Courtesy of Emily Chowning.)

unteered their services. One of the young ladies was very nervous and it was thought best not to take her in the boat. Captain Long quickly secured services of a vehicle to take her to the home of a relative."

On Friday, Jeanette Dudley's body was found on a beach near the mouth of the Corrotoman River. Her body was brought to Urbanna, transferred to Saluda to be prepared for burial in her hometown of West Point. Clarence Gray's body was found in Lancaster County on Sunday. The Saluda Lodge of Odd Fellows, of which he was a member, took his body. Assisted by members of many neighboring lodges, Gray was buried in Christ Church cemetery. Several years later, a monument was erected over his grave in his honor.

His body and the body of Jeanette Dudley came home in a deadrise boat.

On July 14, 1909, Archer Long received a letter of thanks from the Saluda community. For many years, this letter has been in the possession of Jack Long, Archer's grandson. Until recently, Jack was unaware of the 1909 tragedy and the reason surrounding the letter.

It states, "Dear Captain Long, We the citizens of Saluda and vicinity express to you our heartfelt thanks for your kindness to our children and friends this morning and to assure you our heartfelt thanks for your kindness to our shipwrecked children and friends and to assure you that as long as the memory of the terrible disaster which we fear has sent to the grave two of the happy company that left our village on yesterday afternoon and from which the others were saved by a merciful Providence, so long will your kindness in coming to their rescue be embalmed in fond memory."

Twenty-eight families from the Saluda area signed the letter to the captain of the *Calvert*.

twelve
THE LAST STAGE OF DEADRISE CONSTRUCTION

A new chapter in the evolution of the Chesapeake Bay deadrise boats came along in the early 1970s when the first builders of fiberglass boats arrived on the Western Shore of the bay.

These builders began turning out working craft modeled after the traditional wooden deadrise hulls.

Interestingly, three pioneers in this area moved to Virginia about the same time. Hulls Unlimited East, of Deltaville; Gloucester Marine, of Clay Bank; and Glass Marine, of Hayes all arrived on Virginia's boatbuilding scene between 1972 and 1974. In the beginning, all three had to struggle to find direction in the Chesapeake market, where wood had always been king and where watermen were skeptical of fiberglass as a boatbuilding material.

This was an early round-stern fiberglass deadrise built on the bay in 1972 by John Collamore III and Whitey Laurier, and designed from a traditional round stern wooden deadrise. Collamore, Laurier, and Art Helbig were three northern boatbuilders who came to Virginia in the early 1970s and started building fiberglass deadrise boats. (Courtesy of the Deltaville Maritime Museum and John Collamore.)

John Collamore III, of Hulls Unlimited East, moved to Deltaville in 1972 from Rhode Island after an apprenticeship with Allan Vaitses of Bristol Yachts. Arthur L. Helbig of Gloucester Marine migrated from Arnold, Maryland, where he had been production engineer for Revel Craft. Whitey Laurier of Glass Marine was an assistant director for General Dynamics and worked at the corporation's Quincy Shipyard outside of Boston, Massachusetts.

Collamore moved to Deltaville, which was Virginia's self-proclaimed capital of wooden deadrise construction, and Helbig and Laurier moved to Gloucester County, Virginia. All three builders were located in extremely busy commercial fishing areas.

Helbig opened his boatbuilding facility in a deserted fertilizer plant at Clay Bank on the York River. Laurier set up shop on Sadler's Neck. His shop was located just across the southwest branch of the Severn River from Glass, Virginia, near Guinea Neck, whose inhabitants are well known for their skills in harvesting the bay's bounty.

The facility Laurier took over was as renowned as its neighbors. Before the days of convenient transportation, Greenway Railway and Country Store was a booming place, as proprietor Stonewall Jackson Rowe stocked everything from sculling paddles to hairbrushes. The weekly Saturday night hoedown brought watermen from near and far. And when their boats needed work, Greenway Railway was the place to come. When Laurier and his family moved into the old store building in 1972, the operation's heyday had long since passed. But the old railway facility was still operable, and a marina had been added along the shoreline.

For two years, Laurier worked to build up the marina and dry dock business, and then in 1974, a landmark year for boatbuilding on the Chesapeake, Glass Marine and Hulls Unlimited East entered into an agreement that put some of the first fiberglass deadrise-style boats on the bay.

The wooden deadrise after which the new boat was patterned had evolved over years to meet the needs of Chesapeake watermen. Its hard-chine V-hull provided a stable platform for work in choppy seas, shallow draft for shoal-water fishing, and a level of versatility that made the boat suitable for just about every use on the Chesapeake. In short, the bay deadrise had stood the test of time and was what most watermen wanted in a boat. But the question was: Would they buy a workboat made from fiberglass?

Laurier and Collamore teamed up to build traditional-style round-stern deadrise workboats in hopes of selling them to traditional Chesapeake Bay watermen. They formed a partnership called Classic Chesapeake Boats Inc. to market these vessels.

"We still had two businesses in the sense that Hulls Unlimited East and Glass Marine were separate firms," said Laurier in a 1987 interview. "What we did was to form a marketing company. We built and sold three boats."

Laurier designed the "Chesapeake 40," with a round stern that appeared from the side, very much like an elliptical stern built by early wooden deadrise builders. It looked every bit the part of a Chesapeake wooden deadrise, except it was built of fiberglass. Collamore built the boats in Deltaville. The first boats measured 40' x 12' x 3'. Although the forty-footer performed well as a workboat, Collamore and Laurier soon encountered stiff market resistance among traditional bay fishermen. Set in their ways, watermen just weren't sold on fiberglass. Moreover, the round-stern style proved to be a regional feature whose appeal was limited to a handful of areas around the bay. In short, the market was so limited that success was impossible.

As a result, the partnership between Hulls Unlimited East and Glass Marine did not last, but the Chesapeake 40 was truly a bold venture that later spearheaded the fiberglass market that spread throughout the bay.

In August 1976, Classic Chesapeake Boats Inc. was liquidated and Laurier formed his own firm, Chesapeake Work Boat Co. He hired Gloucester Marine and Arthur Helbig to build hulls for his new enterprise, and eight more round-stern forty-footers were sold at Clay Bank.

Collamore had designer Harry Bulifant design a classic deadrise hull with a square stern. He also designed a hull that was to become known as the Deltaville Garvey. Collamore, with the help of his father, went on to build a variety of boats at his shop in Deltaville.

In early 1977, Laurier and Helbig acquired a hull mold of a thirty-six-foot Navy utility boat. They developed a low-freeboard, bay style workboat out of this thirty-six-foot hull. The first of these was built in May 1977 and delivered to a Maryland crabber, clammer, and gillnetter. Between 1977 and 1981, nineteen of these boats were completed. The boats were particularly popular in the Maryland clam fishery because the larger hulls were very suitable for the heavy conveyor dredges used there.

Collamore, Laurier and Helbig all built boats ranging from twenty to fifty-five feet and all three noticed there was more interest in fiberglass boats in Maryland than in Virginia.

The Virginia dream of producing fiberglass deadrise workboats for Chesapeake Bay watermen never reached its full potential. The decline of the fisheries, high cost of building a fiberglass boat over wood in the early years, and the fact watermen would not accept fiberglass, kept the business down.

In the 1990s, as the cost of building a wooden boat rose to all-time highs, the Virginia fiberglass builders found markets in the dive boat, charter boat, research boat, pleasure boat, and workboat businesses. There is now a new twenty-first-century generation of Virginia fiberglass builders, such as Pete Nixon of Norfolk, Bubbie Crown of Deltaville, and Rick Arverson of Exmore, Virginia.

Maryland Builders

About the same time fiberglass builders arrived in Maryland. One of the state's first fiberglass builders to build a bay classic fiberglass deadrise was Chesapeake Marine Industries Inc. The firm got its start in 1974, when Bob Lippinscott Sr. and his two sons, Bill and Bob Jr., opened a branch of their New Jersey-based fiberglass boatbuilding business in Trappe, Maryland, near the mouth of the Choptank River.

The Lippincotts had been building sailboat and yacht hulls since 1955 and were turning out some 300 units annually when they opened the yard at Trappe.

In 1974, Bill and Bob Lippinscott Jr. opened a branch of their New Jersey-based fiberglass boatbuilding business in Trappe, Maryland, and started building fiberglass boats for commercial watermen. In this 1981 photo, Bill Lippinscott looks over the prop, shaft, and rudder system on a recently completed boat.

To get started, the firm approached Ernest Tucker of Oxford, Maryland. Tucker was well known in the bay area for a variety of boats designs. He had also designed several deadrise boats for individuals.

The Lippinscotts told Tucker they wanted an all-around boat that was good in all kinds of weather, could carry a large payload, was strong, and reasonably maintenance free.

The forty-two-foot deadrise that resulted incorporated the classic deadrise shape, which was well known for stability as a working platform and its ability to handle choppy seas. They followed the example of generations of boatbuilders and designers by incorporating the best time-tested features into the boats.

By 1980, the Lippinscotts were turning out twenty-six boats annually, becoming by far the most productive deadrise fiberglass builder of that time.

Interestingly, Maryland watermen seemed to accept fiberglass boats easier than Virginians. Part of that may have stemmed from the fact that several early Maryland fiberglass builders were local folks. Perhaps change came easier because a familiar face introduced it. That certainly seemed to be the case of Eugene Evans of Crisfield, Maryland.

Evans was a Smith Island commercial fisherman turned boatbuilder. He was one of the first fiberglass builders to build and market the traditional barcat, or Smith Island crab scrape boat, as it is called on the island.

Some early Maryland fiberglass builders started out building crab scrape boats. In 1983, noted fiberglass builder Eugene Evans, of Crisfield, Maryland, used his father's wooden barcat as a plug to build the *Twilight*. John Evans's old barcat was originally built as a sailboat. The vessel was one of the first fiberglass barcats built on the bay and had all the attributes of the wooden version. (Courtesy of Eugene Evans.)

He started building fiberglass boats in 1983. His father, John Evans, had an old wooden barcat that had originally been built for sail. It still had the slotted keel for a centerboard, which had been plugged when an engine was installed.

"She was an old boat, but she had features that worked good for working the water in Tangier Sound," said Eugene. "I actually took her and turned her upside down and used her as a plug. She was a slow-going boat because she had a sailing-style tuck stern. I squared the stern on her up and put a twenty-

eight-foot-wide, seven-and-a-half-foot-long tunnel in her for the shaft and prop. It was a feature that made her able to work in twelve inches of water on a soft bottom.

"When we got her done, I sold two more to a father and son. I had no intention of becoming a full-time boatbuilder. I ended up building five that first winter," he said.

Evans Boats, of Crisfield, Maryland, built this fifty-foot fiberglass deadrise in 2005. *Crabs R US II* runs fresh seafood from Tangier Sound to processing houses in Crisfield. (Courtesy of Eugene Evans.)

It was the start of a full-time career for Evans in boatbuilding. Evans later teamed up with Cambridge boatbuilder Gene Travers to design and produce thirty-five and forty-two footers that they called the Somerset 35 and 42. Evans eventually went on his own and became one of the most successful boatbuilders on the Chesapeake Bay. He admits that much of his success has been because his family has taken an interest in the business. His wife Rose, daughter Christine, and son David, all work for Evans Boats at their plant in Crisfield.

C-Flex Builders

Innovations spread further throughout Maryland with the introduction of a new way of building fiberglass boats with a material called C-Flex. This material is a unidirectional fiberglass reinforcement developed by Seemann Fiberglass of Harahan, Louisiana, in 1972.

Consisting of continuous, solid fiberglass rods running parallel to each other in a twelve-inch-wide matrix of cloth, C-Flex was used with great success in building boats throughout the United States. But the main reason for its growing popularity on the Chesapeake was Dave Sintes.

Sintes grew up clinching nails on wooden boats at his father's yard in New Orleans, and later at his own shop. But like so many wooden boatbuilders, Sintes discovered that good lumber was hard to find, and it wasn't long before he turned his attention to fiberglass.

"I fiberglassed over wooden boats, I built molded [glass] boats, and I built plugs for people who wanted to build their own boats," said Sintes. "But when Seemann came out with C-Flex, I could see that this would revolutionize the custom fiberglass boat business."

He explained, "For one thing, a man who wanted to build just one boat no longer had a major investment in plugs and molds or the problem of storing them."

Rolls of C-Flex are used as planking over an open building form similar to the skeleton frames and keel used in traditional wooden boatbuilding.

Sintes himself built numerous boats of various sizes out of C-Flex. He then developed a system whereby a customer could send him a picture or simply describe the type of boat he wanted, and Sintes used his computer to develop a design.

Along with furnishing plans, he builds and supplies frames and provides a four-hour video he commissioned on how to build in C-Flex. In addition, Seemann Fiberglass can set up a manual for custom fabrication with C-Flex fiberglass planking.

In 1986, Sintes was at a commercial fishing show in Maryland, trying to drum up customers for C-Flex, when Jack Koenemann, a St. Michaels, Maryland waterman, requested that he design a forty-four-foot-by-fifteen-foot boat for Koenemann to use in Maryland's soft-shell clam fishery.

When the boat came out, several boatbuilders saw the vessel and started building in C-Flex. One of those who saw her was wooden boatbuilder Harry White, of Rock Hall, Maryland. When a Smith Island waterman contacted White for a twenty-eight-foot deadrise to carry a small clam rig, White contacted Sintes about designing such a boat constructed in C-Flex.

Thus it started. White; Joe Kite, of Smith Island; and Albert Thomas, of Solomons Island were pioneers in introducing C-Flex boats on the bay. All three of these men started as traditional deadrise wooden boat builders, but saw opportunities in a new style of boat.

Harry White, of Rock Hall, Maryland, was one of the first builders on the Chesapeake to start using C-Flex in deadrise boat construction.

C-Flex construction quickly spread throughout the Upper Bay. Kite had Sintes design a classic barcat style. Thomas had a twenty-eight footer designed and White began building forty-four footers. They had an advantage over the Virginia builders who moved from up north in the 1970s. The Maryland builders already had a clientele who trusted their boatbuilding skills and these customers listened to their advice. Today, C-Flex and plug-built fiberglass boats are built throughout Maryland.

Joe Kite, of Smith Island, Maryland, shifted from building wooden deadrise boats to having Dave Sintes design him a hull of C-Flex fiberglass construction. The Christine was one of the first that Kite built.

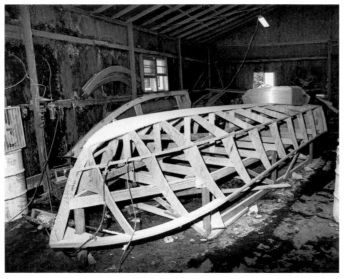

An open skeleton frame is built and covered with rolls of C-Flex. The new fiberglass boats on the bay have some hull traits taken right off traditional wooden deadrise boats.

Interestingly, some fiberglass builders offer both styles. In 2006, Ronnie Carman of Carman Boats of Marion Station, Maryland, built a full line of solid hand-laid fiberglass plug hulls, which include twenty-seven-, thirty-two-, thirty-six- and forty-six-foot deadrise lines, but he also offered Sintes C-Flex boats, which can be built to any length and width.

This roll of C-Flex at Joe Kite's boatshed in Ewell, Maryland, is used as planking over an open skeleton frame.

The fiberglass deadrise is simply an extension of a long history that goes back to the introduction of the V-bottom on the bay. Computers and boat designs and plans have taken the place of rack-of-eye, but features of wooden deadrise and cross-planked boats can still be seen in the new fiberglass boats.

Eugene Evans summed it up when he said, "The only thing we are doing different is using a different material. We are just part of the long evolution of boatbuilding on the Chesapeake. In all my boats you can still see features of my father's sail-powered barcat. They are features that have stood the test of time and no matter what material we build in, those features will always be apart of bay-built boats."

Aluminum Deadrise

Just as the boatbuilding heritage of Deltaville and the Middle Peninsula of Virginia was a draw for fiberglass builders, it was also a draw in late 1970s and early 1980s for steel and aluminum builders.

Davidson Marine arrived in Mathews County, Virginia, and began building steel- and aluminum-hull boats for commer-

Carman Boats, of Marion Station, Maryland, built the *Stephanie Cheryl* in 2007 for oysterman Ronnie Bevans, of Kinsale, Virginia. It took years for bay watermen to make the switch from wooden boats to fiberglass. Although the *Stephanie Cheryl* has lost some of the traditional look of wooden bay-built deadrise boats, her hull carries a distinct V-deadrise in her bottom.

cial fishermen and others. Most of these boats had very few of the traditional wooden deadrise features

However, in 1982, Coddie Carrington and John Fowler, owners of Delta Marine in Deltaville, combined the traditional shape of the bay deadrise into an aluminum hull.

The two men decided to base a style of aluminum boat on the time-tested deadrise, and spent months querying Deltaville wooden boatbuilders Grover Lee Owens, Willard Norris, Alvin Sibley, and Lee Deagle.

"It was a committee design," said Carrington in a 1982 interview. "We decided we wanted to build the best damn workboat on the bay. We spent four months kicking the design

around with the best wooden boatbuilders in this area, and then we took dimensions of some of the best wooden boats and used them.

Their first and only boat was a spec boat, 32' 5" x 10', which looked like a classic Chesapeake Bay wooden deadrise, complete with a "Guinea" steering stick.

At the time, Carrington and Fowler thought there might be a future in aluminum deadrise-style boats. "Worms don't eat it," says Fowler. "It doesn't rust, it doesn't fall apart, and it doesn't crack like fiberglass."

For all its good points, steel and aluminum in traditional deadrise boats made very little inroads into the marketplace.

In 1982, Coddie Carrington and John Fowler combined the traditional shape of the bay deadrise in this aluminum hull. It was one of just a few aluminum boats built on the bay in a similar shape of the wooden deadrise.

By the time Carrington and Fowler completed their aluminum deadrise, a hundred years had passed since the first V-bottom boats arrived on the bay.

The seafood industry that had fueled the evolution of the deadrise had seen better days. Watermen were just trying to survive and keeping what boats they had going. There simply was not much room in the marketplace for an aluminum deadrise-style bay workboat.

Interestingly, the modern builders and designers did not change much from the hull shape of the traditional wooden boats. They didn't have to. Early builders shaping wooden deadrise hulls with a foot adz and broadaxe had already created the right shape.

Chapelle stated in *American Small Sailing Craft* that in the 1880s "the bay became the acknowledged home of the V-bottom." Today's deadrise hull is a tribute to the ability of hundreds of boatbuilders up and down the bay, who took part in this great experiment of refining and building a boat style just right for the waters of the Chesapeake Bay.

GLOSSARY

adz. A tool used by boatbuilders to shape a hull by chopping. It was used extensively in the construction of log canoes and on chunk round sterns on Virginia-built deadrise boats.

bat. Another term for **bateau.**

barcat. Term used on Tangier Island for low-sided frame-built, deadrise, crab skiffs, or boats used to scrape for crabs.

bay-built. A term used in some areas as much as deadrise to designate wooden Chesapeake Bay-built, V-bow, and cross-planked boats.

bay freighter. Another name for a Chesapeake Bay buyboat, which was used to haul freight such as lumber, coal, canned vegetables, and fertilizer.

bateau. The name used for all frame-built, deadrise-style boats larger than a skiff. They are often flat-bottom with a raked bow or stern and some flair in the bow, and can be a powerboat or sailboat. Prior to the term "deadrise," frame and planked boats were often called bateaux.

battens. A colloquial term used in some areas of the bay for frames. See **frame.**

bilge clamp. The timber running from stem to stern at the chine, to which side and bottom planking are fastened.

bilge keelson. See **bilge clamp.**

booby hatch. On a deck boat, a hatch that leads to the forepeak.

booby house. Tangier Island term for a pilothouse on a workboat.

bow staving. The wood used to shape and create deadrise in the bow.

Broad Creek round stern. A round-stern deadrise boat constructed by boatbuilders working on the shores of Broad Creek in Deltaville, Virginia.

brogan. A Chesapeake Bay log-bottom workboat, larger than a log canoe but smaller than a bugeye, usually forty to forty-five feet. These two-masted craft had a small hunting cabin and were used to harvest oysters with hand tongs, dredge, and patent tongs.

bugeye boat. A term used by buyboat captains and crews for sail-powered bugeyes that had been converted to power.

buyboat. Vessel engaged in buying and hauling oysters, crabs, fish, clams, and other seafood. When a captain uses his own vessel to buy seafood from watermen, it is referred to as a **buyboat.** When a boat is owned by a dealer or oyster planter working his own grounds, the vessel carrying oysters back to the processing plant is referred to as a **run boat** or **runner.**

ceiling. Thin boards fastened to the inside of the frames to cover up and finish off the inside of the boat.

C-Flex fiberglass planking. A unidirectional fiberglass-planking reinforcement developed by Seemann Fiberglass of Harahan, Louisiana, in 1972.

chine. Where the bottom and sides meet on a V-bottom or flat-bottom boat.

Chine log. Same as a **bilge clamp.**

chunk bow. Early experimental boatbuilders used chunks of wood, rather than staves, to shape the vee in the bow. This was a style used in shaping pointed sterns and bows on log canoes. See **head blocks.**

chunk stern. Also called a **logged stern.** A construction style that evolved from early log canoe builders. Chunks or blocks of wood were shaped to form the stern and laid in layers one on top of another. The butt joints were staggered so the joints would not overlap. This method also was used in the sides of log canoes to raise the height of the sides. These side chunks were referred to as "raisen wood." In some vessels, chunks were used to shape the deadrise in the bow, but it was not a common practice.

coasting canoe. The second generation of sail-powered log canoe on the Chesapeake. Instead of being completely open like early log canoes, the vessel was larger and had a cabin between the washboards, beginning just abaft the foremast and extending aft some six feet.

coaming. A vertical board on the inside of the washboard or side deck to keep water from coming into the boat.

collar. A bay term for **coaming**, but on deadrise boats it also was used as a structural member.

Crisfield flattie or sharpie. A name used on the lower James River to define a skipjack-rigged vessel.

cross-planked. Bottom planking that is laid crossways so that the outside end is fastened to the chine and the inboard end is fastened at the keel rabbit.

culling boy. A young boy who worked aboard an oyster, crab, or finfish boat culling seafood. It was a term used widely in the oyster business.

culling snot. A culling boy.

cunoe. A pronunciation used to identify a log canoe.

cunners. Term used to identify someone who owned or worked aboard a Chesapeake Bay log canoe.

deadrise. The vertical distance from the keel rabbit to the chine. The line showing the angle that the amidships frame makes with the horizontal plane of the keel. Deltaville deadrise boats have about a two-foot rise at the bow from the keel planked crossways, contrasted to a rise of about eight or ten inches from the keel at the center of the boat. There also is deadrise in the stern of many wooden boats.

deadwood. In Virginia's portion of the bay, deadwood is the wood that is cut and thrown away when shaping the V-bow and the rise in the stern in deadrise, cross-planked workboats. Maryland and Virginia boatbuilders refer to the carved wood in the bow and portions of the stern as "the deadwood in a deadrise." Some traditional bay workboat builders believe that the term deadrise came out of the use of deadwood to shape the rise in the bow and stern.

displacement hull. A hull that will not come up on plane.

donkey skiff. A large skiff, twenty-four to thirty feet in length, used in the haul seine fishery. The skiff had an engine and a winch head. The engine did not power the boat, but was used to turn the winch to haul the net in toward shore. The skiff could carry a hundred boxes of fish and often was towed behind a larger powerboat to carry payload to market.

double-enders. A boat with a vee shape on bow and stern and no transom.

drag basket. A bushel basket tied to a rope and dragged behind a deadrise boat to slow it when hard crab fishermen work a trotline.

dressing a stern. Term used for shaping and smoothing down stern chunks in a round-stern boat and usually done with an adz.

flare. The outward spread and upward curve of the topsides as the sides of a boat rise from the waterline upward to the sheer in the bow.

flat cabin. Term used for a house on a workboat without a pilothouse.

frame built. A boat with longitudinal bottom planking attached to frames.

frames. Athwartship timbers to which planking is attached. Sometimes referred to as **battens**.

Guinea stick. A side-mounted steering stick on a Virginia-style workboat.

Hampton flattie. A sloop-rigged sharpie hull having some deadrise from amidship to stern. One of the early cross-planked vessels on the bay.

hard chine. When the side planking meets the bottom planking at a definite point.

hard driver. A captain of a boat who works himself and his crew hard.

head blocks. Early method of shaping the vee in the bow. When cross-planked bottom staving stops just short of the bow, chunks or head blocks are carved to the desired shape and installed, running parallel to the keelson. The same as a **chunk bow.**

herringbone planking. Cross-planking on a vee angle, not perpendicular to the keel, but on an angle from the keel to the chine. If viewed from below or above, it looks like a herringbone pattern. It provides a stronger hull. This style was used by some bay skipjack builders.

Hooper Island draketail. A boat with a staved round stern with a reverse rake. The design was taken from torpedo boats and adapted to bay deadrise boats by boatbuilders on Hooper Island, Maryland.

hull. The main body of a boat, not to include the deck or cabin.

hunting cabin. A cabin located in the bow of a brogan or coasting canoe, containing two built-in wooden bunks and a small wood stove at the forward end. The cabin occupied all the space between the washboards beginning just abaft the foremast and extending aft some six feet.

inboard rudder. The rudder post and rudder is forward of the transom or stern and usually not seen.

Jackson Creek round sterns. A round-stern boat built by boatbuilders on Jackson Creek in Deltaville, Virginia.

keel. The main timber that goes down the center of the boat.

keelson. An inside timber to add strength to the main keel.

king stick. A fairly straight stick, often made of red cedar, used to point directions from a skiff as to where to set pound stakes. The person most knowledgeable in setting poles for a pound net stands in a skiff and points to where each pole is to be set with a **king stick.**

knee. A wooden bracket or connection joining two pieces of wood that meet at an angle.

launch. Early shallow-draft powerboats used to carry passengers and supplies to and from creek and river landings throughout the Tidewater region.

leg-of-mutton (skipjack rig). A sharp-headed main sail where the boom or foot is longer than the mast for leech of the sail.

lick. Term used by oystermen and crabbers working dredges to denote one drag across a bar.

lighters. Large wooden scow or barge used to carry heavy cargo and usually towed or poled. The boats were all-purpose vessels used to haul lumber out to waiting schooners, tomatoes to canning factories, sand for mixing concrete, and many other uses on the Chesapeake.

logged stern. A round stern on a deadrise boat made of chunks of wood. Also called a **chunk stern.**

lump of oysters. A term used by oystermen to describe a mound of oysters on the bottom of a river or creek. Watermen would say, "I found a little lump over here."

make-and-break engines. An early gasoline engine without a spark plug. Using a coil as a source of high-voltage electricity, the ignition spark is created by quickly disconnecting, or opening, the points, thus creating a spark, i.e., "make" to close the connection of the point to the cord, and "break" to quickly disconnect the point from the coil creating a spark.

monkey rail. A light-style rail mounted above the main rail that runs along the bulwarks of the stern.

net skiff. A skiff used in the haul seine fishery to carry nets to and from fishing grounds.

nor'easter. A storm coming from the northeast.

old fashion nor'easter. Term used for hurricanes before the word hurricane became popular. The August Storm of 1933 was an old fashion nor'easter.

outboard or outside rudder. Style of rudder used on sailboats and early powerboats, usually made of wood. The rudderpost and rudder was attached to the transom or sternpost in the case of double-enders. Portions of the rudder, rudderpost, and hand steering stick can be seen on the stern.

pit-sawed lumber. A pit is dug in the ground, large enough for a man. One man stands above the log and works one end of a rip saw, while the other is in the pit, pushing the saw upward to cut plank boards.

planing board. A platform built onto the stern at the waterline, attached with rods or struts. When power is applied to increase speed this board prevents the stern from squating or sinking.

planing hull. A boat that gets up on plane, or rides mostly on top of the water, allowing it to go faster than a displacement hull.

planked boat. Potomac River watermen refer to a boat with a longitudinally planked bottom as a planked boat, to distinguish it from a cross-planked boat. Most cross-planked builders distinguish between the two as frame built (longitudinally planked) and deadrise built (cross-planked). Builders in Guinea Neck, Virginia, referred to cross-planked bottom boats as planked boats to distinguish them from log canoes.

plug. A term used for a boat mold on which a fiberglass boat is built.

plug rudder. An inboard rudder that is attached to two metal pieces, one with an eye that holds the top rudder mount and another metal piece at the bottom that the rudder plugs into. The disadvantage of plug rudders on skipjacks is that they create more draft than the traditional outboard sailboat rudder.

Pocomoke round bottoms. A style of skipjack with a longitudinally planked and cross-framed bottom. Primarily built around Pocomoke City, Maryland.

Pot Pie stern. A style of stern where the deadrise increases quickly at the transom to give a prounounced "V" to the stern. This stern was common with boat builders from Wittman, Maryland (also known as Pot Pie). Similar to West River tuck stern.

Poquoson V-stern. A deadrise boat with a vee built into its stern as aposed to a round or square stern.

punt. A small boat with blunted square ends on bow and stern.

rabbet. A groove usually cut into the keel or stem for the planking to land in.

rack of eye. When a builder uses his eyes to build the shape or sheer into a boat.

railway. A device composed of two rails and a cradle, used to haul boats up out of the water for repair and maintenance.

raisen wood. Chunks of wood used to raise the height of sides on log canoes.

rake. The degree of slant from vertical that a boatbuilder makes his stem or stern.

round-stern canoe. Before the term deadrise evolved it was the name most used by Virginia watermen and boatbuilders for very early deadrise round stern boats.

run boat. See **buyboat.**

runner. See **buyboat.**

Sampson post. A post made of oak, to which anchor and mooring lines are tied.

schooner boat. Term used by captains and mates on buyboats to describe sailing schooners that had been converted to engine power.

scull. To propel a boat using a single oar over the stern of the boat.

sculling bracket. A wooden bracket attached to the stern that holds the sculling paddle in place while being worked.

sculling lock. An oarlock that the sculling oar handle fits into, and fits into a socket or hole at the stern.

sculling oar. A long oar or paddle, usually made of white oak, used to scull.

sculling paddle. See **sculling oar**.

sculling pin. A pin mounted in the stern to help hold the paddle in place while being worked.

157

settling board. Same as a **planing board.**

sheer clamp. The timber that follows the sheer on the inside of frames, on which the deck beams sit. It helps to maintain sheer and hold frames in the proper place.

shield stern. A tuck stern on a dory shaped like a shield.

side keelson. Same as **bilge clamp.**

skipjack. A single-mast, hard-chine Chesapeake Bay work-boat that carries a leg-of-mutton sail and jib.

Smith Island speedboat. A longitudinally planked skiff, usually about twenty feet by four feet, with an extended bow deck. The boats were built at Smith Island, Maryland, for poling in shallow, grassy waters to harvest soft-crabs and peeler crabs.

soft chine. A boat that does not have a pronounced chine. Usually round bilged and longitudinally planked.

staved round stern. A stern on a deadrise round-stern boat that is enclosed with staves.

step-plank. A tapered plank positioned between the chine and first-side plank on the hull to eliminate squareness in the sides. The step-plank creates a smooth and finished look throughout the length of the boat.

streamlining. A term used on the West River of Maryland for building a sweeping vee in the bottom, which goes aft.

stringer. Timbers (usually about three inches x four inches on a forty-two-foot deadrise boat) attached to the inside of the bottom on each side of the keel, halfway from the chine and keel, to give the boat strength and stiffness. Sometimes referred to as sister keelsons.

strip-planking. The use of narrow strips of wood glued together to shape the sides and sometimes bottom of a boat. When used in the sides, its purpose is to create flare in the bow, a shape easier to obtain with strips, rather than planks.

squat board. Same as a **planing board.**

tow board or drag board. A wide board mounted on the stern of a Chesapeake Bay deadrise boat that can be raised and lowered into the water. Maryland trotline fishermen use tow boards to slow their boats as they work a trotline.

transom. The transverse member at the stern that ties the bottom, sides, and deck together. A **double-ender** does not have a transom.

tumblehome. As the side planking goes aft, it changes from flaring out to leaning inboard as it rises and on powerboats make for a wider bottom at the stern. This helps to prevent squatting. Most Hooper Island Drake Tails have tumblehome as they go aft.

wedge. Small strips of wood attached to the stern to help keep the stern from sinking or "squatting" and to help get the boat up on plane.

West Epoxy System. A particular brand name of adhesive popular with Chesapeake Bay boatbuilders.

West River tuck stern. The stern is flat with a vee shape that runs from the keel to the bottom of the stern. It originated on the West River, near Shadyside, Maryland. Similar to *Pot Pie stern.*

wing board. Same as **planing board.**

worm shoe. A thin plank fastened to the bottom of the keel and skeg to protect it from wood-boring worms.

yoke. Instead of using a steering stick on outside rudders to move the rudder, a yoke was mounted to the top of the rudder and a line was attached to each end of the yoke for steering cable. The rope ran to some type of steering wheel or stick inside the boat, which was used to turn the rudder.

Deadrise Boatbuilders

Tom Abbott	Water View, VA
Charles G. Adams	Crittenden, VA
Fred Ajootian	Ocran, VA
Robert Atwell	Shady Side, MD
Rick Averson	Exmore, VA
Vic Averson	Willis Wharf, VA
Joe Blanchard	Only, VA
D. L. Belvin	Perrin, VA
John Belvin	Dandy, VA
Raymond Bray	Fairport, VA
Wilson Bray	Fairport, VA
Cole Brizendine	Center Cross, VA
Bobby Brown	Rescue, VA
Russell Brown	Wellford, VA
Ernest H. Bryant	Deltaville, VA
Alex Burrell	Urbanna, VA
Winfred Callis	Deltaville, VA
Ronnie Carman	Marion Station, MD
Odell Carmines	Odd, VA
Coddie Carrington	Deltaville, VA
Irving F. Cannon	Fishing Creek, MD
Walter B. Cannon	Fishing Creek, MD
George Cheseldine	St. Mary's County, MD (dory builder)
John Cheseldine	St. Mary's County, MD (dory builder)
Kenelm (Kelly) Cheseldine	St. Mary's County, MD (dory builder)
Walter Cheseldine	St. Mary's County, MD (dory builder)
Carters Creek Railway Co.	Irvington, VA
Dotsie Coates	Bena, VA
George Clark	Deltaville, VA
George S. Chowning	Urbanna, VA
Odis Cockrell	Burgess Store, VA

Tiffany Cockrell	Glebe Point, VA
Robert Conally	Tyler's Beach, VA
Alonzo P. Conley	Oxford, MD
Bez Cornelius	Deltaville, VA
J. (Jim) Bailey Cornelius	Deltaville, VA
B. A. Croasdale	White Stone, VA
Bobby Crockett	Tangier Island, VA
Lester Crockett	Tangier Island, VA
Winnie Croxton	Kilmarnock, VA
Ed Cutts Jr.	Tilghman Island
Charles A. Dana	Crisfield, MD
James E. Daugherty	Crisfield, MD
Lody Davis	Gloucester County, VA
M. M. Davis	Solomons, MD
Ed Deagle	Deltaville, VA
Lee Deagle	Deltaville, VA
Pete Deagle	Deltaville, VA (mostly log boats)
Neal Delano	Fairport, VA
Walter Delano	Wellford, VA
Napoleon Bonaparte (Bony) Diggs	Laban, VA
Edgar Diggs	Mathews County, VA
Edward Diggs	Mathews County, VA
N. B. Diggs	Laban, VA
Bill Dickson	St. Mary's County, MD
Jimmy Drewry	Deep Creek, VA
Rob Dudley	Deltaville, VA
Warren Dunaway	Tibitha, VA
W. F. Dunn	West Norfolk, VA
Jake Dunning	Chincoteague, VA
Jos. Edmonds	Eclipse, VA
Joe Edwards	Crittenden, VA
C. Lyman Ewell	Elliott, MD
Eugene Evans	Crisfield, MD
Noah T. Evans	Ewell, MD
John Fowler	Deltaville, VA
William T. Forrest	Grimstead, VA
Alexander Gaines	Dare, VA (log boats)
Garner Gibson	St. Mary's County, MD (dory builder)
John Gibson	St. Mary's County, MD (dory builder)
Perry Gibson	St. Mary's County, MD (dory builder)
Sidney Gibson	St. Mary's County, MD (dory builder)

William Thomas "Buddy" Gibson	St. Mary's County, MD (dory builder)
Francis Goddard	St. George Island, MD
Wayne Goddard	St. George Island, MD
Maylan Green	Deltaville, VA
Paul S. Green	Deltaville, VA
Paul S. Green Jr.	Amburg, VA
Robert Franklin Green	Deltaville, VA
Robert Franklin Green Jr.	Deltaville, VA
William "Billy Joe" Groom	Shady Side, MD
Luther Hackett	Amburg, VA (African-American)
F. C. Haislip	Harryhogen, VA
Joseph K. (Kenny) Hall	Achilles, VA
Thomas (Man) Hall	Achilles, VA
John H. Harrison	Wittman, MD
J. L. Harrison	Tilghman Island, MD
Emile Alexander Hartge	Shadyside, MD 1860-80s (log canoe and bateaux builder)
Edmond Harrow	Deltaville, VA
Francis Raymond Hayden	Cobb Island, MD
Joseph Haynie	Northumberland County, VA
Walter Hazelwood	Urbanna, VA
Carl Herbert	Tidwell, VA
Bill "Chief" Hooper	Gwynn's Island, VA
Howard & Smith	Crisfield, MD
Mitchell Hubbard	Hudson, MD
Cecil Hudgins	Mathews County
Freeman Hudgins	Laban, VA
Harry A. Hudgins	Peary, VA
William Edward (Ned) Hudgins	Laban, VA
Theopholis (Oph) Hudgins	Peary, VA
R. H. Hudson	Irvington, VA
Harvey Hurley	Wingate, MD
Charlie Huseman	St. Mary's County, MD (dory builders)
Willie Huseman	St. Mary's County, MD (dory builders)
Zach Huseman	St. Mary's County, MD (dory builders)
P. C. Ingram	Palmer, VA
George Jackson	Wittman, MD
Buster Jenkins	Bena, VA
Smiley Jenkins	Gloucester, VA
Larry Jennings	Fairport, VA
Lepron Johnson	Crittenden, VA

J. Watler Jones	Wittman, MD
Orval Jones	Wittman, MD
T. G. Julian	Palmer, VA
Joe Kite	Ewell, MD
Carl Kopel	St. Mary's County, MD
Robert Kopel	St. Mary's County, MD
Herman M. Krentz	Harryhogan, VA
John Krentz	Harryhogan, VA
Maston Krentz	Harryhogan, VA
David Lawrence	St. Mary's County, MD (dory builder)
Ed Leatherbury	Shadyside, MD
Percy H. Linton	Pocomoke City, MD
Bill Lippinscott	Trappe, MD
Bob Lippinscott Jr.	Trappe, MD
John Long	Maddox, MD (dory builder)
David Lowe	Battery Park, VA
Maynard W. Lowery	Tilghman Island, MD
Sidney Lucas	St. Mary's County, MD
Willie Marchant	Deltaville, VA
Stephen Marks	Baltimore, MD
Lawrence Marsh	Smith Island, MD
Leonard (Leon) Marsh	Rhodes Point, MD
Melvin Marshall	Wittman, MD
Samuel T. McQuay	Wittman, MD
Brian Miller	Deltaville, VA
Virgil Miller	Deltaville, VA
Lorenzo Dow Moger	Eclipse, VA
E. J. Moore	Crittenden, VA
Billy Moore	Poquoson, VA
Patterson Morgan	Rappahannock River, VA
Charlie Mothershead	Wicomico Church, VA
Neman Brothers	Shadyside, MD
Pete Nixon	Norfolk, VA
Alfred Norris	Deltaville, VA
Willard Norris	Deltaville, VA
Hugh Norris	Deltaville, VA
Edward Norton	Deltaville, VA
Grover Lee Owens	Deltaville, VA
Creighton Palmer	Abell, MD (dory builder)
Wilbur Palmer	Abell, MD (dory builder)
Lawrence R. Parker	Syringa, VA

Russell Carroll Parker	Wake, VA
Bronza Parks	Wingate, Maryland
Mickey Parks	Tangier Island, VA
O. (Ozzie) W. Payne	Palmer, VA
Carl V. Pederson	Deltaville, VA
Thomas Post	Crittenden, VA
A. G. Price	Mount Vernon, MD
Linwood P. Price	Deltaville, VA
Lioenell Price	Deltaville, VA
Milford Price	Deltaville, VA
Jerry Pruitt	Tangier Island, VA
Phillip Pruitt	Tangier Island, VA and Urbanna, VA (deadrise skiffs)
Raymond Thomas Pruitt	Tangier Island, VA

(Worked in the 1800s before motor power. Built speedy, sixteen-foot to twenty-foot, longitudinally planked, V-bottom sailboats for crabbing in shallow waters. His nickname was Ram Tom.)

Bruce Quade	St. Mary's County, MD
Joe Reid	Edgewater, MD
Charles Henry Rice	Reedville, VA
Edwin C. Rice	Fairport, VA
Emory Rice	Fairport, VA
Luke Rice	Fairport, VA
James B. Richardson	Cambridge, MD
John Richardson	Chincoteague, VA
H. E. Robertson	Palmer, VA
Paul Robertson	Sunnybank, VA
Leonard Rogers	Shady Side, MD
Perry Rogers	Shady Side, MD (1930s)
William M. Rollins	Poquoson, VA
E. H. Rowley	Chincoteague, VA
Bobby Ruark	Dorchester County, MD
Eugene H. Ruark	Ruark, VA
H. W. Ruark	Fishing Creek, MD
Jody Rowe	Newport News, VA
Woodland Rowe	Urbanna, VA
Buddy Sable	Ruark, VA
David Elzie Shreeves	Deltaville, VA
Alvin Sibley	Deltaville, VA
Lorenzo Somers Jr.	Smith Island, MD
Alton Smith	Susan, VA
Harry Steve Smith	New Point, VA

J. W. Smith	Bena, VA
Jack Smith	Perrin, VA
John F. Smith	Dare, VA
Kirby Smith	Dare, VA
L. (Lennie) R. Smith	Susan, VA
Sidney Smith	Bena, VA
W. T. Smith	Achilles, VA
William Smith	Fairmount, MD
Buddy Sable	Amburg, VA
Harry Steed	Mathews County
Sterling & Somers	Crisfield, MD
Marvin Stevens	Lancaster County, VA
Dighton Taylor	Deep Creek, VA
R. D. Taylor	Deep Creek, VA
Albert Thomas	Solomons, MD
Ike Thomas	Deltaville, VA
Reese Todd	Dorchester County, MD (draketail builder)
Rome Thompson	St. Mary's County, MD (dory builder)
William H. (Willie) Thompson	St. Mary's County, MD (dory builder/round stern)
Sommie Trench	Crittenden, VA
Tom Trevilian	Urbanna, VA
B. F. Tull	Tylerton, MD
E. James Tull	Pocomoke City, MD
J. Wood Tull	Irvington, VA
Jabez Tyler	Cambridge, MD
Capt. Lawson Tyler	Smith Island, MD
Winfred Tyler	Honga, MD (draketail builder)
Alvin Walden	Deltaville, VA
Moody Walden	Deltaville, VA
Raymond Walden	Deltaville, VA
Fred Ward	Urbanna, VA
Charles Watson	Deltaville, VA
Buck Web	Lewisette, VA
Earl Weston	Deltaville, VA
Herman Weston	Deltaville, VA
Johnny C . (Big Johnny) Weston	Deltaville, VA
Johnny W. (Johnny Crab) Weston	Deltaville, VA
Julian (Duddy) Weston	Deltaville, VA
Luther Tom Weston	Deltaville, VA
Gilbert White	Palmer, VA

Harry White	Rock Hall, MD
William F. Wiley	Washington, D. C.
William Wills	Glenns, VA
William Wimbrough	Chincoteague, VA
David Winegar	Ocran, VA
Allen E. Witman	Crisfield, MD
John E. Wright	Deltaville, VA
G. L. (Captain Ladd) Wright	Deltaville, VA
Lewis Wright	Deltaville, VA
T. (Tom) W. Wright	Deltaville, VA
William E. Wright	Deltaville, VA

Oral sources from:

George Trice	Poquoson, VA
Jimmy Moore	Poquoson, VA
Grover Lee Owens	Deltaville, VA
Wit Garrett	Bowlers Wharf, VA
Neil Groom	Shady Side, MD
Billy Joe Groom	Shady Side, MD
Jerry Pruitt	Tangier Island, VA
Ronnie Bevan	Kinsale, VA
Arthur Lee Walden	Mathews County, VA
Albert C. Fisher Jr.	Wicomico Church, VA
Pete Lesher	St. Michaels, MD
	Chesapeake Bay Maritime Museum
William C. Hight	Urbanna, VA
John England	Remlik, VA
Billy Hall	Achilles, VA
Bill Keeling	Crittenden, VA
Richard J. Dodd	Solomons, MD
	Calvert Marine Museum

* *Some builders in this listing were log boat builders or fore-and-aft plank round-bilge boatbuilders. They were included because there was an indication they were involved in some aspect of deadrise boatbuilding. An example is Luther Hackett, who was a log canoe builder who specialized late in his career in installing logged round sterns on deadrise and cross-planked boats.*

BIBLIOGRAPHY

Beitzell, Edwin W. *Life on the Potomac River.* Westminster: Heritage, 1973.

Blake, Melvin, in discussion with the author, August 17, 2006, Blake home, Topping, VA.

Bray, Anne and Cynthia Curtis. *The Directory of Wooden Boat Builders.* Brooklin: WoodenBoat Publications, 1986.

Bray, Phyliss, in discussion with the author, August 23, 2006, Bray home, Remlik, VA.

Brewington, M. V. *Chesapeake Bay Bugeyes.* Newport News: The Mariners' Museum, 1941.

———*Chesapeake Bay: A Pictorial Maritime History.* New York: Bonanza Books, 1963.

Burgess, Robert H. *This Was Chesapeake Bay.* Centreville: Cornell Maritime Press, 1963.

———*Chesapeake Bay Sailing Craft: Part 1.* Centreville: Tidewater Publishers, 1975.

Chapelle, Howard I. *The American Fishing Schooners 1825-1935.* New York: W. W. Norton & Company, 1973.

———*American Small Sailing Craft.* New York: W. W. Norton & Company, 1951.

———*Chesapeake Bay Crabbing Skiffs.* St. Michaels: Chesapeake Bay Maritime Museum, 1979.

———*The History of American Sailing Ships.* New York: Bonanza Books, 1935.

———*Notes on Chesapeake Bay Skipjacks.* St. Michaels: Chesapeake Bay Maritime Museum, 1979.

Chowning, Larry S. "Alton Smith and Edward Diggs: Legends of Chesapeake Bay." *National Fisherman,* October 1991, 72, no. 6: 43-45.

———"Aluminum Deadrise Work Boat Sips Fuel at 15 m.p.h." *National Fisherman,* February 1983, 73-74.

Deadrise and Cross-planked

——"Around the Yards (South)." *National Fisherman,* December 2004, 61.

——"Around the Yards (South)." *National Fisherman,* February 2002, 49.

——"Around the Yards (South)." *National Fisherman,* January 2001, 47.

——"Around the Yards (South)." *National Fisherman,* March 2001, 49.

——"At Age 94 Molly 'Crab' Weston Still Vividly Remembers Older, Simpler Times in Deltaville." *Southside Sentinel,* September 18, 2003, 109, no. 25: 1-3.

——"The Belle of the Bay." *National Fisherman,* April 2003, 46-47.

——"The Belles of the Bay." *Bay Splash,* 2006, IV, no. 2: 63-68.

——"Boys of the Bay." *Bay Splash,* 2006, IV, no. 3: 52-58.

——"C-Flex System Sparks Maryland Builders' Shift to Fiberglass." *National Fisherman,* June 1989, 70, no. 1: 66-69.

——*Chesapeake Bay Buyboats.* Centreville: Tidewater Publishers, 2003.

——*Chesapeake Legacy: Tools and Traditions.* Centreville: Tidewater Publishers, 1995.

——"Chesapeake Deadrise Turns New England Trawler." *National Fisherman,* July 1987, 68, no. 3: 44-45.

——"Chesapeake Firm Building Versatile Glass Work Boats." *National Fisherman,* October 1981, 62, no. 6: 62-64.

——"A Craftsman's Ships." *National Fisherman,* September 2001, 34-35.

——"Deltaville Boatbuilder Lewis G. Wright." *Small Boat Journal,* June/July 1983, no. 31: 19.

——"The Deltaville Garvey." *Small Boat Journal,* June/July 1982, no. 25: 58-61.

——"From Classic Deadrise to Modern Work Boat." *National Fisherman,* November 1987, 68-71.

——"From Draketails to Potpie Sterns Chesapeake Watermen Appreciate A Nicely Shaped Rear End." *National Fisherman,* 1985 Yearbook, 65, no. 13: 78-80.

——"Graceful Racers: the Grand Old Oyster Skipjack of the Chesapeake Remind Us that Speed Isn't Everything." *National Fisherman,* February 2002, 82, no. 10: 30-31.

——*Harvesting the Chesapeake: Tools and Tradition.* Centreville: Tidewater Publishers, 1990.

——"Laneview Centenarian Recalls Turn-Of-Century Life Here." *Southside Sentinel,* July 14, 1983, 88, no. 28: 1.

——"L. G. Wright Continues 66-year Career." Supplement to *Southside Sentinel* and *Rappahannock Record,* 1982.

——"Oyster Garvey is Tailor-made for the Shallows." *National Fisherman,* October, 1993, 74, no. 6: 44-45.

——"Rollins Boatyard." *Small Boat Journal,* October/November 1985, no. 45: 37-38.

——"Seasoned by Salt." *Bay Splash* 2006, IV, no. 4: 54-58.

——"Sons of the Fleet: Tony and Ray Kellum Guinea, Virginia." *WoodenBoat* March/April 1986, Number 69: 59.

——"Tangier Island Boatbuilders Combine Tradition and New Trends." *National Fisherman,* January 1995, 75, no. 9: 31, 59.

——"Virginia Builder Still Turning Out Wooden Work Boats." *National Fisherman,* May 1981, 78-79.

Ciotti Chris. *SlackWater: Oral Folk History of Southern Maryland.* St. Mary's City: St. Mary's College of Maryland, 1998.

Culler R. D. *Skiffs and Schooners.* Camden: International Marine Publishing Company, 1976.

Davenport, Cathy Winegar, in discussion with the author, 1993, Winegar's Marine Railway, Lancaster County VA.

Deagle, Ed, in discussion with the author, September 25, 2006, Fishing Bay, Deltaville, VA.

Debusk M. Jessie. *Family Histories of Middlesex County Virginia.* Urbanna: Ralph Wormeley Branch, APVA, 1982.

Dodd, Richard, J. The Potomac River Dory. *WoodenBoat Magazine* February 1996. Issue 128.

Dodds, Richard, J., Pete Lesher. *A Heritage in Wood.* St. Michaels: Tiller Publishing, 1992.

Edson, Merritt. *Ship Modeler's Shop Notes.* Bethesda: Nautical Research Guild Inc., 1979.

Edwards, Stuart, in discussion with the author, January 29, 2007, Edwards home, Gywnn's Island, Virginia.

Deadrise and Cross-planked

Farmer, Weston. "Where have all the old marine engines gone? A bit of history will die if they are not unearthed." *National Fisherman,* November 1971, 4-B,11-B.

Feitig, Paul in discussion with the author, September 1990 and July 1995, Urbanna Town Office, Urbanna, VA.

Footner, Geoffrey Marsh. *The Last Generation: A History of a Chesapeake Shipbuilding Family.* Solomons: Calvert Marine Museum Press, 1991.

Garrett, Wit, in discussion with the author, 2005 and September 2004, Garrett home, Bowlers Wharf, VA.

Garrett, Wit and Neil Groom, in discussion with the author, June 9, 2004, Garrett home, Bowlers Wharf, VA.

Green, Joyce and Paul, in discussion with the author, 2003, Green home, Amburg, VA.

Gregory, Joseph F. *Deadrise Is from Here . . . To Yonder.* Yorktown: Skipjack Publications, 1987.

Groom, Neil, in discussion with the author, April 21, 2006, Shady Side, MD, and May 18, 2006, Middlesex County, MD.

Gwathmey, William Brooke and Caroline Gwathmey Jones, in discussion with the author, 2004, King and Queen Courthouse, King and Queen County Museum, King and Queen County, VA.

Hall, Billy, in discussion with the author, February 24, 2007, aboard his boat built by Grover Lee Owens, Holiday Marina, Achilles, VA.

Harrison, Edward, in discussion with the author, 1989, Harrison home and boat, Smith Island, MD.

Haynie, Francis, in discussion with the author, June 24, 2006, November 2005, Haynie's boat shop, Northumberland County, VA.

Hunt, Ivy. *Memoirs of Ivy Hunt.* March 4, 1958. (Unpublished). Provided by Wit Garrett.

Johnson, Paula, J. *The Workboats of Smith Island.* Baltimore: The Johns Hopkins University Press, 1997.

Kurlansky, Mark. *The Big Oyster.* New York: Ballantine Books, 2006.

Leggett, Vincent O. *The Chesapeake Bay through Ebony Eyes.* Arnold: Bay Media, Inc., 1999.

Madison, Mary. "Master Builder Eases toward Retirement." *Waterman's Gazette,* October 2005, 31, no. 10: 23-24.

Marsland Richard H. *Mathews County Panorama.* Mathews, VA: Mathews County Historical Society, Inc., 1983.

Mountford, Dr. Kent. "Bay Watermen Scrape by with Help of Numerous Workboat Designs." *Bay Journal,* December 2004.

Norton, Randolph. *Old Days on the Chesapeake.* Matthews, NC: The Cedar Press Inc., 1991.

Lee Owens, Grover, in discussion with the author, July 2006, Norview Marina, Deltaville VA.

Pruitt, Jerry, in discussion with the author, 2006, Pruitt home, Tangier Island, VA.

Pruitt, William (Bill), in discussion with the author, October 2, 2006, Middlesex County courthouse, Middlesex, MD.

Ryland, Evelyn Q. *Urbanna A Port Town in Virginia, 1680-1980.* Charlotte: Delmar Printing Company, 1993.

Shackleford, Edna, in discussion with the author, September 29, 2006, Shackleford home, Deltaville, VA.

Shores, David L. *Tangier Island Place, People and Talk.* Newark: University of Delaware Press, 2000.

Snead, V. E. *Boat Modeling.* Hertfordshire: Technical Publications, 1976.

Trice, Latane, in discussion with the author, August 28, 2006, Trice home, Walkerton, VA.

Valliant, Joe. "Maryland Builder Tailors 'Crab Scraper' for the Shallows." *National Fisherman*, February 1986, 66, no. 10: 52.

Vojtech, Pat. *Chesapeake Bay Skipjacks.* Centreville: Cornell Maritime Press, 1993.

Walden, Alvin and Moody, in discussion with the author, January 11, 2007, Moody Walden's home, Deltaville, Virginia.

Walsh, Harry M. *The Outlaw Gunner.* Centreville: Tidewater Publishers, 1971.

Weston, Molly (Crab), in discussion with the author, September 2003, Weston home, Deltaville, VA.

Wilson, A. Bennett. "I Remember Middlesex (Watermelons)." *Southside Sentinel,* January 31, 1991, 96, no. 5: 7-8.

——"I Remember Middlesex (Building a Boat)." *Southside Sentinel,* February 28, 1991, . 96, no. 9: 6.

Wright, William E., in discussion with the author, 2002, Wright home, Hartfield, VA.

INDEX